reality tv

realism and revelation

reality tv
realism and revelation

Anita Biressi and Heather Nunn

WALLFLOWER PRESS
LONDON & NEW YORK

First published in Great Britain in 2005 by
Wallflower Press
4th Floor, 26 Shacklewell Lane, London E8 2EZ
www.wallflowerpress.co.uk

A catalogue for this book is available from the British Library

ISBN 1-904764-04-5 (pbk)
ISBN 1-904764-05-3 (hbk)

Book design by Elsa Mathern

Printed in Great Britain by Antony Rowe Ltd., Chippenham, Witshire

Contents

Acknowledgements

We would like to thank staff at the BFI Library and at Roehampton University TV Services, Eugene Doyen and Caroline Bainbridge for helping to locate videos and other materials. Thanks too to Caroline for her supportive comments on some of the earlier drafts of chapters and conference papers which eventually found their way into this book. Heather Nunn would also like to thank the Department of Media, Communications and Cultural Studies at Middlesex University for teaching remission during 2002/03 which provided much needed time for research.

Parts of chapter 4 also appear in different forms in two short articles for a dossier on trauma for the journal *Screen*, vol. 45, issue 4 (2004). An early version of chapter 7 was presented at the Media Studies Research Group at Sussex University and we are grateful to them for receiving it with interest. An extended version of chapter 7 was also originally published as 'Video justice: crimes of violence in social/media space' in *Space and Culture*, vol. 6, issue 3 (2003). A version of chapter 8 was published in the *Journal for Cultural Research*, vol. 8, issue 3 (2004). Parts of the Conclusion were published in a different form as 'The especially remarkable: celebrity and social mobility in reality TV', in *Mediactive*, issue 2 (2003). We wish to thank these journals for permission to reproduce some of the material here.

We would also like to express our appreciation to Bert Nunn, Kathryn White, Berni O'Dea and Miri Forster as their tireless support and enthusiasm sustained us through the hard times. Thanks too to the anonymous reader commissioned by Wallflower Press who read the entire manuscript with diligence and offered constructive criticism.

Introduction

This book takes reality TV to be a significant development within contemporary pro-gramming and one worthy of close study. It presents a series of case studies that examine each reality TV form closely in order to delineate its distinctiveness and to highlight key issues around ethics, politics, truth-telling and realist representation. It will also seek to make connections between different forms: to track generic evolutions, to trace formal relationships, collisions and disparities among and between different kinds of non-fiction programming. Television in particular, its popular critics and its audiences, seem to have a short memory and where lineage is pertinent to the discussion we will highlight the impact of earlier forms of non-fiction film and television and filmmaking philosophies on current forms. However, the variety of formal conventions employed by this range of programming, the complexity of political or aesthetic agenda adopted by filmmakers and the employment of hybrid filmic techniques all point to the difficulty of establishing clear genealogies and unassailable antecedents. But antecedents do exist; undermining the claims so frequently made that recent reality formats are wholly 'new' or that they have clearly definable and 'unique' characteristics.

Consequently, the book argues that within British television culture especially it makes most sense to understand reality TV within the context of the different but related historical trajectories of documentary film practice. This is not to say that reality TV is in any simple way a commercialised or adulterated or mutant offshoot of documentary but rather that many of its forms owe something to or operate in dialogue with varieties of documentary in particular. And so too, that many of the debates within media and cultural studies about the value, aesthetics, politics and futures of reality TV also owe much to the earlier agendas, manifestos and political commitments of documentary filmmakers.

Reality TV is culturally significant in the sense that, until its arrival, factual programming had never succeeded as a consistently top-rated TV genre on British television. From its outset reality TV addressed huge audiences in innovative ways and it has maintained its hold on the attention of viewers, academics and those in the media industries over a significant period of time. Reality TV altered the terrain of factual programming, drawing on and contributing to changes in television working practices, importing a newly-inflected televisual grammar, establishing new priorities for programme makers and different expectations in viewers. As a resoundingly popular form it has situated itself firmly within what John Corner (2002) has called 'post-documentary' culture. We take this to be a radically altered cultural and economic setting which includes an imperative for playfulness and diversion and the erosion of the distinctions between the public and the private sphere, between the private citizen and the celebrity and between media and social space.

The popularity of reality TV is crucial here. The highly visible presence of ordinary people in 'unscripted' situations is both the watermark of reality TV and arguably an explanation of its success with audiences. The visibility of ordinary people, the increasing audibility of their voices and the possibility of social mobility promised by their appearance on television raise important questions about the provision of space in broadcasting for the representation of ordinary people and their lives. For those critics of reality TV, these new-style celebrities' often voluble, unschooled presence is emblematic of the vulgarity and increasingly shallow values of the newer formats. For its supporters, reality TV may be championed as the vanguard heralding a new, more democratic era of television within a multi-channel environment. Of course, cultural politics is rarely as simple as these positions would suggest and the debates within documentary history studies are a good resource in reminding ourselves of the complex difficulties associated with attempts to represent the 'reality' of real lives.

There are already many overviews of the political and cultural agendas of movements such as Free Cinema or *cinéma vérité* or of innovative television forms such as the observational documentary to which the reader might turn. We provide an account of the generic relationship of reality TV with British, American and French documentary, not simply to map formations of film and then television practice but also to contextualise our discussion of the cultural politics of realist representation of ordinary subjects in factual television. We undertake this here with the explicit intention of complicating any notion that these early forms were either the political bedrock of reality TV or, alternatively, that they were the gold standard of politicised filmmaking to which factual programming should return. Essentially, this book contends that the new forms of reality TV are no less embedded in thorny debates about representing ordinary people, no less politically loaded than their documentary antecedents and no less complex and conflicted as social texts. For these reasons alone it would be wise to treat them with respect.

If a 'politics' exists in reality TV, and we aim to show that it does, it will be differently articulated from the traditional forms of politicised documentary and it often requires different conceptual tools than those employed to unpack the politics of classic documentary genres. The politics of reality TV is a cultural politics. It is usually implicit rather than explicit, concerned with 'social difference' rather than with the 'working class', concerned with the politics of identity rather than with the politics of collective action or group solidarity. Reality TV is more often concerned with parent power or consumer power or girl power than with electoral power or labour power. Sometimes, too, the politics of reality TV will be conservative, retributive and judgemental and this should not go unnoticed. Even where the politics of reality TV is an ostensibly simple one of providing a supposedly non-judgemental, apolitical forum for ordinary people there is more to say. The playing out of social difference, for example in *Wife Swap* or *You Are What You Eat* or *Neighbours from Hell*, is no less incendiary and no less valuable as a social document of classed identity, social hierarchy and status anxiety than, for example, the acclaimed television drama documentary *Cathy Come Home*.

This book's subtitle, 'Realism and Revelation', signals the twin interconnected issues which we take to be key to the success of reality TV and which we consider to be useful points of entry into any evaluation of the development, appeal and futures of reality formats. The book breaks new ground in the analysis of non-fiction forms by linking together the realist enterprise of reality TV and its relationship to the production of knowledges (revelation) in mainstream television. It is a commonplace that the expectations generated by a story are frequently allied to the conventions of realism. In narrative, conventions of realism constrain the ways in which subject matter can be presented and the ways in which ideology can be manufactured and the ways in which messages are received and understood. These conventions, together with the technologies that sustain them, alter over time. Despite these longer-term mutations in realist representation, there is a perception among some viewers that television, especially non-fiction television, should 'tell it like it is'. There is an assumption that television produces a 'realistic', 'common sense' and therefore recognisable and familiar view of the social world; of the family, relationships, personal trauma, class, ethnicity and gender. Reality TV inevitably raises the ante on the expectations made of realist representation. With new scopic technologies that convey a sense of immediacy and intimacy and 'unscripted' material featuring 'real' people, reality TV lays claim to reveal social, psychological, political and historical truths and to depict the rhythms and structures of everyday life with the least recourse possible to dramatisation and artifice.

Reality programming is especially loaded, since by definition, it should occupy a more privileged position in relation to the representation of the 'real' than overtly fictional forms. Its various forms tend to be measured by viewers and television critics against an ideal (and vaguely formulated) conception of the 'realistic'. Programmes are judged to be 'good' – i.e. well-constructed and entertaining – if they offer convincing 'pictures of reality'. It has been said that 'It is hard to define Reality TV other than to say that it has nothing to do with reality and everything to do with TV.'[1] In fact, the production of reality programming and its documentary and factual TV forebears has everything to do with 'reality', although we always have to adopt a posture of scepticism towards any claims that they have fully represented reality and real life. Their formats, technologies, manifestos and professional values frequently strive towards goals of either realist or realistic representation; of showing the 'real', revealing the 'truth' and so on and these goals are too easily dismissed as either naïve or disingenuous. These genres, even in their most radically experimental forms, are always in dialogue with reality as it is commonly understood and in doing so they help to produce current knowledges about what that reality might consist of. In other words, factual programming takes on the burden of *making sense* of reality.

This book addresses the changing technologies and practices of realist representation as necessary but it also attends, more extensively, to the political dimensions of the real: to the changing representation of ordinary people, to the production of knowledges about the real. The impetus to depict ordinary people has been linked by practitioners and critics, both implicitly and explicitly, to often-politicised debates about the real, reality and about the relative value of realist, naturalistic or anti-realist representational strategies deployed to convey real life. Problematically, 'ordinary people' (what used to be called the 'working classes') have been taken *in themselves* as signs of the real and only quite recently with the advent of reality TV have white-collar workers, professionals in the city, in the arts or in medicine, educationalists, socialites and so on been included in this ever-broadening category.

This extension of representation needs to be understood within the context of the changing social and political climate of the post-Thatcherite/Reaganite era in which social mobility and media visibility have become the touchstones of individual achievement. As we indicate later on, it is this climate that has helped to foster the rise of the ordinary person as celebrity and which has licensed the rendering of the celebrity as an ordinary, supposedly knowable person. Its democratising ethos is radically different from the one in which notions of the public sphere supported a conviction that participation in party politics and public debate was the only real avenue for the expression of public opinion. In contemporary late capitalist cultures such as Britain and the United States cultural pluralism, life-style diversity and niche marketing arguably produce fragmented and self-reflexive selves. Here, older forms of authority and security – the law, democratic government, judiciary, medical experts and so forth – have been critiqued and displaced by an increasing public political cynicism and a turn to the self as the only possible marker of integrity (Frosch 1991). So too, new discursive technological forms such as the mobile phone, the video camera and the internet signal the convergence of different media and the increasing emphasis on the individual subject as the guarantor of knowledge and producer of new economies of realism (Dovey 2001). Cultural critics have noted mass forms of popular culture may provide ways of confronting and managing the basic psychic tensions of contemporary urban life (Richards 1994; Elliott 1996). Furthermore, that negotiation of the self within contemporary collective living is arguably infused with therapeutic discourse (Parker 1997).

This brings us to the counterpart of 'realism' in this book, that is reality TV's production of knowledges through tropes of 'revelation', truth-telling and exposure. Histories of documentary practice and current affairs film and television often address the ways in which the politics of filmmaking, at its most radical, could be discerned in the investigative and representational strategies with which social injustices were exposed. The documentaries frequently cited as 'groundbreaking' did not just make the argument for social change but rather they *showed* viewers what was going wrong. In a sense, they helped to bring new knowledges about welfare, racial prejudice, poverty-related crime and so on into the public arena and make them comprehensible. Consequently, their revelations could be read as an often politicised call-to-arms, shock tactics that demanded political change and a modification in social attitudes to support it. The success of established and newer television formats such as talk shows, docusoaps, reality game shows and so on is predicated on a quite different agenda which may well be about a political or more often commercial commitment to providing platforms for ordinary people but is also, much more strongly, about the exhibition of the self and of the psyche. Here the production of knowledges inform and instruct audiences in how to manage the *self* and one's immediate environment rather than the *social*. Audiences often gauge the authenticity or truthfulness of reality TV on a scale of emotional realism and personal revelation. The reality TV subject is enjoined to share their pain, their surprise or their joy in a realm of mediated sociality and the most successful contestants of series such as *Big Brother* are often those who have allegedly remained 'true' to themselves and who have been frank with their audience.

Reality TV had done much to further popularise psychoanalytic discourses in many formats including the 'ego psychology' aired in American-style confessional chat shows and the 'vulgar Freudianism' of *Totem and Taboo* displayed on the survival shows in which combatants overcome personal inhibition and physical limitation to gain enhanced status. Here, the immediacy of the 'real event' is established through images of determination, failure, personal strength and inner conflict. In *Survivor*, for example, the group is presented as a case study in both group membership and individual neurosis. Individual to-camera confessions are edited next to and contrasted with couple and group alliances and conspiracies. In this and other series the clash between individual aside or revelation to camera and group dynamics places the viewer as a 'panoptic' figure able to monitor, judge and punish the participants by banishing them from the television screen. Also, the structuring of these programmes draws on a certain sadistic pleasure in witnessing distress and failure as well as success. Programme makers are arguably very knowing about sociological, anthropological and psychoanalytic discourses in their construction of social bonding as fraught with tribalism, testing of group alliances and the symbolic 'murder' of sacrificial outcasts (Freud 1912/13 and 1921). The use of video diaries, to-camera monologues, shock-tactic interviewing and so on further opens up current critical debates about the shifting parameters of the public and private world. Here, for the reality TV viewer, amateur 'pop psychological' self-analysis and/or amateur or unscripted footage meld the pleasures of voyeurism with the pseudo intimacy of the therapeutic consulting room and a sense of 'democracy of feeling' (Richards 1994) which underpins emotional realism.

In this book we have chosen to focus on the production of certain types of knowledge, certain modalities of revelation and the different ways in which they are articulated in reality TV. We examine, in particular, documentary and reality TV's attentiveness to trauma, personal pain, injury and loss and to its modes of expression through confession, video diary, interview, observational techniques and so on. We point to the embedding of the revelation of trauma and psychological damage in post-documentary formats and its relationship to the broader psycho-social realm of an established therapeutic culture.

As the scope of this book suggests, the kinds of issues raised here in relation to reality TV require not only the harnessing of the conceptual tools of documentary theory but also the deployment of concepts and modes of analysis more commonly used within cultural studies. We aim to show, in particular, through both wide-ranging discussion and more detailed case studies, the value of the strategic use of psychoanalytic and discourse theory in unpacking the cultural politics of reality programming and the relationship between reality genres and the production of knowledges about the self and the social. Post-structuralist psychoanalytic theory has questioned the unity of the subject as depicted within the 'pop' psychoanalytic forums of confessional television. As noted above, the new dynamics of late-capitalist cultures has foregrounded the increasingly visible fragmentation of the self. Instead of examining the 'self' as an integral and essential element, post-structuralist psychoanalysis prefers to analyse the subject-in-process or the subject-in-crisis and to expose the precariousness of the position(s) occupied by the subject. Michel Foucault and other discourse theorists go further still by seeking to understand not the subject itself but rather how *processes* produce subjectivity and subject positions. Much of what we do here is to think through the ways in which reality TV negotiates the subject-in-crisis or else attempts to produce knowable and manageable subject positions including, for example, the criminal subject, the sexual subject, the classed subject and so forth.

The book begins by exploring the ways in which reality TV has sparked popular, academic and media industry debates about the role and impact of popular television in the context of a post-documentary culture. Chapter 1 establishes some of the parameters of current debates, addressing the development of the most recent reality formats and exploring questions of media ethics, democratisation and access, quality and 'dumbing down', truthfulness, trust and responsibility.

Chapters 2 and 3 review documentary practice to establish a historical perspective on the non-fiction filmic representation of ordinary people and everyday life. They seek to identify the lines of connection, affiliation and sometimes disjunction between older and newer forms of non-fiction representation and to highlight the historical commitment exhibited by filmmakers to the representation of the everyday. Chapter 2 aims to foreground the complex and often contradictory political and aesthetic considerations which informed documentarists' depiction of the ordinary and the everyday through examples from British Free Cinema, American Direct Cinema and the French *cinéma vérité* movements. A number of these filmmakers expressed a suspicious scepticism towards the growing popularity and mass consumerism of television, together with a reluctant admiration for its potential audience reach. But the political radicalism of these movements, their diverse filmmaking philosophies and their technological innovations found their way on to the small screen. Hence the chapter ends by addressing the appearance on television of politically radical docudrama and documentary, looking at notable television programmes such as Ken Loach's *Cathy Come Home* and less discussed programmes such as Denis Mitchell's *The Dream Machine* and *A Soho Story*. Chapter 3 focuses on one aspect of the documentary approaches already mentioned – the observational documentary of working-class and family life. It tracks its mutations from the campaigning films exemplified by *Cathy Come Home* and later *Hillsborough* through the less overtly politicised poetic realism of Penny Woolcock's work and the prototypical 'docusoap' observational documentaries pioneered in the UK by Paul Watson.

In chapter 4 the focus shifts from documentary history and its developments to art-house video projects, video diaries and new-style observational and auteur-driven documentary. In doing so it seeks to illustrate how the intimate terrain of the subjective, the autobiographical and the personal has not only been colonised by popular culture but also by new hybrid forms of documentary and factual film practice. Examining a diverse range of mainstream and alternative documentaries it argues that far from distancing itself from the aesthetics and subject matter of popular forms and narratives, much of the most interesting new work has discovered fresh ways to incorporate them into their own practice, forming fascinating points of intersection. Here too the work of John Edginton, Jane Treays and Errol Morris, whose films include disturbing and controversial material mediated through popular conventions and storytelling techniques, is examined to explore the limits of the representation of personal trauma, revelation and of the 'real' within mainstream television.

Chapters 5 and 6 address the ways in which new economies of realism require confession, exhibitionism and emotional revelation to be the conspicuous watermarks of authenticity and ethical commitment to audiences. They explore how these modes of expressive authenticity have come to the fore in a range of reality forms such as *Big Brother*, observational documentary, chat shows and lifestyle programming. Chapter 5 begins by situating confessional television and its emphasis on traumatic revelation within a broader context of a 'therapeutic culture' in which the self is encouraged to speak, to disclose and to narrativise one's life in order to consolidate a publicly recognised and authenticated persona. Examining notions of performance, self-hood and transformation it argues that reality TV lays bare the ways in which subjectivity and subject formation is performative, always in process and inextricably bound up with structures of observation and confession. Talk shows acted as one of the precursors of reality TV, familiarising audiences with a popularised therapeutic discourse and valorising the display of raw emotion within a public forum. Consequently, chapter 6 chooses to address one crucial aspect of emotional revelation, the revelation of trauma, and examines its role as popular cultural script in talk shows and lifestyle programming.

Chapter 7 also examines disturbing and controversial material in its extensive discussion of true crime and law and order reality programming. Whereas the documentaries addressed in the previous chapter constitute intimate portraits of people under pressure who have consented to be filmed, crime reality programming, through its use of CCTV footage, turns every subject into a potential film subject, with or without their consent. This chapter addresses the ethics of displaying violence, lawlessness and victimhood within a popular entertainment-led format. Thinking through the politics of the new formations of media/social space inaugurated by new technologies and popularised by reality TV it explores the pleasures of witnessing crime and anti-social behaviour and the social fears and anxieties that may be imbricated with these pleasures.

Chapter 8 looks at one of the newest forms of reality hybrid – the performance piece as media event. As noted above, the exposure and, more particularly, self-exposure of psychological and bodily trauma has become the central feature of our 'post-documentary' culture. Generally speaking, this showcasing of personal trauma is a gendered one; with many of the established and newer formats dismissed as feminised media culture; with few, if any, intellectual pretensions. This is partly because the domain of emotional suffering, at least, has been conventionally designated a 'feminine' one, with women especially, licensed to speak about bodily or psychological insecurity, vulnerability or damage. When 'masculine' damage or trauma is at stake, its presentation and articulation in media culture takes on quite different forms and meanings. This chapter examines the David Blaine event entitled 'Above the Below', exploring the meanings, symbolics and ethics of the current specularisation of bodily trauma and revealing the multiple ways in which an ethics of the self and of becoming is articulated in a popular form.

'Above the Below' is a rare example of a reality TV media event that showcases an established celebrity and does so in order to enhance his special status rather than render him more 'ordinary', accessible or knowable. Overall, reality programming has provided access and platforms for ordinary people via a plethora of talk shows, reality game shows, video diaries and docusoaps. These now comprise a significant part of the daily viewing of many audiences and their protagonists ('guests', 'contestants', 'housemates', 'characters') have, in turn, become the new celebrities of our age. We conclude by considering the ways in which ordinary people, formerly the sympathetic subjects of social-conscience documentaries, have now been transformed into the 'especially remarkable' celebrity through their new-found media visibility. And also, contrarily, the ways in which celebrities are being encouraged to reveal that they too are only ordinary people. We consider the increasing premium placed on social mobility achieved not through merit, trained talent or the traditional accumulation of cultural and economic capital but through media visibility alone. We also look to the future, identifying new hybrid forms of programming such as *The Club* and *The Salon*. These retain the reality TV emphasis on the intimate and the interpersonal while further eroding the distinction between celebrities and ordinary people, constructing filmed spaces – clubs, bars and beauty salons – where ordinary customers appear to mingle democratically with working celebrities and *manqué* reality TV stars.

Many of the forms of programming examined in this book share one characteristic. They exhibit a commitment, sometimes overtly politicised although frequently not, to the representation of ordinary people and to the provision of a space in which they are made visible and of a platform from which they might speak. As such, reality TV has raised the stakes on television's frequent populist and/or political assertions that it is a central component of common culture and that its main gift is its ability to function as a virtual public sphere. It also frequently claims to offer its audience reality rather than realism, revelation rather than fantasy, authenticity rather than artifice, access to real experience, joy or suffering rather than dramatised emotion. With this promise comes responsibility and the prominence and ubiquity of reality TV continues to inspire serious ethical questions about exploitation, voyeurism and the limits of the representation of the real.

chapter 1
Reality debates

We take television for granted in the same way as we take everyday life for granted … Our experience of television is of a piece with our experience of the world: we do not expect it to be, nor can we imagine it to be, significantly otherwise. (Silverstone 2000: 3)

This chapter outlines some of the recent popular debates that have been triggered by reality TV. In doing so, it firstly attempts to situate reality TV within current preoccupations about the parameters of reality TV and its broader cultural status. Secondly, it signals key generic traits of the genre that have provoked concern and/or support for its role as a democratising formula. Thirdly, we open up the popular ethical concerns with reality TV's claim to veracity and to its ability to document 'real lives' and 'real people'. Whilst we focus on the popular inflection of debates about reality TV, there is obviously no firm and fast distinction between these discussions and their foci and the more academically-framed discussions that inform the rest of this book. Discussions about 'event TV', for example, preoccupy all media analysts now attempting to gauge the media manipulation and marketing of television and its spillage into everyday life. Indeed towards the end of the book we signal that 'event TV' and its profoundly public media spectacle is indeed, as we see it, one of the futures of the reality TV formula.

The intersection of reality packages with older televisual techniques is highlighted in our discussion of 'vox pop'. Again, the relationship between more established and revered documentary forms and the newer populist reality formula is underlined. Television has conventionally been underscored as a profoundly domestic and quotidian medium. The role of the voice of ordinary people on television has been a preoccupation of documentary makers long before its prolific introduction into reality TV. Here, we signal the extension of older media impulses to include ordinary people on screen and to validate their presence in a privileged forum. We discuss the importance of ordinary voices and signal a debate ongoing throughout this book into the potential political nature of that inclusion. Does the voice of the ordinary person on television ensure that a politicised agenda has been met? How does one identify the political: is it merely the older, more pronounced socialist/Leftist/radical impulses of particularly the Griersonian school and its legacy? Does the inclusion of ordinary voices articulating their fantasies and fears on, for example, a makeover programme necessarily mean less than that of a middle-aged couple speaking about their post-war housing conditions? How do we situate and evaluate these claims to everyday political concerns within the cultural and also media contexts in which they occur? As cultural theorists we are concerned to prioritise the 'structure of feeling' that we see as resonating through much reality TV. That said, as politically-concerned media theorists we also bear a certain reverence for older, overtly politicised, forms of media engagement that rooted documentary practice in (albeit flawed) desires to change social policy, uncover invisible lives and challenge an inequitable social system.

These concerns lead into our introduction of ethical debates which have focused on the ability of the camera, in a complex digital, satellite, multi-platform age, to capture the real and to represent it in all its complexity; laying bare the hidden intricacies of ordinary lives. 'Trust' is a key concept here and in our postmodern age trust is a raddled and embattled category. In the discussion of 'faking it', we signal debates covered throughout the book concerning the role and power of the camera and the powerful claims of the documentary modes to capture the authentic moment. As we will argue, documentary has enlivened and indeed informed the more populist reality TV agenda; the moral and ethical claims to authentic representation have been reclaimed by producers of reality TV. Those claims then face moral and ethical opprobrium when visibly undermined and the concept of trust here becomes shot through with the other prevailing postmodern notion of 'risk': 'can we trust what we see?'; 'does the camera always lie?'

In discussing these issues we need to define what we take as the boundaries of 'reality TV'. The term 'reality TV' is a broad one. It is usually taken to refer to the surge in a variety of 'new' or more often hybrid genres which were launched in the late 1990s. It is also used retrospectively by some commentators to refer to programming which first appeared in the 1980s such as docusoaps and law and order formats; some of which would have originated from documentary or current affairs film units and production companies. The term is most commonly used with reference to the more recent group-challenge formats such as *Castaway 2000* (BBC1) and *The Mole* (C4) and '24/7' multi-platform formats such as Channel 4's *Big Brother*, *Eden* and ITV1's *Survivor* which could be followed twenty-four hours a day, seven days a week.[1] We take together as a broad category reality genres which may be said to include video diaries, game shows ('gamedocs' or group-challenge shows), talent shows, talk shows, observational documentaries, dramatic reconstructions and CCTV and camcorder-based programming such as law and order and emergency services programming. As such we suggest that they hold in common an emphasis on the representation of ordinary people and allegedly unscripted or spontaneous moments that supposedly reveal unmediated reality.

Event TV

In Europe, the most famous 'reality' programme is certainly *Big Brother*, which was first launched in the UK in 2000. The original Dutch Endemol format, which was first broadcast in the autumn of 1999, has been sold around the globe and has been adapted to suit the culture and temperament of local audiences. There are now more than forty versions of *Big Brother* commissioned across the world.[2] In the Netherlands and in many other countries (aside from the US), it has attracted unprecedented audience figures. It is also regarded as an innovative landmark in both factual and light entertainment television programming.[3] The importance of the series lies not only in its novel format but in its status as 'event TV'. Event TV is 'high concept', aiming at reaching a critical mass of viewers through high visibility and multi-media choice. As such as it is often stripped across a channel everyday for a number of weeks and is supported by multi-platform media. *Big Brother UK*, for example, not only appears daily as an hour-long 'narrative documentary' on Channel 4 but can also be accessed on E4 with a choice of four different time lapses, on live-stream on the internet, via mobile phone texts, videos, books and radio packages. Event TV merely extends the 'dailiness' of what is already the daily experience of television for most television owners (Silverstone 1994: 2–3).

Referred to in the US as 'water cooler TV', event TV is television that attracts huge audiences and becomes part of the popular discourse of everyday life. Like soap operas, the action in shows such as *Big Brother* is contextualised and *amplified* by excessive media commentary including chat show interviews, tabloid newspaper coverage and the circulation of participants' images as celebrities, which prompts conversation among fans about the characters and their behaviour. The British *Big Brother 5*, for example, broadcast in the summer of 2004, precipitated tabloid and broadsheet debate about media manipulation, broadcaster responsibility, surveillance and expert opinion when violence erupted late one night between housemates after the provocative return of two contestants who had been separated to secretly survey housemates from another room. Here the limits of realistic representation were discussed, one psychologist resigned from advising the show, regarding its manipulation as unethical and media commentators debated the decline of reality TV into increasingly confrontational and staged violent displays by contestants on shows like *Big Brother 5* and Channel 4's *Wife Swap* (sold to the US in 2004). However, these broader concerns are in conflict with the specific pleasures cited by reality TV viewers. For, as Annette Hill noted in her audience research for *Big Brother* 2000, 68 per cent of respondents expressed enjoyment at witnessing group conflict, an almost integral element of highly controlled communal living and 60 per cent also mentioned the pleasure of watching ordinary people do everyday things (2001: 36–50).

The comparison with the violence regularly erupting on soaps and its role as trigger for public debate was aired by some commentators, with both formulas compared for their topical staging of controversial events. But, unlike soaps, the talk generated on reality

TV is not contingent; rather it is an essential part of the series' success. The promotion of talk produces the anticipation, elaborate ongoing evaluations and retrospective judgements upon which the commercial success of the programme depends (Couldry 2002: 272).[4] Shows such as *Pop Idol* and *Fame Academy* encourage intense speculation and identification with characters so that part of the event's success lies in the measurable responses from viewers as they phone or text in their votes to ensure that their favourite stays in the game.[5] Over the first two series of *Big Brother UK* 34 million votes were cast by viewers to eliminate housemates.[6] And like other large-scale media spectacles such as the death of Princess Diana (whose 1995 *Panorama* interview and funeral coverage have been two of only a very few top ten factual programmes aside from the most successful reality formats) event TV involves real people rather than actors within the house itself, but also in the voting process in which the public decides who remains and who goes from the house each week.

Two formal developments set *Big Brother* apart from more conventional observational documentaries (discussed in more detail in chapters 2 and 3). The first is the adoption of a knowing style of production in which the cameras and the scripting of certain events within the house via a competitive game formula put producers and cameras firmly within the frame. This self-reflexivity extends to the housemates themselves, and as the series has developed, contestants have increasingly referred back to events in previous years; enacted minor rebellions calling them 'TV history' or played to the camera. In *Big Brother 5*, housemate Becky (introduced halfway through the series as a newcomer to the established group), was subject of media and web chat room commentary for her overt soliloquies and her posturing to-camera when alone. Somali-refugee housemate Ahmed flirted with the anonymous voice of Big Brother in the solitude of the confessional diary room and housemates Victor and Jason were continually filmed discussing how all the houseguests' 'performance' was to be gauged as 'realistic' or contrived for the camera's gaze.

Secondly, the internet and its prominence in sustaining *Big Brother* as media event has changed the shape of how ordinary people are perceived as media participants. On one level, the crucial role of online, seemingly unedited access to the behaviour of the houseguests 24/7 seems to underwrite the producers' claims to 'realism'. Here, as Mark Andrejevic (2004) has discussed, the promise of internet surveillance is compounded by the promise of full participation available through live chat rooms, official and unofficial bulletin boards, quizzes, opinion polls and often daily voting via newspaper, search engine and fan sites on ongoing aspects of the houseguests' participation. Rather than a democratisation of the previously rather anthropological impulses of observational documentary, this participation illustrates a new level of marketing which involves the mass incorporation of ordinary lives into comprehensive surveillance naturalised as media entertainment.

The gestation of event television begins before production and depends substantially on effective marketing strategies. The American television event of the early 2000s was the heavily marketed *Survivor!* (CBS). *Survivor*, which in Britain followed close behind *Big Brother* in 2001, is exemplary of the kind of co-ordinated public relations spawned in advance of a major reality series. Deploying a PR company specialising in generating tabloid news coverage, the ITV press office inspired 131 stories in the national press in the four weeks before broadcast and newspapers were running double-page spreads about the characters. The producer, Carlton, ran a separate press office to deal with interactive elements such as text messaging and games and the series was trailed with five on-air prime-time trailers per episode of the show, a nationwide billboard campaign and website trailers (Rogers 2001). Ostensibly, in a multi-channel environment, *Survivor* did well in its initial airing with audience figures of between five and six million. But comparatively these figures were very low. Ian Johnson, formerly a public relations officer for Granada, explained that this was because the orchestration of the campaign was heavy-handed. Johnson noted: 'People need to feel like they've discovered the programme themselves. Nobody – least of all the British – like to be told which contestants they should like. It's been over processed' (in Rogers 2001). Johnson has a point. Although event TV is fostered and sustained through marketing and publicity its success *must be seen* to originate from informal mechanisms of gossip and word of mouth recommendations. Furthermore, as Hill's (2001) audience research showed, British reality TV viewers are arguably much more cynical of factual programming in general than documentary viewers of previous decades. There was a strong suspicion voiced by respondents towards the purported 'reality' being filmed and recognition of the performative and highly constructed nature of the genre. While an 'event' is clearly different from a 'happening' which is more spontaneous it must not appear to be overly determined or imposed via the production company.[7]

Group challenge

Survivor, like *Big Brother*, was founded on the group challenge but, with the cast operating under far harsher and more physically demanding conditions, it owed more to the proto-typical *Castaway 2000* than to the domestic dramas of the *Big Brother* house.[8] In the first British run of *Survivor* 16 people were marooned on an island in the South China Seas and pitched against one another to win a million pounds – far more significant winnings than *Big Brother*. Overt competitiveness, strategic alliances and tactical voting were positively encouraged and fostered a vulgar Darwinian game show ethos. The series looked good: showily produced with helicopter shots and time-lapse photography that did little to present the environment as 'nature red in tooth and claw' despite some of the privations endured by the subjects. It was exceptionally filmic, building to dramatic climaxes in an overtly constructed fashion. Any ethnic connotations were soon commodified into an embarrassing melange of drum and pan-pipe soundtrack, gift-shop wooden idols and stereotypical assertions about rainforest living. And any local inhabitants, assuming they had not already been excluded from the shoot, had, perhaps wisely, left the scene.[9]

As such, *Survivor*, which rests on an infrastructure of websites and computer games as well as its televisual presence, is a good example of the 'generalised elsewhere' of 'other places' and 'other people' which is fostered by new technologies that erode a distinctive sense of place. *Survivor* sets the global centre-stage on national television in the home and in this way the 'psychological neighbourhood' takes precedence over one's own locality, if only for a short while (Morley 1992: 280). And as David Morley argues in his account of global/local media politics, there are traceable lines of power operating in this context which promote a 'standardised televisual language which will tend to disqualify and displace all others' (1992: 281). The United States exceptionally favoured the American version over *Big Brother* with the 2000 finale attracting audiences of nearly 50 million viewers (Carter 2000). Its status as a high-audience yield product meant that for the filming of its most recent series it was able to request a no-fly-zone above the production site to further sustain the illusion of desert island isolation. Its environment was no less manufactured than that of the *Big Brother* house but it bore the exoticism and perceived privations of foreign locations and 'primitive' culture that belied its technological sophistication and highly controlled setting.

Series such as *The Trench* (BBC2) went even further in attempting to produce the ultimate group challenge but did so through the pretext of educating audiences (and the participants) about the historical experience and trauma of war. The series, reconstructing the experiences of the 10th Battalion East Yorkshire regiment in October 1916 as they fought on the frontline trenches in Northern France, largely failed in its depiction of World War One trench life. A group of men aged between twenty and forty were assembled to mirror the 24 volunteers who lived and died in the trenches 85 years before. The reality show was presented as commemoration and historical document in its attempt to construct and show the trauma of military service and it was also a group challenge as participants struggled with the simulated wartime routines. The modern-day troops were subjected to extreme cold, lack of food, constant barrages of mock gunfire and shelling, rigorous military regimentation and mild field punishment. This was an attempted implantation of the past in the present that looked to embodied experience as means of realistically recounting past physical and psychological deprivations. The footage of their two-week experience was intercut throughout with interviews with World War One veterans, recalling the real experience of encountering death, frostbite, facing their own mortality and their strategies of survival in the face of recurrent horror. Old newspaper articles and photographs of the war and the battalion were spliced with present-day footage of the volunteers. Images of the troops in recreated trenches were overlaid with sepia-toned extracts from war diaries or government war regulations in attempted authentication of the re-creation.

Bill Nichols has argued that spoken testimony often serves in reconstructions as an antidote to the visibly fictional element of historical re-enactment; the fact is that the bodies of those in the re-enactments appear as 'extras' 'never matching the historical bodies' they represent (1994: 4). The soldiers in *The Trench* were meant to authenticate the authorial voiceover that related the story of the 1916 frontline. The historical footage and documents appended to the current trench experience were supposed to guarantee a congruity between the two, whilst the veterans' testimony was used to anchor the reconstructed trench scenes and provide them with appropriate solemnity.

However, the disparity between the veterans' recollections of war and the highly reconstructed and ultimately safely monitored reconstruction was evident throughout and undermined attempts at veracity. For example, in the first episode, a death in the original battalion whilst under gunfire was reconstructed as one member of the group simply disappeared in the smoke. The effect of this mock death upon his companions was captured on film and resulted in unconvincing footage of a reality TV recruit looking dazed and muttering that the rest would have to stick together and look after one another. The aesthetic filming of the battle scenes – slow motion, sepia tints, melancholic music and hazy imagery alongside hand-held tracking shots of the cramped trenches – unsuccessfully attempted to bestow the trenches with an emotional and physical authenticity.

As these shows indicate the privations and challenges encountered by reality TV participants can range from the moderate to the extreme. Aside from *Castaway 2000*, in which severe weather conditions and enduring isolation took their toll, *Survivor* and *The Trench* viewers could also watch characters shake with fear in a range of studio set-based scenarios. US series such as *Fear* (MTV) (with simulated horror-house conditions) and *Fear Factor* (NBC) saw participants shudder as they faced their worst phobias, while in *The Chair* (ABC) (developed but never screened) their rising heart rates were to be monitored as they tried to answer quiz questions while receiving psychological shocks.[10] Mental stress is further larded on in *US Big Brother: The X Factor* in which the contestants enter the house only to discover that they will have to cohabit with former partners often previously separated in acrimonious circumstances. Perhaps even more extremist still are the shows referred to by Mark Andrejevic (2003) as 'ambush TV'. Programmes such as *Scare Tactics* (Sci-Fi Channel), which owe more to early American prankster television such as *Candid Camera* and guerrilla radio than to game shows, target the unsuspecting. Practical jokes include convincing their victims that they have just been exposed to bio-hazards or that their friend (complicit in the joke) has just died from a parasitic infection which in turn will kill them too.[11] The designation 'reality TV' refers to these new and emergent forms of 'spontaneous' and unscripted non-fiction entertainment despite the obvious contrivances involved in assembling a carefully selected group of people and re-locating them under highly controlled conditions or carefully setting up the prank. Their credibility with audiences is supposedly predicated on the ability to convey reality convincingly and the genuine reactions of 'real people' to highly artificial circumstances.

The controlled but highly demanding conditions of these particular formats are indicative of the connection, not always subtle, between reality TV and psychological or social experimentation. The somewhat controversial BBC series *The Experiment*, which aimed to reconstruct the famous 1971 Stanford experiment which enclosed volunteers in the highly inflammatory conditions of a prison scenario, is typical rather than exceptional in this regard – simply substantiating the description of reality TV as 'manipulated observational documentary' (Mapplebeck 2002: 20). Innovators in reality TV have also credited other, more recent, experiments as an inspiration. The early stages of the conception of *Big Brother* were partly inspired by the North American Biosphere Two experiment in which a group of scientists had to subsist through their own self-sufficiency in a transparent geodesic dome. Critics of reality TV have described these conditions as that of a 'human zoo' or a container under pressure which forces inmates 'inwards', making them deal with one another continually and under highly constrained conditions.

Integral to these forms are technologies that seem to generate a 'less mediated' reality – promoting a sense of intimacy, immediacy, liveness or interactivity by monitoring 'unscripted' and 'unplanned' activity. They emphasise the visual over the spoken word, offering viewers 'the relief of being able to watch rather than be told' (Mapplebeck 2002: 19). Over the longer term, new and newly adapted technologies have frequently been the trigger for the development of new documentary styles. Since the 1960s the relative portability of hand-held cameras, changes in sound recording, the availability of home movie equipment, video and CCTV, the possibility of live web-streaming and DV cameras all appeared to liberate filmmakers, allowing them to represent reality all the more convincingly.

Vox pop in a post-documentary market

The producers of reality TV have drawn liberally from formerly established aesthetics of intimacy pioneered by documentary makers. The tight framing and shaky hand-held cameras of Direct Cinema and *vérité* movements (discussed in chapter 2) have been liberally adopted to signify an immediacy of filming and capturing of the real. Furthermore, the conventions of 'access TV' (to be discussed below) have been imported into the reality TV formula. However, as we acknowledge, the production of reality TV takes place in a television environment which differs significantly from the older emphasis in Britain and significant sections of Europe on Public Service Broadcasting (PSB). Producers of reality TV work in a much altered broadcasting environment from those producing factual genres prior to the 1990s. In the 1990s, the arrival of new cable and satellite channels alongside the emergence of a number of organisations with global markets altered the landscape of media production. Increasingly, factual filmmaking was about satisfying the needs of carefully targeted markets: niche channels, national and international. Countries with a PSB tradition continued to align these broader market considerations with an attenuated emphasis on serious educational programming. Certainly in Britain, up until the 1980s, organisations like the BBC clearly identified the provision of documentaries and factual programming within their PSB remit to inform, educate and entertain.

Post-Thatcher, with the landmark 1990 Broadcasting Act and the resultant increasing de-regulation and marketisation of the television arena, the PSB tradition has arguably been eroded by the impulse to produce popular programmes driven by audience viewing figures. Furthermore, huge sectors of the television production matrix have been privatised, contracted out to independent production companies and subject to market competition and the demands of networks' commissioning editors. As Richard Kilborn (1996: 142–3) has illustrated, in the mid-1990s nations like Britain, the Netherlands and Germany, with established PSB traditions, still produced proportionately more 'serious' factual programming than more market-led countries. However, throughout the 1990s, performance-led criteria increasingly informed decisions by networks on their adoption of factual programming. In consequence, we would agree that more serious or educationally-driven programmes have been supplanted by the more economically driven, less de-manding entertainment-led forms of popular programming. In the UK, the BBC and Channel 4 have been responsible for maintaining a distinctive factual stable. Whilst the BBC has made use of its backlist of programmes to provide specialist factual satellite and digital channels, Channel 4 has increasingly targeted a youth or middle-youth market with programmes like *Club Reps* and *Ibiza Uncovered* as well as the host of makeover or home redecoration programmes aimed at a post-Thatcherite, post-documentary consumerist lifestyle-orientated market.

Alongside this acknowledgment of market changes, we have to signal debates about technological innovation and the possible generation of new, democratised forms of TV footage. This discussion taps into broader debates about the relationship between technology, media form and cultural practice. An overview of technological developments since the 1960s suggests that the relative portability of hand-held cameras, advancements in portable sound recording, the increased availability of home movie equipment and low-gauge video and digital formats have revived the impulse of Direct Cinema pioneers to capture a raw reality. In a broader cultural sense, the spread of CCTV and the possibility of live web-streaming have all appeared to liberate filmmakers.

More lately, there has also been the suggestion that these technologies have liberated the film subject, allowing them, within the more technologically democratised forum of post-documentary television, a greater influence over the filming and editorial process and an opportunity to make more personal, authentically 'real' and revelatory programming. Such arguments tend to marginalise the importance of the alternative video and art-house footage produced since the 1970s by documentary and avant-garde filmmakers (discussed in chapter 4) who were intrigued by the intimate and subjective potentials of new technology.

In mainstream television, the provision of time in the schedules for televising ordinary people originated in the earlier, arguably more overtly politicised, notion of 'access TV' from both PSB and more commercially-orientated television environments. Access TV's proponents regarded the medium as a potential extension of the public sphere and a compensation for the plainly inadequate inclusion of non-elite persons in mainstream factual programming. The early model of such provision was the American nightly thirty-minute show *Catch 44*, a series which in the early 1970s, actively sought to represent the views and lifestyles of those outside of the limited reach of broadcasting professionals (Corner 1996: 166). Following on close behind in 1972 was the BBC's regular access slot *Open Door* created by the Community Programmes Unit (CPU). It was partly inspired by comments from some factory workers who, in a current affairs interview, accused television of manipulating their message and knowledgeably challenged the role of editing in this manipulation. The CPU, albeit with minimal funding and a marginal audience, succeeded in producing a fresh and sometimes controversial strand of programming. People judged to have interesting opinions or knowledge were provided with directorial and technical help in putting their message across and they had a reasonable degree of editorial control. Filming was initially live and studio-bound and later moved out on location and used recorded material (Corner 1996: 167).

From the mid- to late 1990s the CPU invigorated British schedules with new factual initiatives in the form of the BBC's *Video Diaries* (1991–), *Video Nation* (1993–) and (well in excess of a thousand broadcasts) *Video Nation Shorts* (1994–), all of which permitted individuals to speak straight to camera, supporting the ideals of access TV.[12] The earlier *Video Diaries* gave camcorders and training to a broad cross-section of Britons, who would send in films which in turn would generate the programme ideas and themes. Diarists recorded their own stories and had editorial control, overseeing the completed projects with the guidance of a BBC producer. Producers no longer sought to find, by definition, speakers who had strong opinions, although these were certainly strongly represented and diarists were still carefully selected. While many diarists were run-of-the-mill people, others were notably eccentric, chronicling their unusual hobbies or obsessions – pointing to the extraordinary heterogeneity and otherness of a nation often regarded as homogenous. The programmes' appeal lay in their novel format and use of technology and the way in which their use reinforced one of the unique qualities of television – a sense of immediacy. One CPU researcher commented, 'The secret of it is that it's immediate and it does give you one hundred percent access to somebody's life and that's what the charm is' (in Corner 1996: 173).

Video Nation, which followed three years later, was conceived of as a fusion between the *Diaries* and the Mass Observation observational anthropology pioneered by journalist Charles Madge, anthropologist Tom Harrison and artist and film-maker Humphrey Jennings in the late 1930s: 'The aim was an anthropology of Britain in the 1990s seen though the eyes of the people themselves' (Rose 2000: 174). Again the production unit were struck by the number of times that participants said that they felt misrepresented or under-represented on mainstream television and the extent to which this was commonly felt by all kinds of people. Co-producer Mandy Rose recalls:

> Gays, single mothers – sure, but also Christians, and Pagans, and housewives in Cheshire and bikers and bankers – everyone seemed to feel it. At first I wondered whether it was a symptom of … the 'culture of complaint'. But seeing the material that people recorded, I have come to realise that they were articulating something very significant about the gap between television representation and lived experience. (Ibid.)

This realisation challenges the idea that people are predictable and that everyday life is homogenous. These projects licensed greater access of ordinary voices on television and made this type of slot a recognisable and highly visible marker of television's continuing responsibility to its viewers to provide a public space. This commitment is still visible in the form of shorts such as Channel 5's *Vox Pop* (2001) series which chronicled ordinary citizens' responses to war in Afghanistan. While many 'vox pop' programmes relied on 'interesting characters' or personal revelation to carry the episode, others allowed the connection to be made between private concerns and the public domain.

Jon Dovey (2000: 121–32) demonstrates in his detailed discussion of the *Video Nation* project how these forms effectively married the confessional mode of personal revelation to broader debates relevant to the social body. Dovey's examples include an episode in which a junior doctor, exhausted after eighty-four hours on call, expresses her exasperation and distress, saying, 'this is appalling, this is cruelty, this is savage … Why? Why is that allowed?' (2000: 124). For Dovey, her monologue, shot in close-up with a direct address to camera and filmed in her own home after a physically gruelling round of duty, operates in confessional mode, while also successfully intervening in a public debate about conditions in the National Health Service. Moreover, the diary form facilitates an engagement with debates of civic importance over and above what could be offered through more conventional documentary form – the impact and emotional charge of the diary lies in 'the sense of the reality of *that* moment of arriving home in such an appalling state. Moreover this impact … leaves the viewer in the position of having to make the connections' (2000: 124; emphasis in original). These are not overtly expository documentaries. Even where they enable links to be made between personal experience and public interest they do not appear to present an argument or posit a form of action in the light of the information provided. Yet it is possible for personal voices in documentary to also effect a kind of expository function. The doctor's video diary sits on the cusp of personal experience and social reality and the political forces that frame them both. The critical distinctions commonly made between access programming and expository documentary are somewhat challenged in this example as the opposition between the subjective and objective, between empathy and knowledge is called into question.[13]

These formats invite the question of whether and to what degree the presence of the camera alters the 'self' on show. Reminiscent of the claims of the French *cinéma vérité* school of documentary practice, Mandy Rose argues that the camera can instigate frankness and an essentially truthful representation. She describes a *Video Nation Short* in which a drunken couple called Lynne and Craig, arguing about smoking, decide to turn on the camera and record the conversation. During their talk Lynne makes the discovery that Craig is worried that he will lose her to cancer in future years. Lynne, surprised, declares, 'but you've never told me that before'. Rose comments, 'what you see is not what happens despite the fact the camera is there, but rather because the camera is there ... The camera is a catalyst, in this case bearing witness to things that have not been said before' (2000: 179). Her example is thought provoking. The situation is not entirely natural. The couple have to interrupt themselves to set up the camera and pin on the microphone, before picking up the conversation where they left off. Yet the scene feels spontaneous and its import is revelatory – the couple learn something about themselves as we learn about them. Other shows such as *The Living Soap* (BBC) and the subsequent *Flatmates* (C4 2000) tread a fine line between observational documentary and documentary as a catalyst of action. The later series *Flatmates* rendered this balancing act more explicit as it was based on the premise, inspired by the domestic feature-film shocker *Shallow Grave*, that the flatmates should interview applicants to join them in the flat-share. Executive producer Tim Hincks described this rather obscurely as 'adding value to reality' and hence still engendering a kind of truthfulness. He is quoted as saying, 'We've built a format where we can encourage real life, if you like, to happen more quickly. And it guarantees you get real drama' (in Higgins 2000).

The availability and easy usability of recording technologies and their compatibility with confessional-style television has underscored the premium placed on the presentation of an authentic selfhood and the revelation of self within the mediated public sphere. Factual entertainment in the form of reality TV capitalised on the televisual immediacy and investment in ordinary people pioneered by the CPU among others but arguably denudes it of its political values. The look of *Video Nation* had been popularised in commercials and popular programming and has become part of the new visual lexicon of 'real life' on television. No matter how artificial the conditions of filming in reality programming the sense of immediacy generated by the new technologies underpins its authenticity. Audiences ideally expect cameras to capture 'real' reactions to genuine or contrived provocations and circumstances. The premium placed on emotion as a signifier of spontaneity and truth-telling in talk shows, for example, has become part of the broader grammar of reality programming overlaying the more knowing cynicism of the contemporary television viewer.

Reality film subjects also seem happy, on the whole, to invest in this ideal. In the UK's *Big Brother 4*, one of the last five contestants, Scott, was asked whom he thought should win. Seated in the diary room and speaking straight to camera he argues for Ray because he considers that Ray had been the most 'real', that he had 'been himself' most consistently during the previous two months whilst others had been 'themselves most of the time but not always'. By authenticating Ray's persona as real, Scott, with his gaze directed at the audience 'out there' is also authenticating himself. Here, the diary room set-up, which abstracts the interviewee from the communal spaces of the house and forces them to speak directly to 'Big Brother', is the unacknowledged guarantor of the speaker's true feelings and views. Prompted by short questions from an unseen speaker, the ideal diarist should deliver a soliloquy revealing their true opinions or feeling. Scott's observations also refer obliquely to the ideal of the whole, identifiable and integrated self and to the suspicion that success in the social world involves performance and the adoption of personas which by definition would undermine this ideal. In the context of reality TV, performativity is frequently condemned by film subjects and viewers as an abnegation of responsibility on the part of the participants. Part of the friction of interpersonal relations between housemates Jon and Cameron (the eventual winner) in *Big Brother 4* lay in Jon's scepticism about the authenticity of Cameron's behaviour. In interview Jon said of Cameron:

> All his friends tell me I've got it completely wrong, and he is a genuine guy … But my suspicion is that he was very conscious of the cameras. When we had a discussion on whether we would go out with a lap dancer or stripper … Cameron said he wouldn't go out with one because she would work unsociable hours. There's no way that was his real opinion, he was just keen not to offend his target demographic. (in Ritchie 2003: 264)

John de Mol, the co-founder of Endemol Productions, has argued that even the most determined contestant would not be able to mask their persona for more than a fortnight on the show.[14] Being 'untrue to yourself' and cheating by seeking to manipulate the game, breaks the 'reality contract' or understanding between programme makers and audience which underpins its credibility (Jones 2004).[15] This investment in personal integrity is often linked to audience and participant expectations of personal revelation and confession. These expectations operate within the broader framework of television culture which has, in some people's view, valorised a 'culture of narcissism' and popularised psychotherapeutic discourses of personal development. As audience research has shown viewers exhibit deep suspicion towards the reality of behaviour exhibited on reality TV (Hill 2001). Part of the appeal of watching and monitoring the reality TV show then derives from watching and assessing the moments when the television performance cracks and the 'inner person' or 'real self' is unveiled. Spontaneity alongside moments of seemingly unguarded intimacy becomes ciphers of a real self operating in a produced micro-word. From this perspective, as we discuss in depth in chapters 5 and 6, the realism of programmes including soap opera, law and order reality TV, living soaps and talk shows is increasingly calibrated by audiences against the measuring stick of 'revelation', emotional truth and psychological striptease (see Shattuc 1997).

Therapeutic-domestic space

In chapters 4 to 6 we emphasise the crucial importance of 'revelation' as a popular framing discourse for much reality TV. Implicit in these chapters is an acknowledgment of trauma and psychological/emotional damage as core concepts circulating in contemporary culture. The revelation or media unpacking of personal damage is often staged within the domestic space and/or with real family members or temporary families of participants. Domestic labour and emotional labour become melded. The paradox of shows such as *Big Brother* is that in order to satisfy their own ends of achieving media celebrity, of hopefully managing a transition from *Big Brother* house to the postmodern public sphere of celebrity culture, the housemates must agree to inhabit a kind of parodic private sphere of enforced domesticity and therapeutic confession. In this sphere the housemates are forced to interact in contrary naturalistic and un-naturalistic ways; washing dishes, cooking and doing chores but also playing party games, dressing up and talking in the diary room. The pointlessness of the game is emphasised when the housemates have to spend hours cycling on stationary bicycles like rats in a lab in order to win rewards. With the subjects deprived of mass-media entertainment, restricted to one book each for the two months of their stay, audiences are treated to hours of footage of the film subjects over-sleeping, lolling round the pool and chatting in a desultory fashion. Their boredom becomes our diversion and our optional leisure time is filled with their enforced inactivity. As they 'mark time' their essentially boring routine, punctuated by highly orchestrated but pointless activity, becomes an uncomfortable reminder of the essentially modern condition of productive labour which still continues for many citizens. That their 'labour' is actually our entertainment signifies theirs as a late-modern employment rooted in the post-industrial world of service, communications and media industries. This then is not privacy surrendered to the interests of television but an exhibition of manufactured privacy and manufactured *longeur*. The simulation of privacy, over a period of time, feels authentic and indeed, for the housemates, this is their lived reality for the duration of the programme. As a symbolic realm it is very far from 'reality' and much closer to being a metaphor for television itself – intimate, immediate, rooted in the everyday and yet highly produced and packaged for mass consumption. It is broadcast TV produced to be 'the private life of the nation-state' (Ellis 1992: 5) and defying the odds at a time when new technologies and cross-border media ownership should be fracturing television audiences and destroying 'event television'.

The *Big Brother* house is unlike the majority of British homes. The modernist house is open plan, with large windows, encouraging free movement and a psychological openness of personal expression. Brightly-coloured sofas and footstools, open kitchens, dormitory-style bedrooms and the garden filled with low-level seating and a pool which enables play but no serious exercise underline the pre-adult world of *Big Brother*. The only parental figure is, of course, Big Brother, a figure both absent and all controlling through continual surveillance. The house is open to Big Brother's and our inspection and its design underscores this exposure. As Jean Baudrillard notes, the ingeniousness of these modern interiors is that they suggest a simple functionality but examined closely, just like the traditional compartmentalised arrangements of more conventional homes, they also offer a reliable image of current familial and social structures. In contemporary interior design walls have disappeared, rooms are no longer a refuge and the gendered and generational hierarchy of conventional family life is swept away. The housemates, most of them of the 'youth' generation, live in an undifferentiated zone where they share bedrooms, bathroom, kitchen space and leisure space without distinctions of role or responsibility, 'rooms open into one another, everything communicates' (Baudrillard 1968: 313). As a metaphor of Western society, the house points to the current transformation of the public sphere into a realm where respect for hierarchical structures is in decline and where social aspiration and mobility is increasingly ratified through public, media-driven recognition.

The futuristic aspect of the house invokes modernist aspirations of domestic living for the affluent classes – they occupy a faux utopian ideal of a 'self-sufficient sentient space that satisfies all the needs of its residents' (Spigel 2001: 385). Despite the vaguely futuristic and unstructured gloss to the house it perpetuates an inherently conservative ideal of domesticity as inward-looking and privatised. It is congruent with Lynn Spigel's description of developments in domestic architectural design in which 'the home of tomorrow has historically been imagined as a kind of fetish space that typically appears disembodied from the surrounding town and city' (ibid.). As Spigel notes, even the expanse of glass walls in contemporary design are not theorised by architects as conduits of connection to the neighbourhood but rather are conceptualised around voyeurism, exhibitionism and surveillance (2001: 386). This becomes literal in the *Big Brother* house where the large windows emphasise both the housemates' consenting insularity and their subordination to the public gaze.

The boundaries between the house and the outside world are also highly controlled and policed and recall Peter Weir's 1998 feature film *The Truman Show* in which the protagonist Truman Burbank learns that his whole life is being filmed and orchestrated for the benefit of a global reality TV show. When Channel 4 built the external set for the final episode of *Big Brother 4* it masked the noise of construction from the housemates with amplified recordings of crowd noise which further recalled the confined militaristic entertainment of British holiday camps and served to heighten the anxiety of the housemates. The amplifiers outside introduced the world as an extension of their highly-controlled environment and underlined their subordination to Big Brother; like gladiators the housemates waited inside and could only imagine the reception awaiting them. The crowd noise also symbolically reinforced the notion of their future success as the achievement of recognition within *mediated* social space rather that outside of it.

Light entertainment/lite entertainment?

While film subjects are expected to be 'straight up' and 'open' with viewers and fellow contestants the programmes themselves can be elaborately knowing and intertextual. Many of them are overtly self-reflexive; paradoxically drawing attention to their own artifice even as they purport to represent reality. A variety of formal strategies highlight this. The colluding glance between documentary subject and camera, the use of the diary room in *Big Brother* where participants speak directly to camera, the airlifting of contestant Cameron in *Big Brother 4* from the UK to the African *Big Brother* house and the recent appearance of minor celebrities in shows such as *I'm a Celebrity, Get Me Out of Here* and *The Club* are all differently articulated examples of reality TV as a self-conscious project. The unannounced introduction of celebrities into *Big Brother* houses, such as former footballer Diego Maradonna in Argentina and the rock band Status Quo in Norway, also foreground the heightened media status of the contestants themselves and their isolation from normal life.

Audiences have little difficulty in handling the postmodern quality of such televisual encounters as they are, albeit in fresh formats, the natural outcome of the cross-fertilisation of television. Hybridity has always characterised factual filmmaking's re-fashioning of older forms for the modern television market and the boundaries between fact and fiction have never been clear-cut. As early as the1960s, drama series such as *Z Cars* (Granada) deliberately foregrounded their basis in fact and in everyday life, constructing themselves as hybrid drama documentaries. Ground-breaking drama-documentaries such as *Cathy Come Home* and later fly-on-the wall series such as Paul Watson's *The Family*, both discussed in this book, provide evidence of the complex ways in which the representation of everyday life is re-articulated through the changing factual and *fictional* codes and conventions of realist documentary televisual representation. As Janet Jones argues in 'The postmodern guessing game', since the mid-1990s we have witnessed a further degree of experimentation and cross-fertilisation in fictional television formats with drama and factual television freely drawing on one another's lexicon of codes and conventions to create 'new viewing experiences' (Jones 2000: 76). In the early 1990s drama series such as *This Life, ER* and *NYPD Blue* deployed the editing patterns and cinematography usually confined to documentary. The documentary-style was a prevalent motif signalling everything from social realism to psychological realism. This practice continues to flourish with more recent controversial drama series such as Tony Garnett's *The Cops* which further extends documentary codes; indulging in muffled sound, fast editing and awkward framing that forces the viewer to watch the action through frosted windows and the like.

There is also in the UK another tradition of light entertainment whose popularity demonstrates a public appetite for television that has elements of spontaneity and surprise and which is also overtly self-referential. The most enduring of these are shows using amateur or discarded film footage or ridiculous foreign adverts packaged to be talked through by an ironically amused presenter. *Auntie's Bloomer's* (BBC1), *TV Nightmares* and *It'll be Alright on the Night* (both ITV) used television production outtakes that revealed prop failures or actors' gaffes. *You've Been Framed* (ITV) and *New You've Been Framed* (ITV1) pioneered the use of home video footage which also subsequently appeared in leisure and consumer programmes such as *The Real Holiday Show* (BBC 1995). Other top-twenty programmes on terrestrial channels during the last decade included *Before They Were Famous* (BBC1) which showed early, usually embarrassing footage of current celebrities, the *National TV Awards* and the *British Soap Awards*. Nostalgia-based series recalling early leisure programming such as *The Way We Cooked* and *The Way We Travelled* (both BBC2) recycled older programmes from earlier decades. These often critically-neglected programmes suggest a willingness by audiences to view television talking about itself and embrace the knowing complexity and hybrid adaptations of television which point forwards to the substantial success and more importantly to the likely market longevity of reality TV.

Most of the above genres have been subject to trenchant criticism of a lowering of standards. Stepping back from the forms themselves, it is useful to consider what documentary theorist Bill Nichols has referred to as the 'domain' of documentary. He notes that documentary may be located within a broader set of 'discourses of sobriety' (1991: 3). These 'nonfictional systems' which include education, welfare, science, politics, economics and so on, are part of the mechanisms of power; they are 'instrumental' in the sense that their implementation has real effects in the world. By association, documentary has become a privileged form within the media with connotations of seriousness (sobriety), public responsibility and truthful representation. These discourses continue to occupy a primary position in the hierarchy of non-fiction representation including in documentary, news and current affairs. The placement of items on television news, the news values apparent in the 'quality press' and the scrutiny still afforded to 'serious' documentary making are all evidence of this positioning. The 'routine structures' of news and current affairs coverage still depend on 'primary definers'; the institutional producers of news and events such as the courts, parliament, research establishments and industry (Hall *et al*. 1978). These in turn help set agendas in which issues of public concern and the public interest are paramount.

The perceived degradation or 'dumbing down' of documentary and news tends to occur when they partially or entirely occupy, or rather are incorporated into, another domain altogether, not of 'sobriety' but of 'human interest' or light entertainment. In this domain the set of discourses speaks of the private sphere, of individual experience, of the local and the particular, of consumption and even of the excessive, the vulgar and the personal. A number of the features common to reality programming have triggered accusations of 'dumbing down' and more broadly, reality TV has been regarded by some cultural commentators as symptomatic of a culture in decline. Reality TV's lexicon of emotion, intimacy, immediacy and the everyday (much of it derived from soap opera and confessional forms such as daytime chat shows) and its emphasis on the private, previously feminised, realm of home, relationships and service industries distances it from the Reithian ideal of public television. This 'feminine' aspect, together with its playfulness, technological innovations and generally youthful audience appeal, addresses a public often excluded or alienated from 'serious' factual programming. A newspaper journalist speaking on the programme *Big Brother, Small World* (C4, 2001) lamented that the series had not tried to 'push the envelope' in terms of the intellectual discussions undertaken between housemates. He likened its appeal to the experience of listening in to other people's banal gossip on public transport – 'no better' than that. The patent lack of 'seriousness' of *Big Brother* becomes most starkly apparent when, on very rare occasions, the producers decide to inform housemates of events in the outside world. In September 2001, a week before the finale of the US *Big Brother*, hijacked planes were used to attack the World Trade Center. One housemate, Monica, was directed to the diary room to be told that although her close family were fine, it was known that her cousin Tabitha, who worked in the Center, had not yet been found. Monica, clearly profoundly moved, asks viewers and family not to worry about her and said that she would pray for everyone. This scene transmuted *Big Brother* from the commonplace to, the strange, the introduction of a more 'real' reality – that of terrorism and destruction – highlighted the show's artifice and lack of sobriety.

The promotion of factual programming as an 'entertainment', 'diversion' and as part of 'youth' programming rather than serious programming is underscored not only by its distance from the ideal of serious factual TV and its coverage in the tabloids but also through the television channels' own marketing strategies. For example, Channel 4's Autumn 2001 marketing catalogue which was inserted into television listings magazines, promoted the season's factual programming through the humorous (but certainly not witty) re-conceptualisation of documentary as popular culture. A documentary with the working title of *Skinny Birds* was promoted with a mock-advert for a Barbie-style 'Slim Suzy' doll with the sales slogan 'she binges – she vomits – includes: scales – unrelenting feelings of inadequacy'.[16] An alternative series about Tuscany was promoted with the words: 'intimate access to a variety of ordinary and extraordinary Tuscans' lives, this three-part series reveals the often disturbing truth behind the region's romantic popular image'. Here the conventional scenes usually featuring on a holiday souvenir wall plate are replaced by airbrushed images including a priest manacling a women to a chair for an exorcism and police restraining a Nigerian prostitute – all accompanied by the ironic commentary 'cultural scenes from this ancient Italian Utopia'.

As signalled above, this explicit transformation of 'quality' television factual formats and topics into popular programming is symptomatic of the greater transformation of television documentary production departments into departments of factual or even in the US 'alternative' programming. It is also a salutary reminder of the extent to which even more serious documentary has to re-brand itself in the factual entertainment marketplace. Disputes arise about how to understand these changes within the still-influential legacy of the Reithian project in Britain and the continuing debates about the long-term consequences of increased commercial competition in the marketplace both domestically and globally. Perhaps because of these programmes' popularity with audiences they have been heavily debated in the press and on television. They are at the centre of heated discussions on tabloidisation, censorship, media responsibility and so on. In 1998 comedy scriptwriter Andy Hamilton in the Huw Weldon Memorial Lecture queried whether the 'new' phenomenon of docusoaps and hybrid genres arising from CCTV footage represented a dumbing down of British television. His concerns have been echoed by cultural commentators such as Germaine Greer, Salman Rushdie and television industry insiders such as broadcaster Chris Dunckley. Dunckley has gone as far as to assert that the popularisation of reality TV 'has all the attractions of bear-baiting, the stocks and public hanging' (2002: 46); others have referred to it scathingly as 'car crash TV'. More broadly, the perception has been voiced that the sheer volume of reality programmes from the late 1990s onwards has diluted the quality of provision overall. When Lorraine Heggessey took over as controller of BBC1 in October 2000 she marked her inauguration by arguing that too many cheap-to-make docusoaps and makeover lifestyle programmes were leading to a stale and predictable schedule (McCann 2000). As Brian Winston notes, despite the many valid arguments that could be made in defence of the docusoap the industry was remarkably silent and rather shame-faced in the face of accusations about quality in this regard (2000: 55).

Peter Bazalgette, the chairman of Endemol UK, has been the most prominent and influential challenger to the critics of recent popular television genres. Bazalgette already had to his credit new leisure and makeover shows including *Ready, Steady, Cook* (cooking game show), *Changing Rooms* (house makeover game show) and *Pet Rescue* (docusoap) before launching *Big Brother* in the UK. In his 2001 speech '*Big Brother* and beyond', given at the Royal Television Society Conference in Cambridge, he set out to prove, with reference to schedules and film clips, that the provision of quality television and choice has dramatically improved. Moreover, he argued that multi-channel provision could only mean an improved service for viewers. He accused critics (or the 'miserable brigade') of elitism based on a dislike of the popular and of youth cultures and suggested that the 'sheer humanity' of reality TV and shows such as *Big Brother* which featured characters of varying sexualities, ethnicities and classes constituted a celebration of the youth generation's tolerant attitude. Bazalgette's position is that reality TV is the launch pad for a new form of television culture which is 'more real, real people and real language' than its predecessors. Bazalgette's only caveat is that the regulation of multi-media reality streaming into the home is increasingly ungovernable to the extent that parents will need to be their own monitors and regulators.

Bazalgette's nod towards regulation of the reality TV format can be extended to signal the closer scrutiny applied to factual programming in general and documentary coverage in particular since the 1990s. Whilst the proliferation of faked incidents on documentary and current affairs coverage highlighted by journalists since the late 1990s has fuelled a contemporary scepticism of broadcasting realism *per se* (Kilborn 2003: chap. 5), there have been specific public anxieties focused on the potential vulnerability of those appearing in reality TV shows. As the next section reveals, this anxiety has extended beyond the content of the shows to the potential fakery of the pre-production process itself.

The Great Reality TV Swindle

> WANT TO RAISE YOUR PROFILE? New Reality TV show seeks contestants! One year, £100,000. If you're characterful, resourceful and energetic mail nrussian@nrussian. freeserve.co.uk

In early 2002 the above advert appeared in the press. Producer and director Nik Russian gathered 30 contestants together for a year-long reality TV project to be broadcast on Channel 4. During the next two months the contestants, many of whom had resigned from their jobs and left their homes, underwent rigorous auditions and psychological selection processes before signing legally-binding contracts. A camera crew was in place and the auditions were held in an upmarket banqueting suite on a private island on the Thames River. It was not until they discovered what the first challenge was to be that some contestants suspected that the project was a hoax: without food, shelter or financial backing three teams had to compete to be the first to raise £1 million. Some disillusioned team members left immediately and others lingered on, sleeping on friends' floors, not quite believing that there was nothing to it all. When Russian turned up at a team house they locked him in and called a local television news station which covered the story.

Bizarrely, however, this was far from the end of the tale. A production company decided to cover the fiasco as a factual programme genuinely pitched at Channel 4. Broadcast in December 2002, *The Great Reality TV Swindle* revealed the full extent of the deception and charted the reactions of the housemates to their dilemma. The production company Christmas Television drew on archive footage from the fake show, quizzed the contestants about the often heavy financial and social loses incurred by the hoax and finally pursued the culprit to his own front door to confront him with the fraud. Caz Gorham who was responsible for the real documentary was quoted as warning future reality TV applicants, 'when it comes to television, you should be very careful what you wish for, because things can come true in a way that you never imagined' (Smith 2002: 17).

This hoax is exemplary in the way it foregrounds many of the questions and criticisms aimed at the group-challenge reality show in particular and reality formats more generally. Exceptional though it is, it neatly brings together a number of the concerns often raised in relation to the genre. In exaggerated form, it invites discussion about the ethics of factual television and the exploitation of film subjects, and of their aspirations as participants in celebrity culture within a post-documentary context. It also dramatises the ongoing and usually taken-for-granted reflexivity of reality TV itself; which is often a platform for television to talk about itself. Gorham's warning that we should be careful what we wish for spurs the question of what it is exactly that contestants expect from their participation in such enterprises. John Corner (2002) suggests that the appeal of shows such as these is that they provide a new kind of 'experience' for the participants, an 'experiment in living' which offers new challenges and insights. The highly contrived and monitored circumstances of series such as *Castaway*, historical reconstructions such as *The Trench* and *The 1940s House* (C4), and the explicit psychological experimentation of *The Experiment* certainly point in this direction. Adverts for subjects to take part in *The Experiment* asked readers 'do you really know yourself?' and suggested that participation would 'change the way you think' (Brocks 2001). Contestants frequently refer to the expectation of gaining new 'experiences' and insights. A former participant of *The Living Soap*, one of the earliest reality house-share formats, who had reservations about her time in the house still conceded: 'But it was a great experience … I was from a protected, middle-class background but living in the house made me a lot more aware of people's different backgrounds' (in Midgley 2000).

Clearly, the attainment of continuing media celebrity or at least the chance to enter the media industries is part of the attraction for some people and speaks most directly to a youth audience already oriented towards public visibility as a marker of personal success. Several of Russian's subjects wanted to work in the media and had they succeeded, they would have been following earlier precedents. The first UK *Big Brother* winner, Craig Phillips, went on to work in daytime home/lifestyle programming and *Big Brother 3*'s winner Kate Lawler presents Channel 4's breakfast show *RI:SE*. Participants in *Celebrity Big Brother* and *I'm a Celebrity, Get Me Out of Here* spoke openly about how media coverage of their exploits might rehabilitate their image or revive their flagging careers. The perceived importance of publicity cannot be overstated and the paradoxes of reality programming are also the paradoxes of the modern mediated public realm. John Hartley summarises this beautifully when he says:

> while they don't exist as spaces and assemblies, the public realm and the public are still to be found, large as life, in the media … the popular media of the modern period, are the public domain, the place where and the means by which the public is created and has its being. (1992: 1)

From this perspective, the performance of citizenship is only verifiable when it is enacted through the media and contestants' desire to engage with the media at a highly visible level makes perfect sense within this logical framework.

Caz Gorham's warning to be careful what you wish for might well have resonated with contestants in other ways as debates continue about the degree of 'fairness' deployed in the representation of reality subjects. As readers will learn in later chapters, these debates have been ongoing since the onset of observational documentary. More recently, the highly respected current affairs programme *Panorama* (BBC, broadcast 12 November 2000) considered the issue of fair representation in reality TV to be an issue worthy of serious debate (and was itself accused of dumbing down for its pains). When interviewed on the programme, *Big Brother* contestant Melanie Hill complained, 'we had no idea what they were going to do with all the footage and what they did was manipulate it into our little stereotypes'. The use of stereotypes or, more charitably, of a range of representative characters, is part of the casting process. Participants of the earlier and critically-panned docusoap *The Living Soap*, many of whom went on to successful media careers, were selected for a range of stereotypes and placed into a house together. It took some time for housemates to work out why they had been selected. Nadia Agar-Smith recalled: 'At one point the cameras were rolling and the director said "How do you feel about your parents' divorce?" I couldn't believe it, I realised then they wanted someone from a broken home' (in Midgley 2000). This perception that particular types are sought out by producers can lead to a degree of cynicism about the whole procedure of not only contestant selection but also of the editing, presentation process and future media aspirations. Narinder Kaur, a contestant in the 2001 *Big Brother UK*, who felt obliged to leave her original job but could not subsequently break into the media industry, stated, 'I was portrayed as the mouthy, bitchy one. I don't know what's worse: being Asian in this country, being a *Big Brother* reject or being a woman, sadly, I'm all three.'[17]

While media celebrity may be the ostensible reason for the high number of applications to partake in reality programming there are, of course, less clear motivations and these, together with the undoubted pressures of the filming process have led to serious concerns about the well-being of contestants. The psychological complexity of film subjects' involvement in reality television and the potential psychological damage to those taking part was harshly pinpointed by the events of the Swedish prototype of *Survivor*, called *Expedition: Robinson* (SVT) which first ran in 1997. Located in Malaysia, *Expedition* gathered eight men and eight women and left them largely to fend for themselves in the now familiar manner for a cash prize. One amongst the group was 34-year-old Sinisa Savija, a half-Croatian and half-Serbian refugee, who was studying law in a small town in Sweden. Savija was apparently quiet, very keen and, although he was hugely excited about appearing on the show, seemed to accept his rejection after only four days on the island philosophically. Only a few weeks later, in July 1997, he committed suicide, nine weeks before the first edition was broadcast. The show's producers, fending off accusations by his family, implied that Savija already had mental health problems before he joined the show. His wife contends that it was his expulsion from the show that had damaged him. She claimed that he felt degraded as a person. Whatever the case, the fact remains that the programme, like many others, is a kind of popularity contest that a refugee, who only speaks the language haltingly, is unlikely to win. The eventual winner, a policeman from Stockholm called Martin Melin (police officers seem to do very well on *Survivor*-style programmes), clearly articulated the dynamics of the programme. Melin, who became famous overnight following his win, commented:

> It's a social game, that's how it works. I think I won because I was friends with everyone … It works the same way as it does in the country as a whole. If you are a refugee and you don't know the language and the culture – well you're not in the group. You're different. (In Addley 2002: 2)

This corroborates the suggestion that winners usually exhibit a quiet confidence; those that act like winners are most likely to win.[18]

Aside from the problematic exacerbation of individual traumas or phobias etc that are an integral part of incarceration in many of the enclosed worlds of reality game show formulas, there are broader questions here about the way that reality TV highlights and legitimates cultural discourses of interiority and also social interactivity that are a feature of late-capitalist therapeutic culture. Reality TV presents both surveillance and incarceration within a rule-bound micro-world as the mediated route to witnessing or experiencing authentic moments of self-revelation and/or emotional revelation. The opportunity to 'find oneself' or to 'experience' the incarceration and public monitoring is presented as a legitimate justification for appearing on shows like *Big Brother*. When debates about exploitation are raised, programme producers invariably refer to the amnesty of participant consent. However, the ethical concerns of preserving participants' rights and self-respect are balanced with the production's requirements to edit and repeat footage. Here the speed of selection processes for many reality TV shows and the volatile nature of the independent production sector accentuate long-held ethical difficulties of factual treatment of ordinary subjects and their potential exploitation.

Alongside the representation of reality TV participants is the related issue of audience perception of them. Audiences are now over-familiar with the extended debates in which the subjects of *Fame Academy* or *Big Brother* agonise over which of their companions has the most fans. But the film subjects who encountered reality TV as a new genre would have had little idea of what they were taking part in and there is likely to be a sensation of powerlessness in the face of technologies and media coverage over which they had little control. *Expedition* participant Savija was quoted as saying, 'They are going to cut away the good things that I did and make me look like a fool, to show that I was the worst and that I was the one that had to go' (in Addley 2002: 2). The degree of autonomy and editorial control exerted by film subjects over their own image is dependent upon the negotiations between them and the production company and especially in the early years of reality TV both parties might be forgiven for a certain amount of naïvety in this regard. Programme makers themselves might be excused too for failing to anticipate the possible traumas involved in public failure or success.

Individual filmmakers may well be quite scrupulous in their dealings with film subjects. Mandy Rose describes how the drunken couple of *Video Nation* were given the chance to veto the footage that they had chosen to film of themselves. Victoria Mapplebeck, who conceived and directed Channel 4's first documentary/web convergence series *Smart Hearts* (2001), in which the subjects Brendan and Claire who were in the throws of a disintegrating marriage, were filmed for television and the internet, argued that the couple had complete editorial control. Indeed, says Mapplebeck, they would, quite militantly, limit access to filming when they chose. She also provides a number of other examples where film subjects have refused to play the game, including an example from the South African *Big Brother*, in which contestant Brad, frustrated at being unable to walk away from the house, storms into the diary room and yells at Big Brother, 'I'm not your fucking hostage, your playmate, your puppet. Your rules Big Brother, not mine. Open this fucking door or I'll knock it down' (2002: 28). Other incidences include participants undertaking roof-top protests until they are permitted to see their families and a very irritated Fillipo in the Italian *Big Brother* allowing Big Brother thirty minutes to explain why he should remain in the house. It is unclear why this refusal to play in itself constitutes 'control' over the filmmaking process. Participants' ability to foil the production is not the same as being able to contribute constructively to representation and seems a somewhat feeble defence by media practitioners against accusations of exploitation or emotional voyeurism.

This exposure of raw emotion by contestants such as 'Bad Brad', suggests Mapplebeck quite approvingly, is what makes series such a *Smart Hearts* and *Big Brother* 'hard core' and a cut above lesser productions. Like pornography (her analogy) they both provide extensive 'access' and the opportunity to 'look' at their subjects unchallenged.[19] Far from signifying film subjects' control over the conditions of the production these moments of rage, despair and so on, arguably signify a loss of control. It is the sight of film subjects 'losing it' that is the guarantor of raw emotion; the equivalent of the pornographic 'money shot'. Laura Grindstaff, writing about the exhibition of emotion in talk shows, also uses the analogy and unpacks it further:

> The money shot is the focus ... ordinary people's willingness to sob, scream, bicker and fight on national television. The analogy to pornography is both deliberate and fitting. The climax of most sex scenes ... is the moment of orgasm and ejaculation offering incontrovertible 'proof' ... of 'real' sexual excitement and prowess. Pornography thus performs a kind of low-brow ethnography of the body, part of the documentary impulse ... Like pornography, daytime talk exposes people's private parts in public. It demands external visible proof of a guest's inner emotional state. (1997: 169)

Mapplebeck's example of the exposure of Nick Bateman, the housemate who 'cheated' on *Big Brother*, as 'hardcore' reality TV is rich in the detail of his visible humiliation. Having been confronted by his fellow film subjects:

Nick retreats to the bedroom and breaks down. The cameras zoom in. This close-up of Nick Bateman in tears is now a TV icon. He was a broken man, emotionally undressed … To this day I have not seen a documentary subject so exposed in such a sensational way … No voiceover, nothing to distract the viewer, you are looking at a man stripped aware to his lowest point, broken and unmasked and live to the nation … This is emotional pornography with an IOU. You the viewer are implicated. (2002: 28)

And of course, there is more to this than meets the eye. When working-class Liverpudlian builder Craig discovers Nick's duplicity and confronts him (together with the other five housemates) it becomes clear that, whether they wish it or not, Craig and Nick have become emblematic stereotypes of contrasting English masculinities. Nick, who was privately educated and worked in the City, said in his defence:

I just want to firstly apologise to you all for my actions. I'm not going to justify them but will give my reasons. I come from a big family and we tend to compete. I spent ten years at boarding school where people are constantly trying to put one over on you and I worked in an environment where people would stitch you up without batting an eyelid. (Gray 2000)

Following the exchange Craig's sister described her brother as a 'national hero', saying 'what happened could win him the show. Nick is an ex-public schoolboy with all that expensive education and Craig just wiped the floor with him. There is no way he should be voted out now' (in Lister 2000).[20] The confrontation episode generated the highest rating for Channel 4 since 1995. It also revitalised the media debate about the extent to which film subjects might be exploited. John Beyer, Director of the National Viewers and Listeners Association, was quoted as saying, 'the danger of programmes like this is they assume that individual privacy can be cynically surrendered in the interests of novelty television' (in Lister 2000). John de Mol does not deny the exploitation but argues that reality TV is far from unique in this regard:

We only exploit as any programme-maker exploits – be it in a game show, or even a news report which interviews the relative of someone who has just died in a plane crash … The people we cast are carefully selected, 100 per cent capable of understanding what they are getting involved in, and do so to satisfy their own goals. (in Carter 2000)[21]

Nick Bateman recognises this more than most, defending his actions in retrospect by arguing that he thought he was in a game show. It certainly could be argued that just as the contrived format and borrowed televisual grammar of reality programming cannot be condemned for being non-real, neither can film subjects be criticised for being deceitful or untruthful but rather should be regarded as operating on another level of the real, as part of the 'textualisation of public life' (Hartley 1992: 2). While the cases of Savija, Bateman and Kaur are patently different from one another in many respects, their reception by the media (together with others who have attracted opprobrium such as Jade Goody, discussed in chapter 6) has prompted concern about the potential psychological damage of enduring sustained media attention. Speaking at the International Television Festival in Edinburgh in August 2000 psychiatrist and ubiquitous media pundit Dr Raj Persaud observed that Bateman had been portrayed as a 'freak'. He noted that the contestants' 'full complexity' fails to emerge in the shows, which is potentially problematic and psychologically stressful.

Faking it

> 'Can we trust what we see? Reality TV – Real or Rip-off?'
> – Krishnan Gurumurthy on *Think TV*

The Nik Russian 'swindle' discussed above and the assertion by John de Mol that most television is game-playing are salutary reminders of the various levels at which reality TV may be understood as faux, fake or hoax. But stepping back from this we can acknowledge that even at the broadest level of representation questions have been raised about the production of the visual image and its approximation to reality. As Arild Fetveit has argued, there is a growing paradox evidenced in the increasing distrust of photographic images which the public knows can be digitally manipulated and the proliferation of certain visually-dependent fields of representation such as reality TV to which we repeatedly turn for truthful representation. Part of the explanation lies in the 'increased compartmentalisation of credibility' (Fetveit 1999: 797) in which audiences will take programmes on trust within certain generic and institutional contexts. This is fairly indisputable, as audiences must be guided by the truth-claims of programme makers and the contract entered into by the established conventions of genre. Fetveit also suggests that there is a psychological investment in believing in reality TV. We have lost the sense of 'connectedness' that was immanent in the pre-digital (less easily faked) photographic image between viewer and subject as the direct causal relationship between photographic subject and their representation is increasingly undermined. Arguably the appeal of reality TV lies in an attempt to reclaim what seems to be lost after digitalisation, to connect with other subjects across time and space (1999: 798). More broadly, our 'contract' with these formats is that we will accept them on their own terms as successfully realist genres; as representations which are the logical extensions of more than a century of endeavours to mechanically reproduce reality.

Historically, the photographic image, with its assumed indexical relation to the real, foregrounded the ethical status of factual representation: that which claims itself as a record of reality bears a certain weight and duty to the object of its fixing gaze and to its credulous audience.[22] This 'duty' has not always been well served and the public has become increasingly sensitised to fakery and reconstruction. Crucially, the photographic text's status as evidence and as adequate representation of the real has been called into doubt. The onset of digital culture in the 1990s further undermined the assumed relationship between photographic modes of representation and the capturing of reality. Digital culture, for example, challenges fundamental assumptions about the essence and function of the photographic image as 'true' representation. Digital information is essentially malleable and consequently, through techniques of electronic montage and manipulation, can radically alter the reality it represents. What we once trusted as 'pictures of reality' can be seamlessly and undiscernibly edited and modified. The rise of digital culture has fostered a broader scepticism towards factual media representations and their claims. Both the mechanism of representation and the world being represented are revealed as highly managed and intangible: reality is a chimera on the techno-cultural horizon.

Having noted this, it would be simplistic to argue that technological determinism has, in any measurable sense, simply *increased the distance* and lack of connectivity between the pro-filmic/photographic event (referent) and representation. Instead audiences are occupying a differently articulated relationship with non-fiction representations within digital culture, experiencing a 'fundamental transformation in the epistemological structure of our visual culture' (Timothy Druckney quoted in Robins 1996: 41).[23] One aspect of this transformation, initiated by televisual production, has been a familiarisation with the technical possibilities of image manipulation. John Ellis notes the fundamental changes to the imagery of factual programming since the 1980s in television culture. Production staff seized on the graphic and interpretative possibilities afforded by digital image manipulation to layer visual information with the aim of enhancing viewers' understanding and ordering of the incoherent world – the 'raw data of reality' – into interpretative frameworks (Ellis 2000: 100). Television's pervasive use of captions, image mixing and morphing has accustomed viewers to the more graphic aspects of digital image manipulation. The frequent use of digitised imagery has engendered knowing audiences who are visually literate in television's 'working over, placing and processing of the witnessed fragments of the real' (2000: 101). The fact that the televisual image is used as a malleable object rather than a 'picture of something' is an accepted aspect of televisual vocabulary. In news and current affairs, for example, visual tropes and graphic accessories complement narrative discourse and straight photographic imagery:

> Wars become maps, the economy becomes graphs, crimes become diagrams, political argument becomes graphical conflict, government press releases become elegantly presented bullet points … Digital image technology has at last given television the potential to use images to provide more than mere wallpaper (which is still a common term for images which accompany words without adding any further meanings). (2000: 97–100)

Ellis suggests that this signifies a representational maturity in which television is 'no longer tied to its mimetic base', but instead it uses photographic imagery 'as a springboard' to routinely reconstruct and reinterpret the factual referent (2000: 101). The displacement of straight photographic images by digitised interpretations has become one of the defining characteristics of the state-of-the-art factual programme maker, news editor or magazine programme editor. They are characterised by their readiness to adopt digital techniques and their skill in rendering such techniques unobtrusive (2000: 95):

> The frozen image of a refugee is treated to make a high-contrast background to a list of bullet points on the news; slow-motion bleached out images of holidaymakers provide

a background for specific images on the programme menu of a travel show. These are summarising images, encapsulating experiences or ideas for a grazing audience. (2000: 96)

Ellis illustrates one aspect of digital popularisation: an accretion of interpretative discourses of which the image is but a part. Yet, we would contend, people still hold a residual respect for the seeming raw or unembellished image of events – without graphs, morphing and stylistic treatment – albeit possibly accessed by digital means. For, despite the increasing recognition that new media technologies can manipulate and distort the real, they are also looked to as a conduit into other people's real worlds – 'multi-media reality' in Bazalgette's terms. And despite popular scepticism about the representation of reality evident in debates about fakery in factual programming there has not been a wide-scale rejection of realist modes of representation by audiences. Paradoxically, if the proliferation of electronic media platforms has challenged epistemological structures, it has also reinforced the popular investment in ontological realism. For the display of the self on the internet and on reality TV has, if anything, actually re-invoked the cultural emphasis on the individual subject as the guarantor of ontological knowledge. The individual subject is given primacy to the extent that, in some forms of digital culture such as websites and camcorder programming, he/she even participates in the production of new economies of realism.

chapter 2
Real lives, documentary approaches

This chapter charts the development of documentary styles that later, in attenuated form, impact on reality TV. Starting with the now critically acknowledged work of the Griersonian project, this chapter signals the modes we see as most influential on the later development of reality TV which includes Direct Cinema, *cinéma vérité* and Free Cinema. As with reality TV itself, we signal how these forms were in part a reaction to the purported objectivity of the Griersonian documentary makers. In all cases the attempt to faithfully record the real involves the negotiation of the camera's subjects; the use of new technology and its assistance in mobility and engagement with location shooting and the creative use of sound – whether the authoritative voiceover and the symbolic use of ordinary working-class accents to signify and underline authenticity – or the synchronous use of sound on location. We see the development of an increasingly reflexive relation to the camera as crucial to the knowing style of the personalised documentary and indeed the docusoap which we discuss in later chapters. Furthermore, as documentarists abandon their pretence at objectivity, the role of Direct Cinema and *cinéma vérité* informs and/or is in dialogue with the later push towards a more equal relationship between filmmaker and subject adopted by the docusoap (discussed in the following chapter).

What these different documentary styles share is a political concern, differently informed by socio-cultural context, to depict the lives of 'ordinary' people. Whether social realism is depicted in the instructive expositional mode of Grierson and his cohort or in the claims to a scientific observational standpoint seemingly without intervention offered by practices developed in the 1960s, the shared aim is a capture of actuality rooted in the depiction of the everyday. Our discussion of television as the site of a renewed post-war documentary movement highlights once again, in Britain certainly, the importance of class as a signifier of the authentic everyday. Realism becomes measured through the subject matter being reconstructed and that realism depends on notions of suffering, raw experience and personal struggle as emblems of the real. In the discussion of Ken Loach's work, for example, television is the new site for the popular broadcast of factual depictions of the previously *hidden condition* of the working classes. A public service broadcasting ethos is, here, the implicit backdrop to the conditions and opportunities for the depiction, however flawed and manipulated, of the lives of ordinary people; albeit as an educative example for the imagined television viewer at home. Revelation in this context is allied with realism: for all the documentaries we discuss share a common, although differently inflected, belief that to have suffered, to have struggled, to have subjected your life to the camera, becomes the near-guarantee of the production of a new form of knowledge for the viewer.

Showing and telling: *vérité* styles

> Far from being the faithful depiction of reality it is assumed to be, realism, through the various forms it has taken throughout its history, shows itself to be neither window nor mirror but a set of conventions.
> – Robert Lapsley and Michael Westlake (1988: 158)

The impact of the realist-documentary approach to filmmaking, initiated in the 1920s and 1930s, may still be seen in the factual and drama programming broadcast on British television. Despite the presence of other popular cinematic genres in the history of British film, the realist tradition, its conventions and the values commonly associated with it, remain dominant. This tradition privileges actuality and verisimilitude as a mode and working-class lives and social change as its subject matter. Key works of this tradition belong to John Grierson and his collaborators who, during the 1930s, rejected the more voyeuristic 'social explorers' approach which treated the landscape of the poor as an Anglicised 'heart of darkness' in favour of depictions that touched the 'social conscience' (Dodd & Dodd 1996: 42). The aim was to involve viewers in the general social process both at the micro level of the community and the macro level of the life of the nation. In Griersonian films the working class no longer appeared as an inchoate and enigmatic mass but instead was often figured as 'victim' or more frequently still, in films such as *Drifters* (1929) about fisherman and *Coalface* (1935) about mining, as a 'heroic' and usually masculine personification. This tradition contributed towards the project of unifying a nation during the inter-war period and beyond by explaining one class to another (but not affiliating one to the other) and also by helping to forge a masculine national identity on the eve of World War Two (Dodd & Dodd: 49–50).

Grierson, who coined the term 'documentary', happily acknowledged the role of aesthetics in the genre, describing the documentary process as the 'creative treatment of actuality'. The Documentary Movement which he spearheaded, consisted of state-funded films produced by the wonderfully named Empire Marketing Board Film Unit (1927–33) and the General Post Office Film Unit (1933–39), together with some commercially sponsored films, and was underpinned by both sociological and aesthetic agenda (Street 1997: 157). Grierson employed filmmakers with experimental film credentials including Humphrey Jennings whose poetic realism was informed by an interest in Surrealism, Alberto Calvacanti who had also been influenced by Surrealism and the French avant-garde, and Len Lye who had previously employed animation techniques (Street 1997: 157). A film such as Calvacanti's *Coalface*, already cited, is exemplary of the union of the sociological and aesthetic; featuring music by Benjamin Britten and words by the poetic W. H. Auden. Yet Grierson always maintained that this artistic sensibility could only be the 'by-product of a job of work done' and not an end in itself; the importance of the work should lie in its ability to represent the social world (in Kilborn & Izod 1997: 41–2). The influence of these films was such that during the 1940s critics maintained that an *essentially* British national cinema was one that adhered to the poetic realism of documentaries and their kin (Ellis 1996: 71). In the longer term, British cinema and television drama have frequently identified themselves as working in the shadow of this movement.

Following World War Two, the services of the Documentary Movement were less relevant. The Labour government had taken on board many of the social changes advocated by the movement in the form of educational and social reforms and corporate sponsors sought more direct advertising than could be effected in the earlier documentary celebrations of manufacturing and services. Cinema exhibition also increasingly marginalised documentaries in favour of feature films. Instead, it was television that was to revive documentary and sustain it into the twenty-first century (Kilborn & Izod 1997: 64). Griersonian realism, its values and its conventions, had an enduring influence on television's documentaries. Public service values are far more closely associated with the work of the Documentary Film Movement than with any of the other movements addressed below and its ethos was therefore easily assimilated into the declared role of national television to educate and inform its audience.

Griersonian conventions and their ideological import can be identified in contemporary television productions, with the BBC series *The Trial* (1994) cited as a notable example. John Izod and Richard Kilborn's analysis shows how the series, which was the first to gain access to British courts of justice, adhered to the established documentary modes of exposition and example in order to produce a 'responsible' programme which strongly promoted an argument that audiences would find convincing. Their analysis suggests that the adoption of these didactic modes in this instance also helped to protect the series against accusations of voyeurism as they have become signifiers of 'quality' documentary practice (1997: 94–8). Thus even when no longer regarded as the *only* template for ideal documentary filmmaking its 'standards' and aspirations (to give insight into contemporary and historical realities) remain a benchmark of good practice. As such they have also become the measure against which the 'lesser' output of contemporary factual television, in the form of reality television and docusoaps, has usually been found wanting (see Kilborn 2000).

The French *cinéma vérité* tradition and the filmmaking of the American Direct Cinema school have also been identified as influences in the development of British television documentary, particularly observational films (fly-on-the-wall and docusoaps) and other forms which are more properly designated 'reality TV'.[1] In contrast with the Griersonian model, both approaches eschewed the social responsibility agenda that required a degree of propaganda and exposition, preferring a more consistently observational mode. The two approaches do have some elements in common: valuing intimacy, immediacy and the 'real' and embracing the 'flaws' and edginess of more spontaneous styles of filming. Their work exhibited a commitment to the depiction of ordinary people and their lives that was ground-breaking in its sense of accessibility and intimacy. Both movements were aided by changing technologies that allowed a refined sense of immediacy and a sense of 'being there' at the pro-filmic event. In some academic and practitioner accounts of documentary history these two modes have been conflated, as the American school (and later British television documentarists) also adopted the term '*vérité*', but there are major differences between them (see Winston 1995: 148–69).

Direct Cinema, exemplified by the work of Frederick Wiseman, Don Pennebaker, Richard Leacock and Robert Drew, favoured discrete observational filming with no attempt at analysis but instead 'revelation through situation' (Winston 1995: 150). It provided an evidential basis on which audiences would be expected to assess the facts of a situation for themselves. Rather than construct a 'temporal framework' in the form of organised storytelling or rhythmic patterning through a shooting script, observational films chose to rely on editing to generate a sense of lived experience and time passing. In its idealised form they would avoid entirely commentary, self-reflexivity, extra-diegetic music and so on, preferring synchronous sound, long takes, indirect speech and overheard dialogue; characteristics that chime with those of later docusoaps and some forms of reality TV (Nichols 1991: 38–9).

As Bill Nichols notes, these observational techniques are especially suited to the representation of uneventfulness and of time passing, which it should be noted, is a staple of 24/7 reality TV:

> 'Dead' or 'empty' time unfolds where nothing of narrative significance occurs but where the rhythms of everyday life settle in and establish themselves. In this mode of representation, each cut or edit serves mainly to sustain the spatial and temporal continuity of observation rather than the logical continuity of an argument or case … the sense of an underlying temporal or spatial continuity prevails, one which is consonant with the moment of filming, making observational cinema a particularly vivid form of 'present tense' representation. (1991: 40)

These films foster a sense of unmediated connectedness between the space and duration of the pro-filmic event and the film shoot which was to anticipate the sense of immediacy and unrolling of time over the longer time-span of reality TV programming. They shun the structural logic of argument in favour of a temporal logic of continuity and flow. For these documentarists the story and its dramatisation must be inherent within the film and any narration weakens its impact. In the making of these 'cutting edge' documentaries, 'narration is what you do when you fail' (Drew 1983: 273). Writing in the 1980s, Robert Drew argued that the best potential route for the popularisation of documentary lay in the operation of what he refers to as 'filmic-dramatic principles'. Like the movies, the most accessible documentaries should refrain from controlling narration: 'Films that tell stories directly, through characters who develop through actions in dramatic lines – these have the possibility at least of allowing the power of film to build' (1983: 271). This analogy with film suggests a rather simplistic understanding of the filmic principles of mainstream movies. The success of film realism, to which Drew refers, lies partly in the *ideological* realism that masks its naturalising and mythical function by avoiding drawing any attention to its technological construction through features such as camera-work, sound and editing. It sutures the viewer into the text through a realist film grammar of narration, field/reverse field and eyeline match that Direct Cinema is unlikely to achieve with its unscripted filming even if it wanted to. Fiction film's conventions have become so established as to become naturalised and accepted by audiences as a 'realistic' mode of representation. And they are accepted, not only because of these embedded conventions, but also because the films broadly conform to audience's assumptions about 'what life is like' (Ellis 1982: 63); assumptions which a socially-informed radical documentary practice would presumably wish to challenge.[2]

It might well be the case that Drew's analogy with fiction filmic principles is an attempt to bridge the ideological gap between what John Caughie refers to as the 'documentary gaze' and the 'dramatic look'. The 'documentary gaze' refers to the non-fiction modes which 'observe the social space and the figures within it … exploiting the "objectivity" of the camera to constitute its object as "document"'. This stands in contrast to the dramatic imperative which 'orders narrative space and gives the spectator a place within it in a process of quite literal identification' (Caughie 2000: 111; see also Caughie 1980). The 'classic paradox' here is that the two, while both achieving a kind of 'realism', do so in radically different ways: one through the establishment of conventions that become invisible and the other by virtue of the very visibility of the medium: rough and ready filming, and imperfections of all kinds (ibid.). Drew is seeking to formulate the conditions of possibility for a *dramatic* observational documentary practice that refuses to intervene in any explicit way in the pro-filmic event – if achievable it would be the epitome of the dramatisation of everyday life.

It cannot be said, however, that Direct Cinema operated outside of mediation in its presentation of reality. Simply picking up a camera and selecting something to film is an intervention in the flow of real-life events and Drew's filmic-dramatic principles, even if they were achievable in documentary form must, by definition, result in seeking order within the often chaotic flux of the everyday and consequently a modification of the everyday. The promotion of Direct Cinema as 'on the hoof' filmmaking also belies the strategies used to shape programmes in the absence of orienting exposition. Pre-production work can include extensive research and planning of the programming, the choice of subjects such as celebrities or authority figures can in itself generate dramatic tension, opinion can be voiced through proxy figures within the diegesis such as journalists and authorities and post-production work can be used to enhance the 'natural' temporal flow as Nichols, cited above, has observed (Kilborn & Izod 1997: 68–9). All of these subtle strategies assemble an organising grammar of observational documentary that in themselves artificially create a sense of immediacy and 'easy' realism.

These cinematographers certainly achieved works of enduring influence and impact. The main problematic of the observational form arises not because of what was achieved but because the filmmakers' stated intentions to replicate reality have come to be seen as increasingly naïve and untenable. The exponents of this brand of observational documentary were actually very proscriptive, banning, for example, rehearsals, dissolves, film lights and interviews: curiously, 'the filmmaking movement which seemed to stand for iconoclasm and freedom became one of the most codified and puritanical' (Macdonald & Cousins 1996: 250). And while its exponents acknowledged that the filmmaker's perception is itself selective they heavily downplayed the modification of reality activated by the presence of cameras and crew on film subjects.[3] Richard Leacock, for example, contended in interview:

> You can make your presence known, or you can act in such a way as not to effect them. Also, of course, it depends on the intensity of what's happening to them. But we don't think that it effects people very much, at least I don't. (1963: 256)

Leacock is not only downplaying the presence of film crew as actors (i.e. *active* subjects) in the pro-filmic space, he is also, by implication, diminishing the ideological impact of their presence in the unfolding of Direct Cinema's particular brand of realism. Direct Cinema depended for its credibility on an absolute trust in the filmmaker's vision of the truth of any given scenario but, paradoxically, it denied that the filmmaker, *as an auteur*, would influence events. David Maysles, who together with his brother Albert, worked on some of the early classics of Direct Cinema, asserted that, 'objectivity is just a personal integrity: being essentially true to the subject and capturing it essentially' (in Blue 1964: 262). Here objectivity is contrived as a natural attribute of the skilled filmmaker. For these films to be accepted as truthful there is a prerequisite that the audience have an absolute confidence in this personal integrity and in the presentation of footage as 'evidence'. It is, perhaps, for this reason that French *vérité* filmmaker Jean Rouch commented wryly that American-style *vérité* should be more properly named 'cinema-sincerity' (Leven 1969: 265).

In Direct Cinema the consensual relationship or contract between filmmaker and viewer is underscored by technology. From the end of the 1950s the scaling down of the production crew and the miniaturisation of equipment enhanced the viewer's sense of unmediated access (Kilborn & Izod 1997: 67). The vision of the viewer is allied with the film-maker's vision via the camera and synchronous sound. Albert Maysles stated: 'We shoot everything with one camera. You, as a viewer, become one camera. You are not two or three cameras that are impossibly in two situations at one time' (in Blue 1964: 260). Rather than demand that the viewer judge the film on an evidential basis alone, this ideological linkage between viewer, filmmaker and camera demands, in fact, that they also have faith in the perception and judgement of the filmmaker and in the camera's capacity to directly capture reality in an unobtrusive and non-directional manner.

Cinéma vérité, on the other hand, was overtly interventionist; interrupting film subjects, interacting with them and even filming their responses to rough-cuts of film footage. This movement, most often associated with the work of French anthropologist Jean Rouch, worked within a tradition that was more auteur-based and essayistic (Winston 1995: 184). In contrast with the American school, Rouch was more than happy to acknowledge that the presence of cameras affected film subjects but he also argued that their presence prompted them to be *more* truthful and more authentically themselves (an idea that continues to fuel popular fascination with current reality TV). For Rouch, *vérité* does not simply 'show' – it is also a mode that composes an argument, overtly presenting a point of view and even becoming a catalyst for action. Rouch explains this well:

> I go in the subway, I look at it and I note that the subway is dirty and that the people are bored – that's not a film. I go on the subway and I say to myself, 'These people are bored, why? What's happening, what are they doing here? Why do they accept it? Why don't they smash the subway? Why do they sit here going over the same route everyday?' At that moment you can make a film. (In Roy-Leven 1969: 266)

Erik Barnouw (1974: 245) asserted that the difference between the Direct Cinema and the *cinéma vérité* filmmaker was that the former took a camera into a difficult context in anticipation of a crisis and the latter tried to precipitate one. There was certainly a revolutionary aspect to the *vérité* approach and one of Rouch's central criticisms of his American colleagues was that their observational style instigated a mixture of voyeurism and passivity in audiences. In interview, Rouch cites Frederick Wiseman's controversial film *Titicut Follies* (1967) as an example. Wiseman made the film to show his law students the kinds of conditions that their future clients might encounter. In fact, *Titicut Follies'* disturbing depiction of the negligence and brutalities of the criminal justice system's treatment of the criminally insane attracted the wrath of the authorities of the day.[4] But Rouch condemns it: 'There's no hope. Finally it's a film of despair ... There's a fascination with horror here ... it's a certified report, which could perhaps be interpreted as a cynical and sadomasochistic report' (in Roy-Leven 1969: 268). When his interviewer suggests that *Titicut Follies* is merely presenting the truth of the situation, Rouch replies: 'Then you have to speak, you have to say it. I would like him [the filmmaker] to say something, say what the thesis is. Does it mean that we have to suppress this police system ... It's not obvious' (ibid). Brian Winston makes a similar criticism of a key film of the Direct Cinema movement called *Primary* (1960). He asserts that the novelty of the filmic techniques employed masked its refusal to engage with 'social meaning'. The film features a continuous 75-second take of Senator John Kennedy greeting members of the crowd as he makes his way to the dais. The camera, held high and using a wide-angle lens, captures the scene. Winston comments, 'The politics of the situation ... remain hidden. We learn nothing of the issues ... except tangentially because the people being filmed happen, as it were, to be concerned with little else' (1995: 152).

The influences of *cinéma vérité* and Direct Cinema in terms of how they organised the field of vision are perceptible in subsequent television programming, although it was the latter that was destined to motivate, most profoundly, the development of television documentary practice. Direct Cinema, in particular, influenced Britain's National Film School, which fostered in its students a commitment to minimising manipulation and authorial intervention with the objective of replicating reality as closely as possible. Television documentary, benefiting from technological developments which facilitated increased mobility and synchronous sound recording, embraced the impulse to minimise mediation and allowed itself, 'to lay a stronger claim to the real than was possible previously' (Winston 2000: 22). However, the legacy of *cinéma vérité* is also apparent in variants of the interactive documentary in which features of the *vérité* style have become thoroughly normalised. The use of journalistic interview, editing to reveal contradictions in testimony and argument, the conspicuous presence of the filmmaker and/or crew and the use of commentary that reflects on the filmmaking process are among the distinguishing features of the work of documentarists such as Errol Morris, Michael Moore and Nick Broomfield. The economic and cultural requirements of television have reshaped both Direct Cinema and *cinéma vérité* approaches to fit the medium. Exceptionally, some documentarists may make single films for cinema exhibition (such as Moore and Broomfield), others, such as Roger Graef, Molly Dineen and Paul Watson, make series on a single subject and a few make a variety of films for a scheduled slot (such as Morris). But many single documentaries appear in series that organise productions according to subject (institutions, the domestic, individuals) or ways of seeing (observational, interactive or hybrids of the two) and fit in with marketing and scheduling requirements (Kilborn & Izod: 73–4).

The attitude of Free Cinema

> When [these films] came together, we felt they had an attitude in common. Implicit in this attitude is a belief in Freedom, in the importance of people and in the significance of the everyday.
> – Free Cinema Programme 1956

The early British Documentary Film Movement, Direct Cinema and *cinéma vérité* all impacted on the documentary practices of television documentary. Less debated in the history of television documentary has been the place of a British, rather short-lived, movement of documentary film practice known as 'Free Cinema'. Originating in the mid-1950s, Free Cinema favoured hand-held cameras, real locations and a sometimes raw style that echoed many of the techniques of *cinéma vérité* and Direct Cinema. From 1956, the Free Cinema project (which was not as coherent as this label might suggest) sought to make films outside of the established system. It attempted to step outside of the ideological and aesthetic conventions sustained by earlier pioneers of documentary and which were imposed by the commercially-driven film industry of the period. The movement consisted of documentaries, polemical articles and six programmes of organised film screenings between 1956 and 1959.[5] Screenings were organised at London's National Film Theatre by young critics and filmmakers such as Karel Reisz, Tony Richardson, John Fletcher, Lindsay Anderson, Lorenza Mazzetti and Walter Lassally and included not only films made by the group but also foreign films by filmmakers including Claude Chabrol, François Truffaut and Roman Polanski that were considered to be working in a similar vein.

The first programme of shorts included *O Dreamland* (Anderson), which cast a critical and satirical eye on the popular pleasures of the seaside amusement park, *Momma Don't Allow* (Richardson and Reisz) focusing on a jazz club and *Together* (Mazzetti) which focused on the lives of two deaf mute East End dockers. These films, although distinctive from one another, constituted a new style of documentary whose influence was also being seen in television productions (especially on commercial television) by the early 1960s. Their subject matter was popular culture, youth culture and the working classes more generally. Images were allowed to stand without comment and their subjects were closely scrutinised through close-up and sound. All four filmmakers signed the manifesto included in the programme notes cited above and which was drafted by Lindsay Anderson to launch the programme. These screenings attracted media attention, including a spot on television on the current affairs programme *Panorama*. Anderson has described how there was no intention to continue the series; instead the programme had really been put together to showcase the three films. However, as other foreign and British films appeared that were sympathetic to the Free Cinema ideal a one-off event became transformed into a 'movement' (see Anderson 1977).

Free Cinema sounded a call to arms against the conformist social conservatism of a previous generation. The term 'free' condensed several concepts: a rejection of the film industry's commercially-driven constraints (especially associated with Rank) and a consequent liberty to adopt a personal vision in both style and subject matter. In this context it also differentiated these practitioners from 'experimental' filmmakers whose emphasis on technique or on technical innovation could be alienating to audiences and cloud the film's meaning. However, this approach should not imply a disinterestedness in aesthetics and technical innovation but rather an agenda 'driven by aesthetics and attitude' together (Dixon & Dupin 2001: 29) which married a new style with a radical social conscience to produce a new variant of 'poetic realism'. The term connoted a new artistic and *technical* mobility and flexibility in practice; moving filmmaking out of the studio onto the streets, using lower budgets to make more films and using 16mm rather than the more 'professional' 35mm film (see Ellis 1977).

'Free Cinema' then was actually an umbrella term for a variety of outputs including public-relations films such as Lindsay Anderson and Guy Brenton's 1954 *Thursday's Children* (made for a school for deaf children) and Anderson's 1957 Ford Motor Company-sponsored film *Everyday Except Christmas* (see Barnouw 1993: 231). The latter was one of three films made for Ford's 'Look at Britain' series, which also included Karel Reisz's *We Are the Lambeth Boys* (1959) featuring members of a South London Youth Club and John Fletcher's *The Saturday Men* (1962) which looked at West Bromwich Albion Football Club. The subject matter of these films seems commonplace today but was clearly unorthodox at the time, taking ordinary culture seriously and contravening the assumption that documentary should present a selective and ideal picture of national life. Anderson (1977) recalls, for example, how the British Selection Committee refused to submit *Everyday Except Christmas* for the Tours Documentary film festival 'on the grounds that it didn't show an aspect of Britain which merited official publicity' (it went on to win the Grand Prix). The message was clear that the divisions between high culture and popular culture were continuing to be patrolled by the old guard of cultural criticism.

The Free Cinema filmmakers were arguably influenced much more strongly by the European *nouvelle vague* than by the earlier British documentary tradition of the 1930s and the work of John Grierson, of whom they were explicitly critical. Their work was, however, marked by the Griersonian emphasis on social democratic values and the valorisation of the lives of ordinary people. They also infused documentary with their own brand of poetic realism – albeit one not imposed from the 'outside' in the form of extra-diegetic spoken poetry and music (as in *Coalface,* above) but one seeming to originate organically from the editing process. As Brian Winston (1995: 63) convincingly argues, Grierson and his followers failed as mass communicators – despite (or perhaps partly because) of their educational agenda – but they did, arguably, succeed in moving cinema towards a more socially conscious position. The practitioners of Free Cinema attempted to move beyond the overtly pedagogical imperative of their British predecessors and were keen to make socially inclusive and accessible films. In 1956 in an article entitled 'Stand up! Stand up!', which featured in the influential film magazine *Sight and Sound*, Anderson called for a socially inclusive cinema as well as for the pursuit of the filmmaker's personal creative vision.[6] A year later in 1957 Anderson declared, 'The cinema is an industry … But it is something else as well: it is a means of making connections … I want a Britain in which the cinema can be respected and understood by everyone' (in Hill 1986: 128). Having said this, while the later feature films of Anderson and his collaborators (New Wave or 'kitchen sink' drama) did reach out to wide audiences, the intellectualism and sometimes idiosyncratic vision of their documentaries would not achieve the same success.

It was a perpetual struggle to emerge from Grierson's shadow. Even as semi-independent producers they had to contend with external pressures to conform to established practices of documentary filmmaking. For example, the Ford Company insisted on a voiceover for *We Are the Lambeth Boys* which rendered it more conventional and more judgemental, substantiating Winston's argument that the official funding and production of films, together with their romanticism, worked against their potential for *radical* social meaning. Until this point documentaries had been associated with either national or commercial prestige or with the general 'social betterment' of the nation. In 1957 critic John Berger noted with approval how the 'Free Cinema Three' programme had 'triumphantly broken through this propriety barrier'. Importantly, Berger recognised the movement as a timely intervention and identified a new cultural turn to 'reality'. He observed approvingly:

> It reveals a new kind of vision. Every time an art needs to revitalise itself after a period of formalism … artists will turn back to reality: but their attitude to reality, and the way they interpret it, will depend upon the particular needs of their time. That is why realism can never be defined as a style, and can never mean an acquiescent return to a previous tradition. (Berger 1957: 12)

A year earlier, Gavin Lambert asked, in *Sight and Sound*, how it had happened that these images of ordinary people, of the pleasures and alienation of ordinary lives, had been previously so under-represented. There was a clear sense that these films marked a cultural turn in the non-fiction representation of popular culture and everyday life. But there was also a recognition that 'real' does not mean un-constructed or naturalistic or unmediated. The real is all about artifice: 'Here, at any rate, are "real" people in *dramatised* situations, conveying their own truth and illustrating human behaviour in a way that, it is no exaggeration to say, has never (Jennings excepted) appeared before on the British screen' (Lambert 1956: 17, emphasis in original).

The notable British antecedent to this movement, cited by Lambert, was documentary filmmaker Humphrey Jennings whose films such as *Heart of Britain* (1941), *Listen to Britain* (1942) (which has no commentary at all) and *Fires Were Started* (1943) married documentary with allegory and a distinctive, sometimes poetic, personal vision.[7] Jennings was a member of Grierson's GPO Unit and his best-known films were made as wartime propaganda. Yet in 1954 Lindsay Anderson was to describe him as 'the only real poet the British cinema has yet produced' (1954: 53). In these early films Anderson spies the fashioning of a distinctive style:

> A style based on a peculiar intimacy of observation, a fascination with the common-place thing or person that is significant precisely because it is commonplace, and with the whole pattern that can emerge when such commonplace, significant things and people are fitted together in the right order. (1954: 54)

Bearing this description in mind, the debt to Jennings may be seen, for example, in the opening sequence of *Everyday Except Christmas*. Two men are filmed loading their truck, in the middle of the night, with produce from a Sussex market garden. As they drive through the empty, but brightly-lit roads and streets into London the soundtrack moves from the final moments of the BBC radio light entertainment service with its national anthem to a continuity announcer wishing everyone a safe night. The sequence forms associations between an 'imagined community' and its sovereign, between the reassuring voice of the BBC announcer and the quiet suburban streets where those who will buy the groceries that are passing by their doors in the delivery truck are already sleeping.

The sequence stresses the continuities and routines of everyday life. The narrator, speaking in a lilting Welsh male voice, describes the journey to London as one of many that will be made that night and every night. The journey and the subsequent Covent Garden market scenes give primacy to the visual over the spoken word. Visual patterning and repetition is achieved by lingering shots on boxes of flowers and produce as they are unloaded and stacked for elaborate visual displays. The rhythm and the busy-ness of the marketplace flows through the film, with porters, buyers and sellers all working with apparently unthinking regularity like worker ants. Towards the end of the film market porters are slumped tiredly after twelve-hour shifts and at the end of the day elderly women who sell flowers on the streets and raggedly dressed old men arrive to sift the discarded leftovers for anything salvageable. But these and other voices are smothered beneath the soundtrack that segues from music to authorial voice. Where voices are heard commenting on prices, food quality and so on; these voices are usually disembodied, patched into a montage soundtrack.[8] The film focuses on everyday life and ordinary people but its aesthetic dominates any social commentary. The poorest people who live on the fringes of the marketplace, making-do on what others have left behind are given no voice; neither are the porters who seem to stride so stoically throughout the day with heavy boxes on their heads. In this sense *Everyday Except Christmas* is not about individual lives but about the life of commerce, trade and the marketplace, and its servicing by individuals. Through its use of music, visual patterns and recurring motifs it presents an abstract and emblematic picture of the nation's commercial life.

The observational documentary and its aesthetic philosophy promoted by Free Cinema continued in the films of the television production company Unit 5/7, whose mainly Manchester-based members were allied to the Free Cinema movement. Their work is exemplified by *Tomorrow's Saturday* (1962) which was sponsored by the British Film Institute. Directed by Mike Grigsby, the film was strongly reminiscent of *Everyday Except Christmas*, presenting a montage of sound and images, impressions really, of a typical Saturday at Blackburn, a milling town in the North of England. The only commentary, if so it could be described, is a patchwork of voices and some street songs that explicitly critiqued those in power. Regarding it now, it seems shocking that such obvious poverty existed side by side with the growing affluence of the period. But no comparisons or juxtapositions are presented in the film between rich and poor and it seems to be devoid of social comment in spite of its visual revelations. The heritage of the lyric poeticism of Humphrey Jennings is prominent, together with a Griersonian attention to the social conditions of ordinary people. If the function of documentary is political then its politicisation is apparent mainly in this centrality of ordinary people. Grigsby has commented, 'I think it is incumbent on us … to be looking at our society and trying to find those resonances, trying to hear those voices, to give people space' (in Kilborn & Izod 1997: 7). The film is intrinsically observational and it does afford a representational 'space' for its subjects but it is hard to imagine, even in 1962, how it could generate political debate without some form of commentary. Also, like most documentary practice, it precluded the possibility of its subjects having some autonomy over the filming process and offered no chance for them to express a point of view. Instead subjects are treated as always already there in the manner encapsulated by John Caughie: 'the rhetoric of the documentary … constitutes its object – the community, the social environment, the working class – as simply there, unproblematic, always already complete, "extras" waiting to be filmed' (2000: 122).

These ordered scenes of everyday life and the 'silence' of some film subjects, trigger the question of how the treatment of the subjects of this documentary movement should be understood. Free Cinema documentary and the New Wave feature films that followed certainly placed ordinary people *centre stage*. The feature films were distinguished by both filmmaking techniques and subject matter; preferring location shooting, unknown regional actors, some improvisation and a new emphasis on the experiences of the industrial working class in the context of a socially-committed cinema (see Hill 1996: 127–8). Anderson himself asserted, 'I want to make people – ordinary people, not just top people – feel their dignity and importance' (in Hill 1986: 128). And indeed, films such as *Everyday Except Christmas* afforded its subjects a significant role in the life of the community. Film critics such as John Berger (1957) acknowledged this, regarding Anderson as achieving a more easy relationship between filmmaker and subjects who are neither overly scrutinised nor patronised but treated 'humanely'. But the phrase *centre stage* is used advisedly, because Free Cinema produced a *dramaturgical* depiction of ordinary life, as ordered and visually pleasing *and as distant* as any theatre choreography.

Other, more cautious, contemporaries noted a certain distanciation between filmmaker and subject in these films. In 1969 Ray Durgnat wrote of *O Dreamland* and *Momma Don't Allow*: 'Anderson's vehement ambivalence to the common people and Reisz's cool calculated tact dampen one's enthusiasm a little. We're too obviously in the presence of outsiders to the society they claim to be revealing to us' (in Dixon & Dupin 2001: 29). *O Dreamland* was especially scathing in its depiction of ordinary people and their apparently enthusiastic embrace of cheap and transient entertainment. Like Richard Hoggart's *The Uses of Literacy* (1957) (which extended literary criticism to the criticism of working-class popular culture and questioned the 'shiny barbarism' of modern popular pastimes) but without the affection and respect that tempered it, Anderson's film was fiercely judgemental. John Hill's description of the arcade scene in which visitors are shown viewing re-enactments of executions and so on, sums up the film's attitude and the manner in which it created 'the overall pattern of degrading spectacle and lethargic spectators':

> This disdain is further marked by composition, fragmenting the spectators' bodies and imprisoning them behind bars, as well as editing, whereby model dummies and spectators are intercut in the suggestion of a parallel ... the raucous laughter of a model policeman is heard ... it quickly becomes something of a motif, punctuating the film at a variety of stages and accumulating thematic significance, mocking the spectators. (Hill 1986: 152)

It seems that as one of the interpretative approaches to the working-class culture of the period, observational documentary fell short of its social democratic aims, even as it made a space for the representation of ordinary people. In the case of Free Cinema, and the New Wave feature films that followed, their representation of ordinary life was firmly placed within the context of a cultural critique that was already being articulated in the intellectual debates of the day. As Carolyn Steedman's (1986: 10) eloquent exposition of a gendered working-class life demonstrates, the cultural criticisms of working-class life written in the late 1950s (and indeed much later in the 1980s), while ground-breaking, were flawed. Accounts such as Hoggart's, cited above, may have put working-class culture on the intellectual map but they also served to consolidate the absence of psychological complexity which had always been a problematic feature of working-class representation from 'the outside'. Within this framework it was perhaps inevitable that filmmaking would sometimes slip into perpetuating the picture, which Caughie draws above, of the great mass of people and their lives as unchanging and homogenous and always already there – only waiting to be filmed.

Television and the 'unconsidered corners'

Free Cinema nonetheless exhibited a respect for working-class culture; albeit bound together with scepticism about the mass entertainment they consumed and a politicised critique of the social and economic conditions of the period. The catch-phrase for the era was the assertion by Prime Minister Harold Macmillan to his electorate that they 'had never had it so good'. For a few years at least, it seemed that Britain was becoming more confident, more stable and more affluent. It was suggested that the unemployment and class struggles of a previous generation had been overcome (Davies & Saunders 1983: 20–1). The standard of living was rising and within a few years it became an expectation among ordinary people that they would own washing machines, refrigerators and television sets. By the mid-1960s, however, the growing realisation that social problems continued to reproduce inequalities instigated a 'revolt against complacency' among academics, writers and those in the entertainment industries whose productions, such as Ken Loach's television docudrama *Cathy Come Home*, informed a national audience about social disparities (Davies & Saunders 1983: 39).

Cinema's main rival, television, also came in for criticism by the new radicals, along with the older forms of mass entertainment pilloried in *O Dreamland*, as an emblem of complacency and enforced passivity. Television featured as a signifier of claustrophobic domestication, consumerism and enervating mass culture in a number of the New Wave films which followed in the wake of Free Cinema (see Hill 1986: 153–4). The 'angry young man' railed against the capitulation of his father's generation to cosy domesticity. Television was thereby figured as a feminised form, part of a broader smothering of masculine working-class radicalism, that conflated class struggle with the battle of the sexes and which led to the fashioning of working-class heroism as intrinsically masculine and naturally central to the narrative of class struggle. Steedman notes that the working-class stories of the late 1950s and early 1960s, such as John Braine's 1957 novel *Room at the Top* (reworked as Jack Clayton's 1959 film of the same film), failed, in this sense, to provide a framework with which women could identify: 'That framework was itself ignorant of the material stepping-stones of our escape: clothes, shoes, makeup ... [Women] could not be the heroines of the conventional narratives of escape' (1986: 15) because they were somehow rendered classless (and thereby invisible) by the assumption of their social mobility that was underpinned by consumerism.

Ironically perhaps, it was television that was to become the most commonly used and most accessible arena for both the screening of documentary and as a space for the representation of ordinary people – men and women. There were practical reasons for this transition from big screen to television set. In interview, Karel Reisz has commented that there never really was an effective distribution system for the movement's documentary films and that television, especially in the form of the commercial company Granada, provided a far better forum for innovative filmmakers (BFI, 2001). Producer Tony Garnett has commented on the timeliness of television and its appropriateness as a medium of socially-orientated communication in the days just prior to the launch of commercial television in 1955:

> Television was the most exciting place to be ...There was just two channels, but the whole nation, it seemed, was watching and talking about it the next day. Our families did not go to the theatre ... and British cinema was dead in the water. Several of us entered television ... because we were politically motivated. We wanted to occupy that screen to show the Britain we knew, to incite, to express our anger. (Garnett 2000: 12)

Garnett's recollections support Penelope Houston's (1963) view, expressed in her book on the contemporary film industry, that there was a perception in the early 1960s that cinema was no longer *the* mass medium. She notes, for example, that the influential Griersonian cinema documentary *Housing Problems* (1935), which revealed some appalling living conditions, would easily be matched in impact and audience reached by a single episode of the television documentary series *Panorama*. The moment of Free Cinema was actually timely in the sense that it was able to contribute to the style and tone of both television documentary and social-issue drama. Its attention to the representation of ordinary lives intersected not only with radical theatre (which also went on to influence television drama and documentary) and critiques of ordinary culture such as *The Uses of Literacy* but also with the changing cultural scene of television. The advent of programmes such as *That Was The Week That Was* (1962), which broke the unspoken codes of respect by satirising the establishment, and *Coronation Street* (1960), which borrowed the conventions of British New Wave feature films to present a recognisable 'social realist' picture of working-class life, suggested that the public was ready for more challenging and more 'realistic' explorations of social and cultural relations (see Houston 1963: 115–16).[9] *Coronation Street*, in particular, was conceived of as a realistic portrayal of working-class northern life. Although sometimes humorous and often nostalgic, it seemed to convey a less mediated reality by, among other things, harnessing the rhythms of everyday life, with multiple characters and storylines, to the continuous serial format. Television was becoming increasingly important as the medium of representation of ordinary people *to* ordinary people. In Houston's view, filmmakers were battling against the British film industry's 'natural conservatism' and outmoded industrial working practices that meant films could not be made on the very low budgets employed by the French *nouvelle vague* filmmakers. Consequently, television could come into its own in challenging accepted ideas and ways of working. She suggests that television documentary series such as *Monitor* allowed more scope for creativity than the 'sponsor-dominated world' of documentary cinema and that this autonomy was crucial. Houston comments: 'simply by getting about, moving easily up and down Britain, and poking its cameras into some unconsidered corners, television loosened things up all round' (1963: 116).

The late 1950s and early 1960s was also the time when television became firmly established in working-class households as both a sign of respectability and as a pastime leading to ever-increasing audience numbers. The proportion of the adult population who owned a television set increased from 4 per cent in 1950 to 80 per cent by 1960 (Gorman & McLean 2003: 132). Michael Young and Peter Wilmott's 1957 study of working-class families in East London noted that for women especially, the television mast was a status symbol and the outward appearance of respectability (1957: 156).[10] Television also compensated for a lack of amenities in poorer areas so that, in this study, researchers discovered that the possession of television sets was far higher on a relatively culturally isolated council estate than in nearby Bethnal Green, which had a greater variety of facilities and entertainment. The authors note:

> Instead of going out to the cinema or the pub, the family sits night by night around the magic screen ... In one household the parents and five children of all ages were paraded around it in a half circle at 9pm ... the two-month-old baby was stationed in its pram in front of the set. The scene had the air of a strange ritual. (Young & Wilmott 1957: 143)[11]

At this time, viewers such as these could access a growing number of documentary and current affairs programmes and 'live' events as well as the mainstream light entertainment that had characterised BBC radio and television broadcasting for some time. And recollections of the period suggest that it was not the apparatus of television but its transmission of these events and programmes, as well as the shared experience of watching, that remains with viewers over time. Audiences interviewed years later about their experience of television tended to dwell on the programme rather than the medium, bearing witness 'to the power of the medium in presenting itself as transparent' (O'Sullivan 1991: 163).

The influence of Free Cinema's scepticism about the place of television was also in evidence on television itself. It is ironic perhaps that one of the most fascinating debates (which does however roundly prosecute popular television) about the importance of television in national life took place in a documentary called *The Dream Machine* (1964), directed by Denis Mitchell. Mitchell was one of the Free Cinema exponents (writing the script for Fletcher's film *The Saturday Men*) who went on to work in television. *The Dream Machine* debated, in a style owing as much to Grierson as to Free Cinema, the impact of television on culture and its chronic critical neglect by academics and critics alike. The impact of television was only slowly being addressed within the scholarship taking place in universities and was not yet an area of consistent and serious attention on the arts review pages of national newspapers. At that time television had 40 million viewers but no one wanted to write about it, preferring to write about the established arts which were consumed by a far lesser number (40,000) of people from more 'cultured' backgrounds. The film's long opening sequence is overlaid with a montage of voices signalling the debate to come: 'television is and will be a main factor in shaping our society'; 'The living reality of a twelve million audience [for a programme] is compelling', and so on. The programme emerges as a juxtaposed debate about the value and role of television between lecturer Roy Knight and a light entertainment producer for commercial television Francis Essex.

Knight is filmed holding a seminar for a small group of all-male undergraduates to launch his new course about television. He is emphatic, speaking with a belligerent confidence and conviction to his audience and punctuating his reasoning with a cigarette clenched in his fist. He presents the kinds of arguments with which media studies students are now familiar but which were then fresh and unexplored. He suggests that television was taken for granted, not sufficiently critiqued and therefore of dubious quality. Audiences only had the illusion of choice, had no say in television provision and they were erroneously regarded as a 'mass' by those who worked in television, when they should be understood as families and individuals.

The film crew trails Francis Essex behind the scenes as he develops a one-off variety show called *Six Wonderful Girls*. Essex, far more suave than Knight, is depicted spieling the 'girls' and their agents and selling his concept to his colleagues. Interviews with Essex partly substantiate the notion that the television industry viewed audiences as undiscriminating; with him suggesting that as a mass they required little more than 'distraction and diversions'. Essex adds complacently, 'I don't require audiences to think or contribute.' The programme aimed to showcase singers such as Shirley Bassey and Milly Martin with spectacular sets and costumes. Mitchell's selection of the variety show, with its frothy rehearsals and mini-dramas over artists' schedules, is heavily loaded. He juxtaposes its 'showbiz' busy-ness with the unforgiving earnestness of Knight's serious engagement with the 'problem' of television. With commercial television typified as feminine spectacle and diversion the debate about the quality and consumption of television once again becomes a gendered one and although Mitchell presents two opposing arguments it is not difficult to ascertain whose side the filmmaker favours.

Mitchell had worked extensively in radio prior to his television work; he had an ear for voices and allowed popular speech patterns a new centrality in television documentary. During the 1950s and 1960s he became one of the most influential documentarists in television. Mitchell was an important innovator who experimented with full-scale outside-broadcast television units in order to make small-scale domestic documentaries (Winston 1995: 207) and introduced the tape recorder as a mode of recording a more spontaneous popular speech. He imported into radio and then television the sound of real people talking rather than real people reading a scripted version of what they had already said. In recalling his early radio work he states, 'I got launched with a series called *People Talking*. It was an astonishing success mainly because for the first time ever they were listening to real people saying whatever came into their minds.' This immediacy thus facilitated a subjective mode of actuality which privileged the 'consciousness' of his subjects through speech recording initially called the 'think-tape' method (in Corner 1991b: 49–50).

Mitchell's entry into television occurred when he worked on a report entitled 'Teenagers' (1955) for the current affairs series *Special Enquiry* (BBC 1952–57), repeated two years later in 1957 with the title *On the Threshold* (see Corner 1991b). His experiments in sound recording were used to produce a tape-recorded soundtrack as the lynchpin of the programme. Tape recording enabled the film crew to use the more portable silent camera and his collaborator Norman Swallow, who was initially sceptical about the process, commented that the programme managed to get close to the 'hearts and minds of those teenagers' (in Corner 1991b: 48). Mitchell's intimate style of observational documentary was acutely apparent in his attention to the voices of ordinary people; oddballs and outsiders, radicals and hobos. Films such as *In Prison* (BBC 1957) and *A Soho Story* (1958) delighted in the sometimes rambling but always revealing monologues of their subjects. *In Prison*, like some of the British Free Cinema documentaries, organised its narrative around the cycle of prison life, including entry and release. An observational style is married with an impressionistic soundtrack that begins with a prisoner's voice and a snatch of the well-known Ewan McColl song 'Time On My Hands'. The soundtrack frames the topic, building 'an "inner" structure of feeling, closing the imaginative distance between prisoners and viewers right from the start' (Corner 1991b: 50).

In Mitchell's most intimate portraits, he avoided lecturing his audience but instead chose to refract social commentary via his subjects. Reisz said of Mitchell, 'he uses "untypical" characters … because he tries to find those who are most vulnerable to the social pressures he is describing' (in Barnouw 1993: 234). In this sense, Mitchell's portraits of those with most to fear from the majority community say as much about that community as they say about the ostensible subject of the film. This is crystal clear in the remarkable film *A Soho Story*. The film begins with a reflective voiceover in which Mitchell recalls how he had wanted to make a film about buskers and had been seeking a character called Mack who could show him around. He discovers that Mack has left the streets to try to make a new life as an artist. When Mitchell does find him he decides, instead, to make him the subject of the film. Appositely, Mack who was also an artist and a bohemian, had made his living for twenty years orating Shakespearean soliloquies for theatre queues in London's West End and he proves to be a hypnotically attractive speaker to camera. In an extraordinary piece of early confessional television, Mack sits on a bar stool nursing a pint and a chaser or stands by his easel with paint palette and bottle of beer, while he chronicles his life as 'one of society's outsiders, an intellectual bum', as one of his Soho companions puts it. It is an intimate scene and we, the audience, feel as though we are seated with him by the bar. Mack's story turns out to be a poignant one. Told straight to camera and quite frankly, with very little in the way of self-indulgence or self-pity, viewers hear about his youthful rebellion against middle-class values, his alcohol abuse, his failed marriage and his recent attempt to live a more mainstream life. His account is intercut with colourful scenes of Soho life; mainly bars where artists, poets and other outsiders amplify or illuminate Mack's diatribe against society. Mack's eloquent critique of mainstream society is extended by cuts to speech-makers at Hyde Park's 'Speakers' Corner' and the defiant voices of other Bohos who refuse to conform. Their critiques are explicitly ideological. The film suggests that Mack has made a 'cult of being an outsider' and he asserts that even though he has been beaten by the middle classes, 'I'll never believe in the idea of them.'

Mack's autobiography is also a chronicle of Soho and its inhabitants since he arrived there in the late 1930s. And with an elegant reciprocity other characters are brought in to comment on Mack's life. The most touching of these is when Mack's former wife Marie tells, in voiceover, of her affection for him, how they met and why they could not continue together. There is very little in the way of authorial comment or intervention here and it is never explained whether Marie refused to be filmed, whether she speaks her words or whether they are read out by another on her behalf. It is as if she is simply sitting off-stage, close by. More direct and more awkwardly placed, is the scene in which a policeman is filmed confidently declaring that Mack will never make it and will soon be back on the streets. Seated formally behind his desk, and speaking rather stiffly straight to camera, his attitude recalls an earlier era of the public information films and makes a nice counterpoint to the laxity of the bizarre-looking Soho inhabitants whom it is difficult not to regard sympathetically.

Cathy Come Home and the dramatisation of everyday life

From the late 1950s a number of factors contributed to a socially-committed observational style on British television. The political inflection of Free Cinema, the style of Direct Cinema, the influence of individual directors such as Ken Loach and a growing televisual commitment to the depiction of social issues and the representation of ordinary people was increasingly evident on the BBC and on the new ITV services. Even drama, partly inspired by the success of the 'angry young man' stage dramas of the Royal Court produced between 1956 and 1958 and exemplified by the work of writers such as John Osborne, embraced the issues and the filmic techniques that had formerly been the purview of documentarists.[12] Influential television producer Tony Garnett has also indicated how the cinematography of Jean-Luc Godard and the radicalism of the East End Theatre under the aegis of Joan Littlewood influenced the style of filmmaking that eventually imposed itself onto the BBC:

> I wanted us to go out with a 16mm camera on the shoulder and just grab these films. The BBC film department at Ealing ... thought it was 'lowering standards'. Those 16mm cameras were for news, not drama ... Anyway I fought the battle and we won. Indeed within two or three years no one wanted to work in a studio anymore. (Garnett 2001: 74)

The arrival of Harold Wilson's Labour government in 1964, after thirteen years of a Conservative administration, also corresponded with a growing radicalism among writers and directors within the BBC. Canadian Sydney Newman, already responsible for ITV's successful *Armchair Theatre*, move to the BBC in 1963 with an agenda of refreshing television drama and directing it away from filmed theatre towards a more uniquely televisual form. 1964 therefore saw the inauguration of a series of plays in a new slot known as the *Wednesday Play* which ran for six years until 1970 and which, during that period, reconfigured both the televisual and ideological grammar of drama. Inroads were made into a television culture that had drawn most heavily from stage theatre, which was well-suited to programming that was studio-bound, used tape (as opposed to celluloid) and deployed live rather than recorded and edited drama. The *Wednesday Play* aired for about forty weeks each year at 9pm following on from the evening news. Director Ken Loach recalls how its placing in the schedules was crucial to the image of the plays that he and others wished to project:

> We were very anxious at the time for our plays not to be considered dramas but as continuations of the news. The big investigatory documentary of the time was *World in Action* ... and we tried to copy its techniques and cut with a rough, raw, edgy quality, which enabled us to deal with issues head on. (In Fuller 1998: 15).

Television producers, directors and writers increasingly aimed to depict a 'history from below' that could give a voice to working-class experience and touch the social conscience of their audience. Documentary drama (or 'docudrama'), in particular, enabled filmmakers to unite a political agenda and social comment with an engaging, watchable drama.[13] The fresh new perspective afforded by these programmes, on those often categorised as outside of respectable mainstream society, was contextualised within a social responsibility agenda (Caughie 2000: 103). By the time that the *Wednesday Play*, the *Play for Today* series (also BBC) and *Armchair Theatre* had come to an end, the arena of documentary drama especially had been colonised by the left. Moreover, it was championed by television professionals such as Leslie Woodhead, from Granada TV, as 'one of the few art forms pioneered by television' (Woodhead 1981: 105). The documentary drama was also borne of necessity. Filming was mainly studio-bound and limited by the use of 35mm cameras, which meant that heavily researched and scripted material was a natural way to express information; when these plays also managed to include outside and location shooting as well they represented the best of both worlds. The term 'documentary drama' itself also points to the perceived importance of dramatic realism at this time, which, together with an emphasis on truth-telling as the foundation of productions, led to the cultivation of a uniquely televisual lexicon of conventions. Even soaps like *Coronation Street* and *Emergency Ward 10* and crime dramas such as the BBC's *Z Cars*[14] were referred to as drama documentary.[15] It is certainly arguable that it was British television, more than cinema, that gave mass audiences a taste for realism as the primary organising structure of contemporary storytelling.

Cathy Come Home (BBC, 1966), directed by Ken Loach and produced by Tony Garnett as part of the *Wednesday Play* series, is widely recognised as a landmark docudrama that successfully married the chronicling of events and social realism that characterises British documentary form with fictional devices, filmic and radio techniques. Loach, like the exponents of Free Cinema and together with the subsequent Granada producers of docudramas from the 1970s onwards, was committed to an intensely observational style of realism. This is not to say that *Cathy Come Home*, albeit in observational fashion, did not formulate an argument; indeed it is frequently cited as an exemplary campaigning film and more broadly as evidence of good television practice. Shot in monochrome, with shaky camera work and plenty of exterior and location filming, the film has become a touchstone of British documentary drama filmmaking. It also acted as a rejoinder to the commercial cinema of the British New Wave which had come to the fore with films such as *Room at the Top* (Clayton, 1959) and *Look Back in Anger* (Richardson, 1959); putting on the small screen working-class voices and attitudes. But unlike films such as these, *Cathy Come Home*, with its central female protagonist, also gave a real and sympathetic credibility to the social aspirations for consumer goods and the comfortable life that was so frequently coded as problematically 'feminine'.

Cathy Come Home contributed towards the development and re-fashioning of television drama as a form in its own right rather than a form heavily indebted to theatre and theatrical conventions. There was a growing sense in the industry that television drama in particular needed to change and formulate its own identity as a mass medium. It needed to 'forge a unique representational and discursive model … which was capable of validating the upstart medium as a form in its own right' (MacMurraugh-Kavanagh & Lacey 1999: 60). Alongside this there was an acceptance that television drama needed to be more accessible and relevant to viewers' lives. When the BBC invited Canadian Sidney Newman to run the Drama Department it called in a man whose background in documentary and commercial television signalled a sea-change in attitude towards what was representable on television. He advocated topical dramas that 'dramatise the lives of ordinary people in matters that are relevant to their times' (MacMurraugh-Kavanagh & Lacey 1999: 61).

This commitment to move from classical dramaturgy to a more topical realism demanded corresponding changes in form and technique. It prompted the development of a filmic methodology that increased the narrative pace, the use of an extra-diegetic soundtrack, multiple cameras, and so on. It also adopted the 16mm film which was regarded as uniquely televisual, already associated with the realist genres of documentary and news and which enabled the removal of filming from the studio to the world outside. Madeleine MacMurraugh-Kavanagh and Stephen Lacey describe the radical outcome of these initiatives in the broadcasting of Ken Loach's 1965 drama *Up the Junction*. The drama, a contemporary story of working-class experience, gained currency by following on from the evening news and by articulating a realist aesthetic supported by natural lighting, street-sound, location filming and the busy backdrop of everyday life. It also replicated working-class voices, well captured in Nell Dunn's script which exhibited an 'ethnographic ear for fragments of the everyday' (Caughie 2000: 120). The dialogue was so naturalistic that some accused Loach of allowing his actors to ad lib (Fuller 1998: 18). The 'play', so different from its predecessors, re-figured viewers' expectation of television drama and established what were eventually to become the new conventions of television realism.

But even so, *Up the Junction* was partly studio-based and the few productions that were all-film during this period tended to be documentary dramas, with *Cathy Come Home* being the most notable example. The story, written by investigative journalist Jeremy Sandford, privileges Cathy's point of view as it follows her throughout her social and personal downfall. The opening shots find Cathy hitching a lift on the motorway, escaping her 'respectable' home in the country to seek a new life in London. The story cuts to shaky footage of street scenes with her new boyfriend Reg Ward. Popular music, including the song 'Stand by Me' sets the tone as the couple court, playfight, chat and begin to talk about a future together. A tramp, sleeping rough on a nearby bench, is barely noted by the couple courting in the park but his presence is used to undercut these scenes and anticipate the disaster that will follow.

Cathy and Reg, both earning reasonable money, plan their wedding and choose the flat they will live in together. They have aspirations with which contemporary audiences can identify – they admire the central heating, parquet flooring and the tin opener fixed to the kitchen wall. The couple's detailed discussions about money at this moment and throughout the film provide an accessible and detailed insight into the practicalities and pitfalls of contemporary life. Gradually, Cathy and Reg are overwhelmed by a series of events both externally imposed and of their own making. Reg is injured at work and receives no compensation and Cathy falls pregnant. The rest of the film charts their downwards moves: staying with Reg's mother in a crowded tenement block in Islington, moving after a dispute to a house in a run-down area, evicted and turned onto the streets, turned away from the council, living in a caravan and squatting. Finally, Cathy and her children are separated from Reg and lodged in temporary half-way houses until, in a final traumatic scene, her children are forcibly removed from her as they shelter in a railway station.[16]

The backdrop to this story is an urban landscape that encompasses the leafy park of the couple's opening courtship, the grim tenements, crumbling blitz-damaged houses and the dank sticky marshes of later scenes. It capitalises on the freedom to move from television studio to location to give the play a filmic quality and to establish a fresh verisimilitude in the form of landmarks and buildings. As Andrew Higson argues in his discussion of landscape in British New Wave films, scenes such as these construct not only a 'narrative space' for action but they also 'authenticate the fiction' (1996: 134) and underpin its claims to realism. Moreover, the townscape can offer viewing pleasures in this context quite different from the grim gratification of recognition. In one scene Reg drags and cajoles Cathy up some high steps to see the view across a building site; we, the television audience, are dragged up with her to gaze across a landscape in which new houses are rising from the rubble. Cathy follows reluctantly, before collapsing with laughter in his arms. The scene is emblematic and loaded with symbolism, depicting Reg's youthful optimism and confidence in the modern world which turns out to be fatally misplaced, as well as their own jointly-held aspirations to create a life together.

Cathy's centrality to the story is underscored by her strength of character; she retains her dignity and her respectability (which is important) throughout the narrative, only succumbing to tears towards the end of her ordeal. She refuses to be 'pushed around like so much litter'. Reg is an easygoing, family-centred man who tries to make the best of a catastrophe so incremental that he refuses to recognise its full implications. When they move into the caravan site situated on a rubbish dump in marshland he maintains, 'we may have dropped a peg Cath but we'll be a lot contenter [sic]'. He registers their increasing exclusion from mainstream society with bemusement and, bewildered, he wonders how they 'sunk somehow out of the race'. Their story is also a gendered story, with Reg increasingly mortified at his inability to keep his family together and Cathy, forced to occupy the bitter role of the maternal protector in desperate circumstances, made to fight for her children.

This narrative, although linear in its account of the decline and fall of a family, is imbued with a cyclical, repetitive quality that enables Loach to build up a sustained argument about social welfare within the context of one fictionalised and actually highly artistically constructed story. What is distinctive here, is the primacy of voice and its relationship to images (Caughie 2000: 118). For example, an educated male voiceover punctuates each stage of the narrative as Cathy moves from place to place. When Cathy tries to find lodgings following her husband's accident the voiceover adds not only a commentary on homeless statistics but advocates political action, stating, 'we need a government that realises that this is a crisis and treats it as such'. When Cathy is installed in temporary accommodation the audience is informed that the situation produces 'problem families by the time they leave' who have suffered from the 'punitive attitude' of local authorities.

This commentary also has an interventionist function. When a white resident in an argument with a black woman accuses immigrants of taking too much housing allocation the voiceover contradicts this assumption, referring to the Holland Report and explaining that more people leave the country than enter it. In this way it prevents or tries to prevent viewers from consenting to the white woman's perspective and her understanding of the pre-conditions of her own situation.

Finally, the voices of ordinary people at each of the locations – tenement block, run-down street, caravan site, dormitory – provide a chorus; speaking about their own experiences of living in difficult circumstances. A collage of voices add their own observations: 'there's disease here', 'we all get on together', 'it's as low as you can go', even 'our own' are prejudiced against us, 'I feel like a refugee' and so on. This allows people to speak from within their own setting. In interview Ken Loach has identified a key problem in the representation of working-class people on television. Whether studio-based or even on a location such as a picket line the setting 'works against people being articulate' thereby countering the essence of good drama which should be precisely about fostering expressiveness (Rowbotham 1997: 84). This bricolage of voices may be somewhat disembodied but at the same time it amplifies the setting and enriches viewers' understanding of the experience of inhabitation in these conditions. The final text, superimposed as Cathy hitches a ride (having lost her husband, her children and her home) back to her original family home states: 'All the events in this film took place in Britain within the last eighteen months.' The film ends by asserting the essential truthfulness of its revelations. For its director, Loach, it was this collision of drama and statistics that gave *Cathy* its vitality and, surprisingly perhaps, their inclusion prompted a greater attention still to the dramatic realism of the piece: 'The complementing of a fictional story with a factual context places a responsibility on the fiction ... the fictional elements you put in the film have to be as authentic as any bit of actuality' (Fuller 1998: 23).

The trauma and de-humanisation of social inequality are underscored through this tri-partite structure of dramatised narrative, commentator as advocate and information-provider and multi-voiced chorus. The rhetorical power of the film resides in the inter-weaving of voices; a strategy which allows the commentary a gravitas which is funda-mentally important in a film that advocates change without diminishing the importance of Cathy's story and the stories of the ordinary people that she encounters. The dramatic impact of the piece is rooted in traumatic scenes such as the one in which Reg's grandfather is coerced into an old people's home to ameliorate overcrowding in the tenement flat or where Cathy clings to her children as they are dragged away from her; but also in comic scenes of comradeship and mutual support through hard times. The dramatisation of real life allows the viewer a usually forbidden glimpse into the painful negotiations between social worker and client over the terrain of respectability but a script populated by defiant and resilient voices arguably precludes a more voyeuristic engagement with events. It also reveals the ways in which the ideal of the self-supporting nuclear family was being placed under intolerable strain, undermined not by decreasing personal commitment to its ideals, but by social and political factors beyond one's control. The tensions between Cathy and her mother in law, the ejection of the grandfather from the family home and the splitting up of Cathy's children are engendered by poverty, poor social planning and unsympathetic officials. The breakdown of the family unit is rooted here in structural inequalities. Author Jeremy Sandford is quoted as saying, 'Cathy is Everywoman, Everymother ... coming up against state machinery, which results in the decimation of her family. Her natural instincts and desires are destroyed by the institutionalised violence of a state' (in Paget 1999a: 76).

The montage of image and voice can produce some non-naturalistic effects, sometimes blurring the lines of authority within the narrative. In one crucial scene towards the end of the film the camera follows Cathy as Reg speaks at length about their difficulties. He sounds distanced, more closely allied with the voice of the documentarist than with his own character. This moment signals perhaps the couple's growing estrangement as they consider the benefits of him seeking work in Liverpool where the housing is said to be cheaper. But it also foregrounds the limitations of seeking to understand the film solely in terms of its commitment to realism and to a socialist realist aesthetic. At this moment Reg's voiceover and ensuing dialogue with his wife foreground the constructedness of film, pointing to the non-naturalistic and paradoxical moment when a private conversation about the couple's relationship must also be a public conversation about social welfare.

The oddity of this moment is embedded in the tensions of a form that pulls in two directions; between dramatic engagement and investigative journalism. Some of the criticism levelled at *Cathy Come Home* suggests that the problem inherent in the 'social problem' film lies in the centrality of an 'exaggerated human interest' (Paget 1990: 87) that may weaken the overall argument about policy, governmentality and social change. Also, the continuing 'marketability' of films about social class and poverty in modern times, while politically admirable, may be rooted in what Derek Paget condemns as 'cultural tourism'. He argues that the claim to immediacy that is built into factual-based drama may actually mask the distancing mechanisms that construct audiences as entertained spectators within documentary drama. These spectators are also actually consumers and the act of filming to a lesser or greater degree objectifies its subjects. This is not to say that the politically motivated film is founded on questionable intentions but rather that in its name 'an *attitude* of concern' is also being marketed and consumed and that the individual consumer is, in any case, fairly ineffective should they wish to make a political response to the film (Paget 1999b: 49).

This caveat not withstanding, *Cathy Come Home* was arguably 'the first dramatic political statement on television in terms of form and content, congruent with its channel of communication and with the power to change thought, institutions and situations by the time it had finished transmission' (Hanson 2002: 59). A grand claim perhaps, but the form is especially significant in televisual terms – its hybrid aesthetic points forward to the increasing blurring of boundaries between performance, dramatisation and documentary form. As John Corner demonstrates, the play's formal distinctiveness is characterised especially by its interplay between 'story' and 'report' – between the viewer's sense of an involving dramatised narrative and their understanding of the play as an 'account' or document which provides a 'bigger picture' than Cathy's story can provide alone (Corner 1996b: 99–100). As a document too, plays such as this, come in for criticism. Playwright David Edgar argues that *Cathy Come Home* is characteristic of docudrama in that it has a *thesis* and that as such it attracts concern because of an anxiety that viewers will fail to recognise that they are being presented with an argument rather than a statement of fact. Indeed, on the occasion of the second broadcast of *Cathy Come Home*, the statistics were removed, following queries about their accuracy and their interpretation. But for Edgar, the advantages of the form, its unique capacity to present arguments in an authoritative and credible manner is paramount. He adds, 'the form also needs to be defended because the presence of docudrama in the schedules is an active encouragement to audiences to think critically and seriously about the programmes they watch' (Edgar 1988: 187).

The success of *Cathy Come Home*, however, was rooted not only in its presentation of an eloquent and accessible argument but also in the convincing depiction of ordinary people and everyday life. *Cathy Come Home* broke new ground in this regard and demonstrated that the working classes could be far more than simply a *sign* of authenticity and of the real; they could be complex characters negotiating a complex world. Chapter 3 moves on from *Cathy Come Home* to track a number of subsequent routes in the documentary portrayal of ordinary lives, including the campaigning films that worked in the shadow of Loach's film and those that broke away from this highly politicised arena through either poetic realism or observational documentary.

chapter 3
Just being themselves:
from docudrama to new observational documentary

Class-based documentary: from campaigning voice
to the withholding of judgement

Since the 1960s variations of the drama/documentary form have continued to find a place on television. The docudrama's influence extends to contemporary forms of reality TV as well as contributing to the 'standard rhetoric' of factual television more generally (Kilborn & Izod 1997: 87). Its new emphasis on the voices and experiences of ordinary people, in particular, was to be powerfully revivified in the observational documentaries that followed in its wake, but arguably without the overt campaigning voice or political critique. Following *Cathy Come Home*, the docudrama and related forms went from strength to strength during the 'golden age' of television drama; sometimes maintaining a campaigning edge and at other times remaining broadly politicised simply though its commitment to the representation of the lives of ordinary people. Irene Shubik, a drama producer for both the BBC and ITV, has observed that much writing for television is 'dramatised journalism' (2000: 72) and *Cathy Come Home*, in fact, fits this description well, for all its filmic attitude. Television has demonstrated a continuing ability to adapt and to take on board documentary and journalistic polemic; and many of the plays that followed on from *Cathy Come Home* merge journalistic characteristics with their fictional form. They depict ordinary lives, often through composite representative characters, not simply to afford them recognition but also to make a point. The 1969 drama *Mrs Lawrence Will Look After It*, written by Tony Parker and commissioned by Shubik to launch a new series of the *Wednesday Play*, is a good example. Parker's earlier journalism was distinctive in that it arose from detailed taped interviews with criminals which led to riveting books such as *The Unknown Citizen* (1963), which revealed the life of a recidivist criminal and *Five Women* (1965), which was a portrait of women law-breakers. Shubnik describes Parker's perspective as one of 'pure external observation'. He even lived in a prison for three months with the permission of the Home Office to research a book on the penal system. *Mrs Lawrence Will Look After It* was intended to highlight the precarious existence of illegal childminders and to reveal the inadequate provision of childcare for lone mothers. Based on interviews, the drama was shot on film rather than in the studio by director John MacKenzie, who had training in documentary production and had worked with Ken Loach. Although the drama was stylistically different from *Cathy Come Home* it attracted a number of favourable comparisons and, in Shubnik's view, pointed to a continuing audience demand for 'realistic and identifiable subjects, treated in realistic terms' and which was to become an established characteristic of British television fiction (2000: 81, 86).

Issue-based docudrama, still seen intermittently on television, remains an important form which is frequently controversial and can attract national attention through extensive media coverage. This programming continues to exhibit a commitment to the representation of ordinary people in the face of unnecessary bureaucracy, negligence or corruption. Dramas such as *Hillsborough* (1996), which re-traced the events that led to the stadium disaster in 1989 and *Fighting for Gemma* (1993), which investigated the long-term effects of the nuclear fuel industry on the health of its workers and their families, sought to convey private grief and trauma within a campaigning framework that voiced national concerns and challenged the authorities. Unlike *Cathy Come Home* or *Mrs Lawrence Will Look After It* these do not fictionalise characters to explore, in a representative manner, social issues but choose instead to dramatise the lives of real individuals. *Hillsborough*, written by the outstanding television dramatist Jimmy McGovern, was a classic of its type. The two-hour documentary deployed detailed research to present its case and combined this with a close focus on the dreadful experiences of just a few of the families affected by a disaster that led to the deaths of 95 football fans. McGovern himself stated that the intention was to tell the truth of the situation and to reveal 'the things that were done, before and after the tragedy, by our public services in our name' (in Scraton 1999: 158). Like *Cathy Come Home*, it contributed substantially towards the formation of public opinion, and in this instance, specifically to the demand for the government of the day to investigate claims of police negligence and cover-up. Tabloids referred to it as the 'most shocking TV drama ever' (Scraton 1999: 160). Such was the impact of the drama, that although the story was nearly eight years old, it helped re-ignite media coverage, making the issues newsworthy once again and placing those particular families in the media spotlight (see Paget 1998: 207–8; Scraton 1999: 158–63).

While the campaigning voice of films such as these is crucial to their construction it bears repeating that their distinctiveness also lies in the privileging of ordinary people, their voices and perspectives and their prominent insertion into events of national impor-tance is paramount. McGovern himself said in interview that he did not think that the film would effect change in itself but rather reveal the 'truth' of the situation. The 'truth' in this context, although later publicly substantiated, is one rooted in a partisan commitment to its subjects' perspective (such as the fans and their families) over and above the views of other protagonists (such as the police or football club). This commitment is especially apparent in the example of *The Stephen Lawrence Story* (1997). This dramatised documentary traced the events and aftermath of the death of Stephen Lawrence, who was killed in South London as the result of a racist attack. Focusing heavily on the experience of Lawrence's parents it did not bring new evidence to light but explored multicultural relations through the lens of the incident. In doing so it presented a dramatic and highly effecting portrait of an ordinary couple trying to grieve while fighting for justice; all the time besieged by news hounds, lobbyists and police investigators. For some, its presence proved that there is still a place for passionate political documentary amid the crowded market of the docusoap and its like (Owen 1999: 203).

The lens through which the Hillsborough and Lawrence cases were focused was of the family as a social unit and the dynamics of these relations in times of intolerable stress. As Diana Gittens points out, 'What actually goes on in families is conveniently dismissed as "private" until it becomes "public" by creating a nuisance or a financial responsibility to the state' (1993: 153). The narratives invited viewers to identify, in both cases, with parents in mourning, but also with parents who are forced to become 'public' in order to challenge authority and orthodoxy. Here the families are ordinary people, who through no choice of their own, are forced to breach the threshold of media visibility. As an idealised social grouping the family also becomes the touchstone or marker of authentic feeling and righteous conviction in the face of institutionalised intransigence and political obfuscation. This opposition between family (posited as natural and given) and bureaucracy (posited as faceless, cumbersome, overwhelming and unnatural) is also evident more broadly in media culture, as in television drama such as *Edge of Darkness* (1985), 'real life' movie stories such as *Lorenzo's Oil* (1993) and *Ladybird, Ladybird* (1994), dramatised documentary such as *Cathy Come Home* and *Fighting for Gemma* and popular journalism such as the features in *Reader's Digest*.

As already noted, not all forms that conflate drama with documentary realism sit within the campaigning tradition; some make a less overtly 'political' intervention simply by choosing to depict extensively and sympathetically the lives of ordinary people. The films of Penny Woolcock (documentarist and later feature-filmmaker) deal with the economically deprived neighbourhoods that were decimated by the closure of heavy manufacturing industry. These are communities fractured by the unemployment and alienation that hit the estates which had grown up around the steel works and mines of Britain's industrial north. In mainstream press and television reportage, such communities were made visible in the early 1990s by a series of riots, which spread across the municipal suburbs of Cardiff, Oxford and Tyneside. In some cases the riots involved racial attacks as young white youths laid waste to community buildings and targeted Asian shops. In other cases, the target was the police or the other inhabitants of the estate or the scrubland and streets which became a stage for ritualistic burnings, joyriding and violent behaviour.

These forms of public protest were the excessive and violent expression of defeat and exile. The protesters were 'neither legitimate citizens nor consumers', adrift from all the recognised forms of authority (Campbell 1993: 97). In dominant representations, the otherness of these estates was underlined; these were 'demonised domains', places where undesirables had been transported, places where people did not pay their rates, who were often excluded from the electoral register, did not have their vote and whose status often slipped from symbolic victim to symbolic culprit: the unemployed male, the single mother, the 'problem family' (Campbell 1993: 172). These people were often crudely united and caricatured by the theorists of the 'underclass'. Woolcock's films, made in collaboration with Channel 4, entered these 'no-go zones' and revealed a world of hardship made tolerable by humour and an extensive involvement in the black economy. There were three innovative documentary films scripted and directed by Woolcock which addressed white working-class estate life in the post-Thatcher era. The films are all the result of independent production work and examples of innovative new-realist representations of class: *When the Dog Bites* (1988) deals with the dynamics of space and power, community and individual adaptation to the broader de-industrialised landscape. The focus is the town of Consett, in County Durham, and the film offers a series of accounts of how the inhabitants of the town have survived after the closure of the main industry, the steelworks, in the early 1980s; *Tina Goes Shopping* (1999) and *Tina Takes a Break* (2001) focus on the residents of a Leeds housing estate. In the *Tina* films the dramatic reconstruction of estate life involves the improvised acting of real-life estate inhabitants themselves who take on and perform the everyday dramas of estate survival.

The documentaries provoke political as well as aesthetic responses to their form and content. Woolcock employs ordinary people instead of professional actors whom she selects from local inhabitants.[1] But she also inserts fictional characters which has attracted criticism from the 'real' people who were members of the cast. Her research for the films involves embedding herself within the community and slowly uncovering the alternative networks of black economy, crime, fleeting consumerism, personal relationships and gendered patterns of responsibility. But the films are very far from the working-class realism that this preparation might suggest. *When the Dog Bites*, begins, for example, with a homage to Orson Welles' film *Touch of Evil* which signals the experimental 'dreamy' effect that Woolcock sought to incorporate into the narrative (Corner 1996b: 151). In contrast to depictions of estate life as drab, mundane and disempowered, Woolcock's films construct a layered depiction of the local unofficial structures of power and exchange and their production of winners and losers. Her filmic technique mixes a range of documentary and fictional discourses, together with a postmodern attitude embodied by what John Corner calls 'hallucinatory realism' (1996b: 123). In *When the Dog Bites*, she mixes a sequence of interviews with unconventional *mise-en-scène*: one interview takes place in the local swimming pool with the interviewee providing commentary whilst appearing to be chest-deep in water. There are also various sequences of observational footage which combine to produce a symbolic as well as naturalistic tone: for example, the recurring imagery of a local escapologist attempting to release himself from a strait jacket or a padlocked bag.

In all these films, the estates are represented as grimly realistic, the raw underside of an iniquitous class system, but they are also the sites of complex celebratory cameos of almost exotic menace and the risk of everyday existence. In *Tina Takes a Break* Tina, the unemployed mother of two children with an alcoholic partner, takes a break from the family to recover from her heroin addiction. The resulting chaos of the family home as it descends into dirt, disorder and almost carnivalesque inversions of power as her two young children survive with their drunken father, combines naturalism and almost hallucinatory realism. This is a world where only women's networks or powerful male criminals can survive; the unemployed white male is absent from the frame, only fleetingly caught in the image of the ineffectual drunken father. The film achieves a tenuous poise between comedy and tragedy; the humorous or even exhilarating moment is carved out of a lifetime of despair or banality and, at any moment, the ordinary threatens to turn into the exotic. *Tina Takes a Break* ends with a powerfully tragi-comic scene in which, quite surreally, a local ice-cream vendor hands out ice-creams to the children and drugs to the local women – and a good time is had by all.

These films stretch the boundaries of both fact and fiction and through experimentation further explore the 'complex politics of the everyday' (Corner 1996b: 122–3). Unlike the work of the early 'social explorers' who condemned their subjects, Woolcock's films refrain from making judgements. She refuses to condemn the class-based decisions of parents that keep their son at home when he could leave and take up a scholarship or the canny reluctance of neighbours to call an ambulance for a badly beaten adolescent on the estate. Woolcock reveals and valorises the alternative systems of care and different codes of behaviour which structure these communities during hard times. And unlike the work of Ken Loach, Tony Garnett or Jimmy McGovern, for example, her films make no explicit political comment and do not adopt a campaigning agenda. What they do achieve is a re-invigoration of factual/fictional forms through a mixed marriage of journalistic investigative research, dramatised narrative and filmic experimentation. The films may offer a strange and engaging hybrid of the everyday and the outlandish but at the same time they place the marginalised 'underclass' centrally and afford its constituents a real psychological complexity. The complexity of Woolcock's work reveals the unrealised potential of many of the reality TV docusoaps that were produced in the same period to provide a voice for ordinary people in an entertaining fashion.

Docusoap and the drama of the domestic

> The home as theatre is an idea that survives on and through television, but it is a family theatre, in which families participate both as audiences and as players. (Silverstone 1994: 41)

There are clear differences in the forms employed and the spectator positions offered by drama-documentary, the more traditional expository documentary and observational documentary. At its best, observational documentary liberates factual filmmaking by adopting a more casual, non-interventionist style and by focusing on the topical and the everyday in ways which not only refresh the genre but may also make important social statements (see Bruzzi 2000: 68). But as such, they arguably leave behind any pretensions to *political intervention* in the lives of those they portray. Where they do undertake a kind of implicit social commentary it is through a commitment to revealing *social structures* and challenging the preconceptions of viewers through the revelation of the patent 'humanity' of its film subjects. Whereas some dramadocs and most expository documentary may be regarded as constructing a 'spectator' who adopts a critical distance on the documentary subject, observational forms construct a viewer/voyeur who gains a sense of looking in on other people's lives. Stella Bruzzi suggests that the successful advent of the docusoap or 'new British observational documentary' signalled a growing discontent with the authorial absenteeism of the more conventional fly-on-the-wall programmes. It answered the 'pervasive modern concern with the notion that documentary's most significant "truth" is that which emerges through interaction between filmmaker and subject in front of the camera' (2000: 76).

The best docusoaps, which may be regarded as a sub-genre of observational documentary, with their detailed attention to family and personal life, are especially adept at exposing the fractures in the social structures that maintain social cohesion. Attracting high ratings, these shows came to dominate the early-evening schedules from 1996 to 2000 with some of them regularly attracting audiences of between 8–12 million viewers. Broadly speaking, docusoaps are multi-part series, each episode featuring strong recurrent 'characters' engaged in everyday activities, whose stories are interleaved in soap opera style. In the late 1990s the format became a resounding popular success and was familiar enough to have its characteristics open to parody. Rich with melodramatic moments, cliff hangers, hyperbole and personality clashes, the series focused predominantly on the service industries, entertainment and white-collar workers – estate agents, nurses, shop workers, traffic wardens, families, holiday reps. A mixture of commentary, edited narrativisation, observational filming and direct address to camera structured what were often fairly banal happenings (see Winston 2000: 55). In some, focusing on hospitals and vet practices such as *Pet Rescue* (1998) and *Animal Hospital* (1995), the drama of the illnesses of children or animals was rooted in an unashamed sentimentality that could not help but invite the charge of dumbing down, tabloid voyeurism and an uncritical complicity between host institution and programme makers (see Kilborn, Hibberd & Boyle 2001).

Paul Watson's series *The Family* (1974) is often referred to as a landmark in the new observational documentary and as the precursor of the docusoap. Directed by Watson and Franc Roddam and produced for the BBC, the series took viewers into an ordinary working-class family home in Reading, England. During twelve 30-minute episodes it tracked the relationships between matriarch Margaret Wilkins, her husband Terry, daughters Heather and Marion and Marion's rather reluctant fiancé Tom. It contained many of the elements that would become trademark features of Watson's filmmaking, albeit differently weighted in later productions: a strong central female character, a focus on the institution of marriage, and more subtly, an interest in Englishness, domesticity and social class. It also attracted a substantial audience of an average of 5.5 million viewers per episode (Winston 1999: 2).

Documentary maker Bernard Clark foregrounds the radicalism of Watson's venture by contrasting it with Richard Cawston's 1969 BBC documentary *The Royal Family*:

No one pretended this would reveal a natural real-life portrait of the Queen, just that we would glimpse a few more informal 'set-ups' than previously ... even the royal corgis appeared to be playing to camera ...Three decades ago this was typical documentary – class-conscious, polite, unobtrusive and modest – an art-form that knew its place. (2002: 2)

In contrast, *The Family* demanded to be taken at face value as a genuine filmic intrusion into the day-to-day interactions of the Wilkins's. As such it probably owed more to the change in approach of current affairs programmes of the 1960s and 1970s such as *This Week* and *Man Alive* than to the more 'official' documentaries characterised by *The Royal Family*. Examining 'problem' issues around social and sexual life, *Man Alive* conducted highly personal interviews with ordinary people and provoked tears often enough to attract the labels 'sob-umentary' (Root 1986: 99). They were certainly compulsive viewing and when accused of voyeurism their defenders argued that if audiences were shocked it was not because the topics were shocking in themselves but mainly because representation of real life on television was so very limited (Root 1986: 100).

The opening sequence of each episode signals and anticipates, quite explicitly, the viewing pleasures to be had from an observational form that seeks out the private and the domestic. After a brief voiceover or discussion between two Wilkins family members the sequence begins. A camera pans across the roofs of rows of small houses, enters through the window into the living room of the Wilkins' home before focusing on the mantelpiece. Here, in a framed family photograph flanked by domestic knickknacks, still images of the various members of the Wilkins family appear. The camera then pulls back to show the real family standing in front of the fireplace. This opening gestures towards an iconography of the realist cinema established by the British New Wave discussed in the last chapter and popularised in the long-running television series *Coronation Street*. Andrew Higson talks about a similar sequence, too, in the 'Sunday morning' section of the film *Saturday Night and Sunday Morning* when the camera moves from the general to the particular, from the townscape across terrace houses to an interior shot. He notes: 'The movement from one image to the next rapidly impregnates the space, after each transition, with increasing narrative significance and dramatic purpose, until finally the individual is placed in his environment, the figure in the landscape' (1996: 139).

The photos on the mantelpiece are rich in connotation. Ideologically they invoke the idealised cohesion of the family unit, each in his or her place, centre stage in the communal heart of the home. Formally placed, they make a public statement about the Wilkins's as a social group. As documents they also seize a moment, their verisimilitude seeming to capture the reality of that time. Finally, they suggest a sentimental attachment to the family which is of personal importance and underscores the emphasis on the private, personal and domestic in Watson's film. As Patricia Holland has noted in her historical overview of personal photographs, 'the fact that private photography has become *family* photography is itself an indication of the domestication of everyday life and the expansion of "the family" as the pivot of a century-long shift to a consumer-led, home-based economy' (1997: 106). Historically, 'social explorers' of working-class life focused precisely on the questions of how the poor conducted their domestic lives. The expansion of middle-class domestic values and behaviour was to be adopted by the respectable poor and the family realm became the main forum for the expression of emotion and the conduct of close relationships (Holland 1997: 106). In this context, both the behaviour of the family and the appearance of the domestic realm (in terms of taste, consumer goods, maintenance and the pursuit of leisure) became the object of fascinated speculation in photography and later in documentary film.

Home as dramatic centre

In *The Family* the privatised setting of the domestic sphere becomes the dramatic stage for family interaction. Just as television has become centre stage in the home, so too the home takes centre stage on television. And unsurprisingly, perhaps, in this series the mother Mrs Wilkins seems to be most in control of her setting and most confident about the place of television in their lives. Speaking to the camera about their decision to be filmed, she said, 'It gives us a chance to portray ordinary people. Our opinions are probably what 60 per cent of people in this country think but can't put over – they've got no media to put it through' (Collins 2000). In this context *The Family* seems to offer opportunities to be represented, to see oneself on the small screen, to enable the gratification that comes with public recognition.

It also offered riveting viewing; revealing domestic strife, prolonged arguments about money, relationships, emotional commitment and the viability of marriage as an enduring institution during a period of 'permissive populism' when older forms of respect, family values and sexual propriety were dissolving (Hunt 1998). If voyeurism was an engaging element of audience involvement in the programme, then it lay in watching the Wilkins family's apparent 'indisciplinarity', in viewing their incontinence with money, language and emotions.[2] The family's behaviour is excessive from the perspective of the bourgeois ideal; pub sessions, the hen night and even small domestic disputes seem to connote a hyperbolic emotional setting. At the same time, Mrs Wilkins' attachment, in particular, to family life and to the already crumbling institution of marriage, resurrected earlier images of the white working-class family and especially the matriarch maintaining old-fashioned family values. This early series itself became a media phenomenon which focused especially on the on-off wedding of Marion and Tom. Mrs Wilkins seems to have handled the media attention with grim pragmatism. In one episode prior to her daughter Heather's marriage she doggedly turns away a persistent local reporter while telling him in no uncertain terms that she is unhappy with press treatment of her family.

Watson himself has argued vehemently against the attribution of *The Family* as a proto-docusoap. He would contend that his series inhabits a more respectable realm than the more entertainment-led work that followed in its wake. Following the production of his documentary *A Wedding in the Family* in 2000, Watson stated of docusoaps, 'They sneered and didn't enrich our lives or understanding, even when dealing with serious hurt in *Neighbours From Hell*. Most of the time it was middle-class media people taking the piss out of people performing for the 15 minutes of fame' (in Collins 2000).[3] *The Family* was strongly resonant in its depiction of the limited aspirations and proscribed lives of its subjects. It exposed the limitations of a range of gendered, ethnic and class differences and, in this sense, it made a statement about contemporary social life.

That the family-based observational documentary could attract large audiences with characteristics such as multiple story lines, domestic drama and strong central characters invokes a comparison with British soap opera. The popular success and critical notoriety of Desmond Wilcox's BBC 1986 series *The Marriage*, which he contended at the time, showed that 'real life *is* soap opera' provides a good example. Wilcox compared the series to the US prime-time series *Dallas* but it was more akin to the modest scenarios of British soap opera. The series, which traced a young Welsh couple called Marc and Karen Jones through their first year of marriage together recorded petty squabbles and prosaic chat, sounds unpromising. In fact, as Jane Root recounts, their lives were tabloid topics and if they could be regarded as at all ordinary, it could only be as 'extra special' ordinary people – ordinary people as media celebrities. Moreover, the pleasures of viewing their unfolding relationship were structured through soap-opera motifs of emotion, small-scale drama and a realism that invites recognition and identification.

Paul Watson's later series *Sylvania Waters* (1993) more obviously invited comparisons with the affluent prime-time dramas of American soap opera. Watson produced the twelve-part series, which premiered on Australian television in 1992 and attracted a great amount of media attention – it was also the first programme to inspire the press description 'docusoap'. Taking its name from the wealthy harbour-side suburb in Southern Sydney, it observed the lives of couple Noeline Baker and Laurie Donaher and their largely adult children. It filmed them for ninety hours over six months. This 'new money' family, while superficially easy-going, had all their interpersonal conflicts and individual values exposed: the family's investment in material goods, Baker's alcohol consumption and Donaher's white Australian racism seemed to be writ large across the screen. The series is narrated by Baker's 16-year-old son, which fosters a closer, less objective engagement with the characters than is usual in documentary and introduces a more reflexive and performative element to the observational documentary form.[4]

Baker's growing notoriety as a 'larger than life character' (the press simply referred to her as 'Noeline') became the subject of much media criticism and was also criticised by the family themselves. Her media presence as a celebrity after the series was broadcast in Britain and presaged later 'entertainment and character-led' docusoaps. More broadly, there was a perception from Australian audiences and critics, at least, that their national image had been deliberately stereotyped. The *Sydney Morning Herald* critic Richard Glover wrote scathingly, 'Meet Australia's new ambassadors: a family whose members are variously materialistic, argumentative, uncultured, heavy drinking and acquisitive' (in Lumby 2001). There was a sense here, as with much earlier documentary criticism, that documentary makes not only particular observations but generic ones; that the truth about one family might be read as the truth about an entire nation's identity. As Jon Stratton and Ien Ang have noted in relation to the series: 'The intimate connection between television and family suggests how the two institutions interact – are mutually complicit – in contributing to a unified national culture in the modern world' (1994: 1). As the private sphere merges with the public sphere and the symbolic load on the family becomes more onerous and more untenable it was perhaps inevitable that the family itself would come under intolerable pressure. Despite Watson's refusal to acknowledge the connection between his work and the soap aesthetic found in television drama serials, *Sylvania Waters* was marketed with reference to soaps and bears a number of soap opera conventions (see Stratton & Ang 1994).

Stratton and Ang point out that it is not only the marketing circuit that linked the documentary programme to soap opera (through promotional leaflets, press and television coverage) but the 'collusion' between the two genres in that the family is rarely seen interacting with the external world. Whereas *Cathy Come Home* graphically illustrates the links between official culture, bureaucracy, politics and the private realm, series such as *Sylvania Waters* seem to evacuate socio-political context. There is little sense of how the family's social attitudes to money, to ethnicity or to social status can be more broadly understood except as the idiosyncrasies of one family grouping. This presented little difficulty for British audiences, unfamiliar with Australian culture and over-familiar with Australian suburban soaps such as *Neighbours*, who could regard the series as real-life soap opera. But for Australian audiences the decontextualisation of the Baker/Donaher family produced serious ideological problems and rendered it difficult to digest. As Stratton and Ang suggest, 'in the Australian context the distinction between self and other, subject and object, could not so easily be maintained' (1994: 9) and consensus about what constitutes the ideal Australian family came under scrutiny.

In *A Wedding in the Family*, Watson stated that he wanted a wedding involving a nurse so that he could touch on 'the core establishment of middle England. Those that keep the fundamentals going – teachers and nurses' (in Collins 2000). He wanted, in contrast to *Sylvania Waters* it seems, to forge links between the individual and the social, the private and public spheres. Nurse Anna Hutton, who featured in the documentary with her future husband, recruitment consultant Stuart Hutton, saw Watson's advert in Harefield Hospital. Although the couple was happy to trust Watson, Anna Hutton felt that his focus altered during the programme:

> Paul's original agenda was to document a family at the turn of the millennium. He wanted to present social issues so he wanted to attract someone who was involved with the NHS ... I think the agenda changed. It seems to me now that it's all about the marriage. (In Lacey 2000)

The wedding, together with an interrogation of the concept of marriage as a life contract, is indeed central to the film and arguably, Watson fails to make a larger statement about social structures. The wedding ceremony itself is central; the event and its emotional and ideological load deferred throughout the programme by being inter-cut with family interviews and other footage of Anna and her father (who is a doctor) at work. As such the drama is inevitably a family one. It is also difficult as a viewer not to focus overly on the accoutrements of family life and their signification of middle-class aspiration and ideals. Weddings are about display and consumption as well as a declaration of feeling and commitment and by directing the viewer towards this event it is difficult to come away with any larger nuanced understanding of the institutional context in which Anna Hutton and her father are employed.

Watson is not exceptional in trying to distance himself from the docusoap label. There is certainly a stigma attached to the label for those working within the industry and generally speaking producers are apologetic about the term. *The Secret Life of the Family* (2000), for example, tracks a 'typical' Saturday for Paul and Janine Bentall and their four children; counterpointed with a commentary from behavioural researchers, nutritionists and doctors. The show, in by now typical hybrid fashion, linked social experiment to family observation. Producer Jeremy Turner commented:

> I didn't set out to make a docusoap here – that came about as part of its evolution … the original premise was to look at a 24-hour period and dissect every event from a scientific point of view as we go through it. (In Higgins 2000)

The couple are professional actors, so there was, argues Turner, a greater degree of control and mutual understanding and co-operation. The show even includes interviews of them talking about being documentary subjects. Turner is one of many who seek to distance their work from the docusoap label. Joe Houlihan, a television producer for London Weekend Television, described his dismay when the documentary series *School Days* broadcast in February 2000 was referred to by many critics using the 'dreaded D Word' docusoap. His concerns were two-fold. Firstly, that despite the earlier critical successes of docusoap series the term was now being used in a derogatory fashion. And secondly, that was a somewhat lazy and confusing catch-all term for a diverse range of work and that it was being used retrospectively and wrongly to describe the earlier work of documentarists such as Paul Watson and Roger Graef. Houlihan called for tighter definitions and argued that viewers themselves differentiate quite clearly between fly-on-the-wall and docusoap formats. His own attempt at differentiating between the two is, however, less than convincing and only highlights the subjective nature of categorisation; he argues that fly-on-the-wall is recognisable because of its greater emphasis on 'the darker, grittier side of life and had subjects more directly connected with public and social policy'. He notes that *School Days* producer and director Rukhsana Mosam regards a series based in a school and addressing issues such as sex, exclusions, bullying and admissions policy as being in a 'different category from life on a cruise liner' (Houlihan 2000). There is an imputation here of a lack of seriousness in the agenda of docusoaps. This is complex territory. For to distance Paul Watson's work from docusoap, using Houlihan's criteria, we would have to argue, for example, that much of his work overtly, or even implicitly, addresses public sphere issues of public or social policy – which is not the case. Yet who could deny that many of Watson's programmes invite serious questions about social relations and the place of the family and the domestic within it? Equally, many other docusoaps could be defended on similar grounds. John Willis, for example, who commissions factual programming has noted:

> Just look at the BBC series on the opera house which laid that institution completely bare. Even *Neighbours from Hell* contained a more powerful portrait of brutal racial harassment than any number of editions of *Panorama* or *Dispatches*. (2000: 101)[5]

So, perhaps the most voyeuristic docusoap may also lay claim to exposing issues of social and political import and to affirming the central importance of ordinary voices and the conduct and structures of everyday life. Indeed chapter 4 aims to show how even the most personalised of documentary forms such as the video diary and the subjective auteur-driven documentary can engage in challenging ways with controversial social and political issues.

chapter 4
Personalising the documentary:
from video diary to Errol Morris

This chapter begins to chart what we see as a significant shift in emphasis for documentary modes. This shift – a personalising of the form in terms of its aesthetics, address
and representation of subjects – marks the increasing attention to the subjective in
documentary television and video. What holds together the seemingly disparate formats
we discuss is an attention to the subjective in both style and content. We examine, in
particular, documentary and reality TV's attentiveness to trauma, personal pain, injury
and loss and to its modes of expression through confession, video diary, interview,
observational techniques and so on. Over this and the following two chapters we
point to the entrenchment of the revelation of trauma and psychological damage in
post-documentary formats and its relationship to the broader psycho-social realm of
therapeutic culture.

In the early 1970s Stuart Hall gave a valuable account of the specificity of televisual
discourse and the types of transformation it operates upon 'raw materials'. A number of
the key points that Hall established are still pertinent to our analysis of reality TV. Hall
importantly highlights the increasing interplay between non-televisual productions such
as arts events, theatre, cinema and seminars which are relayed fairly unmodified through
the television to a domestic audience and material produced either in a studio or on location for TV. The 'technics of television' he describes are relevant to this interplay and are
predominantly defined as relay, proximity and intimacy. Television material tends to be
fragmented and serialised, but also mediated through either a presenter or the production-
editing process. But this mediation is obscured through the intimate, profoundly domestic

nature of the medium. Also, as Hall indicates, television in its content has prioritised actuality – 'pictures of people, events and places in the "real" world, transmitted to us via the medium of the set' (1971: 5). The question of form seems indivisible here from content. Whilst television favours the documentary mode; it tries often to produce the sense of 'live actuality'. Allied with the rapid transmission of pictures which lends to the 'natural-istic' reportage of 'everyday life and events' television bolsters a sense of first-hand transmission whilst appearing to offer visual realism (ibid.). Importantly, Hall highlights television's affinity with documentary: both are popularly thought of as 'reproducing the reality' with which they deal (his emphasis).

Crucial for our analysis here is the cross-over between 'high art' forms and those produced with the television arena in mind. We focus then on the more culturally privileged art-house projects as well as video diaries and 'auteur-driven' documentaries. Those that privilege cherished cultural distinctions here may well throw their hands up in horror. But our discussion of the work of Andy Warhol, for example, alongside the television-created video diary, aims to link the creative impulse in both 'elite' and popular forms to prioritise the personal. This prioritisation is more to do with cultural shifts in thinking about and through the subjective and signals the increasing popularisation of the therapeutic as an avenue for filmmakers to explore the contemporary moment, the formal properties of documentary and the realistic capture of the complex individual subject.

In this chapter, then, we discuss the use of video diaries, to-camera monologues, and shock tactic interviewing to signal the increasing importance of the private world over the public in video and televisual forms. For the reality TV viewer amateur 'pop psychological' self-analysis and/or amateur or unscripted footage meld the pleasures of voyeurism indicated in previous chapters with the pseudo-intimacy of the therapeutic consulting room. Here the emphasis is less on capturing the rawness of an unmediated event played out before the camera and more on the hidden or secret emotional realism suggested by confession, individual close-up engagement with the camera and popular therapeutic knowledge that suggests even the layman or woman can unpack personal trauma because we all have personal histories that score our identity. This notion of a shared competency at the level of subjective history lends to the dominant function of the representations we discuss: revelation on screen as the route to a new emotional realism.

Video diary and the performative

This chapter looks at the development of the personalised documentary. In these docu-mentaries subjective experience is central and informs both the documentary subject matter and frequently the dominant perspective; the form of address is frequently subjective, framed as therapeutic and confessional. This emphasis signals a shift in the grammar of documentary from an association of the word with factual explorations of the social world and its external structures to an association with uncertain knowledge, the impressionistic and personal world. This has resulted in documentaries that are constructed around memory, personal beliefs or individual dilemmas that are not necessarily intended to exemplify broader social issues although they may do so indirectly. Alongside this, the use of ordinary people who nonetheless have a general 'savvy' about media construction and media influence result in individual stories that have an idiosyncratic quality that arguably arises out of a culture that prioritises the newsworthy twist on self-inquiry. Both filmmaker and subject in a sense acquire a stylistic mark: the subject to legitimate their role in the documentary as extraordinary subject and the filmmaker as one who knowingly suggests their controlling, manipulative presence.

One key influence on the development of the personalised documentary is the use of the video diary. The entrance onto television screens of the first-person confessional in the video diary is well charted by documentary theorists (Corner 1996: 185–6; Dovey 2000: 55–77; Keighron 1993: 24–5; Kilborn & Izod 1997: 81–3). The biographical narrative has gained a distinct prominence in many forms of contemporary documentary, a strategy they share with a range of light-entertainment studio-based programmes as discussed in the previous two chapters. The video diary, a form arising from the spread of low-gauge videotape formats in easy-to-use camcorder technology, has become a commonplace sign of filmed intimacy or the captured moment on our television screens. The technical characteristics of the camcorder – its lightweight transportability, synchronised sound, easy editing facilities and relative cheapness – help produce a format that emphasises the intimate, spontaneous, exposing and endearingly amateur or superficially guileless moment. The video diary, for example, has become an essential element of the makeover/lifestyle programme and the survival/competitive reality show. These formats, with their clearly demarcated rules, challenges and group or couple dynamics frequently contain video extracts embedded within a structure that, for the most part, is highly regulated and policed. The seeming contrasting intimacy of the to-camera disclosure of the ordinary individual signifies a switch of power relations, as the 'real' individual speaks to the audience without the interference of camera crew, television hosts or coaches, and so on. The emphasis on the individual pointedly speaking to-camera at moments in the show taps into the current cultural preoccupation with the uninhibited and authentic emotional self being given media space and also being a stamp of authentic communication.

The life narrative that is told to-camera is obviously culturally and linguistically shaped. The power to structure perceptual experience, to organise memory and to segment and construct significant events in one's life is highly dependent on the cultural tool kit of metaphors, symbols, myths and so on that the self-story teller can draw upon that will chime with his or her audience. In the post-war era in many affluent Western cultures, the language of psychotherapy has shaped notions of failure and success, inadequacy and need in a psychological model of interpretation. Dreams, family history, minor pathologies, fears and defences – these are the narrative criteria that make sense of and judge personal landscapes – common mythic themes on which individuals draw. The 'intimacy' of the video diary is mapped onto a cultural sense of 'home' as private, forgiving, predictably safe but also secret, hidden and possibly troubling or transgressive. Correspondingly, the way this cheaply produced video footage is widely used on contemporary mainstream television reveals a cultural emphasis on the subjective and embodied. As Jon Dovey notes, such miniature and highly mobile technologies could have been used to efface the filmmaker (as in Direct Cinema). Instead, the opposite aesthetic emerges in which 'the contemporary video document is nothing *but* an inscription of presence within the text':

Everything about it, the hushed whispering voiceover, the incessant to-camera close-up, the shaking camera movement, the embodied intimacy of the technical process, appears to reproduce experiences of subjectivity. (2000: 56–7)

Work that foreshadows current developments in video diary documentary includes experimental or avant garde praxis from the 1960s and 1970s. During this period artists concerned with interrogating social and media practices used video and performance to consider the individual subject as part of a complex of social practices, discourses and systems of representation. The role of public persona and private self was often explored. For example, the current emphasis on personal disclosure and the inner self in a range of reality TV programming was anticipated in Wendy Clarke's *The Love Tapes* (1977) and the experimental work of Andy Warhol.

In *The Love Tapes* project, individuals from a variety of backgrounds are given three minutes of tape in which to deliberate on the intensely personal experience of what love means to them. Each individual is seated in a booth with a self-activated camera and the theme of 'love' as a catalyst to their discussion to-camera. Each video diary, whilst the same in length and subject, announced the multiple differences of the individual subject, for the repetitive formula counterpoised by the highly individual performances of each subject rendered each monologue unique (Renov 1999: 90).[1] The abstract notion of 'love' is revealed to be both cultural and also individual: notions of love as private, emotionally intense, euphoric, damaging, and so on are part of the shared imaginary that the speakers draw upon. Yet their accounts also reveal their individual stories of meeting, notions of love, personal enterprise, beliefs, expectations of a relationship and so on.

In Warhol's *Outer and Inner* Space (1965) he continued his ongoing artistic examination of the role of the mass-produced image in commodity exchange. In this work, Warhol combined experimental technology and a multi-screen framework with the conventions of portraiture and performance. The piece is a film and video portrait of Edie Sedgwick shot in August 1965. Sedgwick is seated in front of a large television monitor which is playing back a pre-recorded videotape of her. She is positioned so that her head is about the same size as her video image which gazes as though looking out of the frame. The filmed Edie sits to the right of the video image in three-quarter profile as though in conversation with the videoed Edie placed slightly to the right and behind her. Warhol shot two 33-minute reels of Edie and then projected them alongside one another. The videoed Edie is front-lit, with a mask-like flat quality to her profile giving her an enigmatic quality whilst the filmed Edie has nuanced lighting which, accompanied by the glow of the video screen, gives her a three-dimensional quality. The televised Edie has the sculpted quality characterised in Roland Barthes' analysis of Garbo's image as: 'the temptation of the absolute mask' (1972: 56). The filmed Edie appears unsettled by her video companion and the juxtaposition of the two images suggests perhaps the outer carapace of the video persona – a public persona – and the inner vulnerability and multi-dimensionality of the filmed Edie.

Importantly, for the later use of videotape, Warhol experiments with the role of video and film in capturing public persona and inner self as the film of the two reveals Edie's increasing discomfort as she encounters and tolerates her televised self. This can be read as an interrogation of the role of the moving image in concealing and disclosing the inner self. The filmed image of Edie is, of course, a media construction as much as the videotape version framed by the television. However, the seemingly greater, natural and more vulnerable quality of the latter, whilst intending perhaps to underline the superficiality of the video and mass-produced television image, in fact highlights both as media productions of equal weight. The more naturalistically-presented filmed Edie can be read as much as a performance as the harshly-lit video self. Both predict the masquerade offered by some film subjects to the video diary from the 1990s, in which surface identity and vulnerable interior are equally placed before the camera for the benefit of an audience.[2] This process of examining the multiple self is also captured in much experimental work coming out of the feminist movement and its interaction with artistic practice in the 1970s and 1980s.[3]

Both Clarke and Warhol anticipate the performative documentary that came to the fore in the late 1980s and 1990s. Bound up with the moment and ethos of identity politics, a significant number of documentaries foregrounded the subjective matrices of identity fashioned by the cultural markers of class, race, ethnicity and sexuality. For example, the work of Pratibha Parmar, Gurinder Chadha, Isaac Julien, Marlon Riggs, Rea Tajiri and Trinh T. Minh-ha drew upon an expressive, poetic, rhetorical and multi-dimensional style that often melded conventional fragments of historical or popular narratives with an intimate personal account of racial violence, ethnic legacy, sexual encounters, class consciousness and so on. Often the patterning of memory and expressive colours, music or voiceovers is juxtaposed with more conventional documentary material such as archival footage or interviews.[4]

As an extension of the feminist project of personalising the political, video diaries can be read as part of this larger media project to destabilise the masculinised all-controlling rational ego and to allow the inner private self to be acknowledged. They offer avenues towards undermining binary oppositions between evidence and experience, objectivity and subjectivity, the public and the private: categories that have underpinned much factual media work. As already noted in chapter 1, the BBC's *Video Diaries* series provided a more mainstream space for the first-person documentary, with ordinary people given video cameras to record for broadcast their personal views (see Kilborn & Izod 1997: 81–4). The launch of this new format by the BBC's Community Programmes Unit heralded the advent of a new format for confessional culture in which ordinary people produced subjective footage of their lives on cheap Hi-8 footage. As one *Times* newspaper reviewer of the 1992 series noted, many of these resembled 'DIY psychoanalysis' (Barker 1992: 353). For instance, in *Searching for a Killer*, Geoffrey Smith returned to Haiti to relive the traumatic experience of being caught in a bloodbath on polling day as a gunman sprayed bullets at Haitian voters, injuring Smith and killing his friend. Smith described his return as a means to purge the old nightmares and, as he faced fresh dangers, this self-help therapy appeared to work. He described his video diary in therapeutic terms: 'The camera was my only companion ... I needed a friend that would listen' (in Barker 1992: 354). He described the process of filming as 'a cathartic device' in which he became attached to the camera, overcoming the trauma of the experience by burying himself in filming.

Also of particular note is Willa Woolston's *My Demons: The Legacy* (1992) which shifts through a process of self-discovery via a journey which is 'both a recovery of autobiographical history and a self-administered therapy' (Kilborn & Izod 1997: 104–9). Woolston's documentary records her journey from London across North America visiting her children and sisters. This is no travelogue, but video footage with an explicit therapeutic aim:

> The record of her travel across the States becomes the trail of an inner journey in which she goes back to get the psychological roots of the physical and mental torture she and her sisters suffered at the hands of her stepmother. That mistreatment has left her with a life ruled by savage apprehension and relentless traumas. (Kilborn & Izod 1997: 105)

In the diary Woolston's voiceover narrates her drink problem and suicide attempts as well as her damaged relationship with her own children. Crucial to the film are the long takes in close-up in which Woolston or other family members relate to the static camera their experiences of physical and mental abuse and the inaction of their father who was terrified of losing his new young wife (ibid.). Professionally edited in post-production the diary retained its amateur quality and included home movie footage taken by Woolston's father of her and her sisters, seemingly happy with their stepmother. Richard Kilborn and John Izod argue that this mix of amateurishness and professionalism underwrites the documentary's status as 'deeply personal' but also 'acceptable (even trustworthy)' in the way it is paced and edited (1997: 107). They argue that the professional qualities of the film complement the therapeutic symbol of a journey into 'the realms of repressed memory', but add that the inexperienced aspects of the filming signify Woolston's isolated persona as she attempts to track back to 'what she must perceive to be her unique and wounded self' (1997: 109). In September 1992 the screening of the second of Woolston's video diaries followed her revelation of family secrets and how her family coped with the public nature of this process. Woolston, a portrait painter, describes her diaries as 'extremely distressing at first … A painted portrait is objective. Here you are being subjective. I was unaccustomed to looking at myself like that' (in Barker 1992: 354).

Woolston's video diary fits within the broader move within documentary and factual filmmaking since the 1990s to seize upon the personal and 'human interest'; a move which has, in turn, produced an ambivalent response amongst feminist critics. The filmic pursuit of intimacy and the personal arguably corrected a skewed prior emphasis on the masculinised rational debate of public issues and events at the expense of affective or personal affairs. In fact, the displacement of the politics of social movements by the politics of identity and a recognition of the personal as political were legacies of the second-wave feminist movement in the 1960s and 1970s and partly enabled the current 'effusion of documentary subjectivity' (Renov 1999: 89). However, the focus on the personal tended also to divide off this area into the 'feminine' and thereby to ghettoise it as trivial (van Zoonen 1991). Myra MacDonald (1998), has examined the interventions made by feminist television documentary makers since the 1990s which attempt to engage positively with the personal whilst resisting voyeurism and trivialisation; aiming instead for emotional and intellectual discomfort. She contrasts the 'confessional' mode of presenting women's stories with that of the 'testimony'. In the confessional mode, the woman confessing on screen is objectified and spectatorial pleasure comes from the viewing experience of detachment from the events being described by the film subject. She locates both television talk shows and video diaries in this mode; with the film subject being constructed ethnographically as the observed 'other' (1998: 109–10). MacDonald chooses to highlight examples from a number of 'quality' documentary series in this context – such as BBC2's *Modern Times* and Channel 4's *Cutting Edge* – confessional-mode documentaries in the respective series that tracked jilted female lovers and working mothers, locating each within a formula that foregrounds the individual emotional journey and dilemma, rather than emphasising the broader connection to women's lives and surrounding social structures. In these examples, suggests MacDonald, the women are reduced to an exemplar of narrated experience. In contrast, the testimony mode made women's subjectivity and social or political issues 'textually available' (1998: 114). Testimonial documentary allows the 'possibility of *access as exposition*' (1998: 112).

In Jane Treays' *Men in the Woods* (2001, Channel 4's *True Stories* series) the documentary retains subjective experience but arguably adopts a testimonial mode. Here Treays narrates her childhood trauma and its long-term effects while also exploring women's fear of masculine threat more generally. Much of her film involves her speaking to-camera, or in voiceover, narrating the events that have marred her adult life. She was walking in the woods as a six-year-old child with her mother when a masked man brandishing a stick leapt from the bushes and masturbated in front of them. Treays either speaks directly to the audience of these events or the film is shot as though we are walking alongside her as we explore the interlinked intimate geography of the woods near her childhood home and her internal fantasy woods in which she frequently returned to the scene of the crime. This auteur-centred approach uses a poetic wander through the woods, which borrows occasionally from the uneven tracking of horror films intercut with grainy cine-footage of Treays as a windswept child laughing or staring trustingly into the cine-camera. The aesthetics stress this as an individual person-to-person exchange: there is no other point of identification but with Treays. When the camera turns on Treays' mother towards the end of the film as she is confronted and challenged for silencing this woodland encounter in the name of family propriety, a generational and ethical gap emerges as Treays wishes to expose the incident and her mother wishes to let old demons remain buried: the past is past. Consequently, Treays connects her personal sense of alienation with the broader structures of middle-class self-containment, stoicism and respectability that shaped her family's response to her trauma, pressurising her to bury the incident and get on with her life. Here, the power of the camera is revealed as the daughter refuses to turn it off and the viewer witnesses, and perhaps feels for the mother and her discomfort at facing long-repressed events dealt with through her own discourses of decorum, privacy and common-sense rather than through Treays' therapeutic ones.

Men in the Woods meets MacDonald's criteria for a testimonial work. It prioritises memory and is in keeping with the recent feminist autobiographical practice of linking individual recollections built around personal and familial autobiography and to broader debates around gender and identity (Kuhn 1995; Steedman 1986). An interactive co-operative mode of communication is present at points in the documentary as Treays interviews women with similar experiences of random sexual assault, many of whom spoke of their disbelief at their ordeal:

'There must be a mistake,' thought one, who was flashed at in a bookshop. 'What has gone wrong?' thought another, at the complicity of the rest of the world in keeping the experience as one to be laughed at dismissively. (McLean 2001: 18)

Whilst self-indulgent perhaps in parts, with a nostalgic view of prelapsarian childhood before the assault, the documentary exhibits the provisionality and locatedness of experience characteristic of testimonial work (MacDonald 1998: 115–18). The reviewer who criticised this as 'a wade through Treays' psyche' and a programme in need of 'objective analysis and information on the sex offenders who were briefly interviewed' missed the point (McLean 2001: 18). This was a story based in fact, but the lines between fact and fiction were muddied and the fantasy nature precisely depicted the act of telling and retelling a traumatic childhood event. The aesthetics complement the journey of self-discovery. And there is a broader self-reflexivity in the use of popular cultural myths to signal the way childhood and its dangers and fears – in this case the danger of a rogue male – are encapsulated in fairy stories and urban myths. For both the *Men in the Woods* and *Our Father the Serial Killer* (2002), discussed below, are accounts of intimate injury and also, in keeping with this style of personalised documentary, a process of accusation: of naming the abuser as part of publicly reclaiming the self. In many cases, the documentary presents the pathology of its subjects in a form that lurches between horrific, damaging or intense recollected events and representational strategies that elide such intimate confession with popular cultural myths: the bogeyman in the woods, the killer under the stairs.

Inside/out – private trauma and public knowledge

Witnessing is also the discursive act of stating one's experience for the benefit of an audience that was not present at the event and yet must make some kind of judgement about it. (Peters 2001: 709)

In *Our Father the Serial Killer*, which featured as one of the British *Everyman* documentary series and was broadcast on Court TV, journalist John Edginton investigates claims made by Steve and Dianne Griggs that their father, Steven Griggs Sr, committed numerous acts of atrocity during their childhood and subsequently. They accuse their father of being a long-term serial killer of children and later of adults, too. These memories return to Steve Griggs as an adult and when he turns to his younger sister Dianne she corroborates his recollections. They report their father to the police who take their accusations seriously. But they are concerned that all the investigations are going to come to nothing. Having seen a documentary on criminal justice by Edginton they invite him to tell their story. He meets with them and like the police he finds them highly convincing. The documentary trails the pair as they investigate and challenge their father. The film is an account of intimate injury and also, in keeping with this style of personalised documentary, a process of accusation: of naming the abuser as part of *publicly* reclaiming the self. In this case, the documentary presents the pathology of its subjects (i.e. the harm they incurred and the case history of that harm) in a form that lurches between horrific, damaging or intense recollected events and representational strategies that elide such intimate confession with broader popular cultural myths of trauma: the bogeyman in the woods, the killer under the stairs, the mobile serial killer.

The Griggs are relentless investigators of their father. They unearth old newspaper evidence of children missing at the precise time and location of their father's alleged murders; they offer highly detailed and convincing accounts of children that they saw murdered, of scenes of crime and the disposal of bodies. The difficulty for the police is that while they are unable to find evidence in support of the Griggs' accusations neither are they able to disprove them. Much of the mythology of the serial killer 'profile' seems to fit their parent: he was in the army and was trained to commit violence. Furthermore, he was very dominant in the home which was situated in an isolated location, he dug out a huge cellar, he was mobile and had opportunities to kill. In addition, as the police noted, there are missing people whose disappearances remain to be accounted for in the surrounding area. Also, after the death of his wife the rest of his children moved away and failed to keep in touch. Only Steve and Dianne remained in the vicinity, seemingly not out of affection but to stalk their parent and safeguard the community from his predatory habits.

Edginton's classic investigatory documentary technique reveals these facts, using interviews, documentary evidence and photographic stills. Its narrative structure is one of continuing investigation with minor revelations on the way. The audience follows both Edginton and the Griggs' from those intense first moments when their horrific accusations are voiced, through their increasingly frustrated attempts to produce the evidence, to a growing realisation that whatever terrible crimes were committed by Griggs Sr they were unlikely to include relentless and continuing serial murder.

This more conventional process of documentary representation is intercut with the subjective perspective licensed by confessional programming formats in which the siblings, often highly distressed, recall to camera the horrific scenes which they either witnessed or in which they were forced to participate. They are shown recalling these events and making accusations to the documentarist, the police and media experts. Edginton re-visits the scenes of crimes as remembered by the siblings; remaining firmly off-camera but present through controlling questions and a voiceover that is increasingly sceptical of the factual status of the Griggs' surfacing memories. Towards the end of the film they meet with a psychologist who confirms that they have undergone serious traumatic experiences but doubts their recollections of serial killing. It emerges, as Steve's stories become increasingly unlikely, hyperbolic and contradictory that their memories are also connected to their own experience of abuse as children. Other siblings confirm that Steve and to a lesser extent Dianne were shockingly and consistently abused. One sister even says that she would not be surprised if their father was a killer. It is through these personal disclosures, inconsistencies of evidence and moments of intense confession-style revelation that the alternative crime story unfolds; not of serial killing but of child abuse. The initial investigation of a public and community-based crime becomes an investigation of psychic states in the aftermath of some terrible private and hidden traumatic event or series of events.

What is certain by the conclusion of the film is that the Griggs have undergone classic psychic trauma. They underwent events defined by their intensity, their incapacity to respond to them and by the long-lasting upheaval that this brings to their psychic organisation. They were unable to fully master or to work through the excess of traumatic experience successfully (Laplanche & Pontalis 1973: 465). If trauma can be understood as the compulsive return to the scene of a crime (Seltzer 1998: 260–1) then their remembering of abuse (it dominates Steve's life to a debilitating degree) through the metaphor of serial killing constituted an apposite kind of working through. For the figuring of Griggs Sr as 'serial killer' is nothing if not a figure or trope of endless repetition; his crimes according to his children's stories are innumerable and still unending; elaborate variations on a theme. And it is this trope of serial killing, with all its attendant mythology already established through film, drama, novels and reportage, that speaks to the viewer of something greater than individual trauma and which forms the connection between private suffering and the public narration of that experience. The serial killer, then, is a familiar and powerful cultural trope used by both Edginton and the Griggs in different but related ways to re-present the ultimately unrepresentable events of an abusive family past. Whilst the Griggs siblings clearly underwent extremely violent experiences as children, their trauma *as trauma* lacks clear origins that can be unearthed. As such the documentary does credit to this, perhaps inadvertently, by revealing the disjuncture between journalistic practice (embodied by Edginton) with its clear narrative structure, chronological time and factual reference and the Griggs' memories which are marked by absences, gaps in chronology, fragments, flashbacks and repetition. The serial killer then becomes a familiar and powerful cultural trope used by both Edginton and the Griggs in different but related ways to re-present the ultimately unrepresentable events of an abusive family past.

As such, rather than understand the trauma of what are, after all, from the perspective of the viewer, highly mediated subjects of documentary practice, *Our Father the Serial Killer* can be read for its use of contradictory discourses of private distress and public crime story, personal memory and public history and the precarious manner in which these are yoked together. For example, in one scene Steve finds a newspaper clipping of an old unsolved child murder and 'recalls' that his father was the perpetrator of the crime. We follow Steve and his sister, together with police officers, to the scene of the crime near a river embankment where Steve describes in convincing detail how their father killed and disposed of the child. Eventually, the police realise that Steve is unable to recall any details which they could corroborate with the information they held back from the press. This is one of many inconclusive scenarios in which public facts and fears about crime in the community seems to connect with private recollections only to trail off into loose ends. By allowing Steve to declare publicly his recollection of these dreadful acts the documentary taps into the narrativising of private events popularised in the confessional forms already discussed and does so in a way that ultimately objectifies the film subjects rather than empowering them. Steve's and Dianne's crises, in which they bear witness to various atrocities, are increasingly undercut by the lack of evidence and the growing scepticism of law enforcers and medical experts so that they become spectacles of declining credibility.

In the riverside scene, among others, Steve concentrates, gazing into the distance as he focuses on his recollections, rather like a medium in a séance. As he gazes beyond the camera into the middle distance, the camera's point of view locates him as overly intense, excessive and unsound. Edginton's authorial voice, present through commentary and editing which guides the viewer into a more 'correct' understanding of the Griggs' predicament, shifts the emphasis much more firmly onto the documentarist's encounter with and investigative search for the 'truth' of his story. The siblings' story of the search for evidence of the truth of their father's criminality ultimately becomes subordinated to Edginton's story of the search for the truth of their trauma.

This story is captured in a form, documentary, that is far more highly regarded than true crime or talk show confession but shares with such popular programming an attempt to construct a topography of un-representable elements such as interior states: memory, trauma and fear. And also, just as importantly for a public form, it reveals the ways in which trauma documentaries across the spectrum from the 'serious' to the 'popular' attempt to represent individual and also collective fantasies: mythological structures that explain culture to itself, structures which viewing subjects will recognise and with which they will connect. Like Treays' film, it renders private trauma via public narratives.

One might ask what kinds of documentary forms are most effective at delivering these seemingly unrepresentable interior landscapes via broader mythic structures. We are talking for the most part about documentaries that are internally rich in representational strategies such as condensation, displacement, symbolism of all kinds. John Corner calls these 'thick text' documentaries; formats which incorporate the aesthetics and narrative devices of fictional and art film forms which speak to and incorporate structures of fantasy and the unconscious (Corner 2003: 94). These documentaries are rich enough to provide pleasure over and above the overtly informational and invite and merit a second viewing in the ways that, for example, a news programme does not. While *Our Father the Serial Killer* is not *wholly* in this league its composition is sufficiently thick to bear the burden of fantasy and trauma through the slow revelation of facts and the deferral of knowledge but also through the use of extra-diegetic music, its attention to landscape and locale, its fleeting use of horror film aesthetics. Its narrative builds suspense. It is partly a psychological and partly a genre-based detective story which builds to a climax in which the filmmaker confronts the by now very elderly father/serial killer in his own home and descends with him into the cellar.

This scene begins with the mobile camera circling the house, peering into the porch and through windows; drawing on a horror film lexicon of camera movement to disorientate the viewer, not only through its mobility, but by positioning the viewer as the intruder in the domestic space of the Griggs' former family home. Griggs Sr is discovered sitting in an armchair and called to the door. The shock of this moment, for the viewer, lies partly in the frailty of this now elderly man whose shocking exploits loom so large over his children's lives and the film itself. After a discussion in which the father denies everything and is both dismissive and bemused, he agrees to take Edginton into his cellar and proudly shows him round the dug-out and reinforced room. Such is the power of horror film iconography that it is difficult not to imagine the bodies immured within. They are an absent presence in the sense that even if they do not exist literally they do exist within the logic of the film. The film ends with the camera's point of view, filming up the stairs and showing Griggs Sr looming at the top, fleetingly a photographic still of his younger face is transposed onto him to malevolent effect. The tenor is one of menace; a signifier of the monstrous father buried within this seemingly benign character and within the home. The filming in this encounter rather heavy-handedly signals the uncanny, the camera peeping through the window to discover the killer in his lair. The sinister extra-diegetic music accompanies the unveiling of Griggs Sr's photograph, this black and white image of the uniformed father is only teasingly revealed, like a striptease, from the feet to the head, deliberately invoking a horror film genealogy. The viewer is left in little doubt that Griggs Sr is a bad man.

This dramatic and highly impressionistic climax, however, sits awkwardly in a format that operates more conventionally in investigatory and interrogatory modes and which is, overall, far more subtle than this moment suggests. One of the disquieting elements of the film is the contrast between established investigative documentary technique and the staging of distressing confessional scenes which are almost therapeutic in their intensity. These usually occur at the alleged scenes of crimes.

In one example, Dianne Griggs drives to the location in which her father allegedly lured a young boy to his death. She recounts her childhood memory of her father persuading the boy into the car and then sexually abusing him in front of the two siblings. Her father then drove to a desolate well and threw the young boy down there having taunted her brother to kill him and made him pull a knife on their captive. In an intense and claustrophobic scene Dianne convincingly recollects this event in a faltering and shaking voice punctuated by moments of complete breakdown. She sits in the front passenger seat while the camera films from the rear – in the position and point of view of the filmmaker (and of the two Griggs children as recalled). Dianne does not face the camera throughout this recollection. She is shot in near silhouette. Her placement in the intimate but de-personalised space of the car seems to jar alongside the clear surfacing of violent and disturbing memories. The filmed encounter clearly suggests the therapeutic encounter: situating the journalist and the viewer as therapists listening in on another's private disturbed history.

At the corner of the frame, through the side window of the car, her brother is clearly visible, walking the ground where the well is supposed to be. Agitated and distracted, he seems to represent the recollected father as much as himself. Intense and driven in appearance he becomes a reconstructed illustration of Griggs Sr and an extension of the therapeutic scene of memory and/or fantasy. We, for a moment, are made to appreciate the relative safety of the enclosed vehicle as Steve roams around about outside. In this, and other scenes, Steve himself becomes an elided figure whose meaning is increasingly multivalent (child victim, adult survivor, crime witness, dangerous individual). The imputation unfolds that Steve is potentially dangerous; that he is someone who not only bears his father's full name but whose identification with his father is as strong as his revulsion for him. Other scenes, such as one where Steve obsessively digs into a vault newly discovered on his land (reminiscent of his father's cellar) or the episode where the police reveal that they are nervous of being alone with him, reflects the growing insinuation on the part of the filmmaker that it is Steve himself who may be disturbed rather than (or as much as) his father.

This is very much a landscape of trauma in which the scrub-like terrain seen frequently throughout the documentary comes to signify the anonymous killing ground, suitable for the concealment of serial killers' victims and emblematic of the spaces where child abuse could be enacted without disturbance. Edginton follows brother and sister to what are presented as isolated lakesides, scrubland, the river's edge and vacated houses all of which were alleged scenes of crimes and constitute a form of psychic topography. The scenes are charged with emotion as the camera records Steve patiently fishing for body parts in the lake or pacing agitatedly through woodland with a spade in his hand. As Corner notes, television documentaries of this type embrace the 'impact of the picture not simply to be looked through, but to be looked at'; here landscapes and buildings require to be 'read as a discourse about the world rather than a depiction of it' as landscape becomes imbued with meaning; in this case memorials for traumatic events, possibly deaths (1996b: 96). The siblings claim that many journeys were made in their father's car and that ostensibly happy family trips were actually taken to stalk victims, bury body parts or molest his children. Both the car journeys that Edginton and the Griggs's take as the documentary is filmed and the anonymous scrubland they cover constitute fetish objects that stand in for the absent evidence. As the Griggs siblings drive or pace the scrub they tell a story of slaughter for which there is no concrete proof – no bodies, bones, murder weapons, witnesses – yet throughout the documentary they insist on the truth of their account: they reiterate to the journalist 'I know there is nothing there but nonetheless...'. And every now and then the police manage to corroborate some small detail of their recollections – there was once a well in this isolated location which few people knew about; children do go missing. It seems nearly impossible to read the Griggs family drama as anything but contemporary family gothic horror; with the paterfamilias reminiscent of Tobe Hooper's nightmarish *Texas Chain Saw Massacre* (1974): disposing of bodies beneath the porch, in wells and in rubbish dumps as he travels with the children along the country's highways and byways.

Erik Barnouw asserted that the difference between the Direct Cinema and the *cinema verité* filmmaker was that the former took a camera into a difficult context in anticipation of a crisis and the latter tried to precipitate one (1974: 245). In terms of Direct Cinema Stephen Mamber explains how the Drew films, for example, operated within a 'crisis structure' in which the film's momentum and its organising principle is provided by an 'anticipated crisis moment' (1972: 115). This structure is not a 'given' of documentary form but inherent already in fiction and at its worst 'the story would be a fictional element to support a non-fiction result. At best the story would be a true representation of an exciting period' (1972: 117). The ideal story, then, is one in which there are a number of possible outcomes, some of them resulting in real crises; crises that do not need to be manufactured for the filmmaker. In Edginton's case, the situation of publicly-made accusations would be fertile ground for the generation of crises. However it would seem that not all crises are filmically equivalent. Steve's revelation of the importance of his experience of abuse to his accusation of his father as a serial killer may well be a crisis moment for Steve but it is arguably insufficiently filmic to constitute closure within the organisation of the documentary. It is never explained why we do not witness the Griggs children confronting their father but it seems clear that a confrontation must take place, albeit a relatively manufactured one between filmmaker and the accused.

In this context, Steve's moment of realisation is reduced to one of a number of 'less Important' crises that punctuate the film; emotional breakdowns or 'confessions' with which television audiences are already more than familiar from both observational documentary and popular factual programming. Nikolas Rose has tracked what he refers to as the increasingly dominant 'therapeutic imperative' to heal ourselves which is evidenced in such confessional and autobiographical representations (1990: 214; see also Lasch 1978). He points to the ways that nineteenth-century disciplines prefixed with 'psy' – psychology, psychiatry and psychoanalysis – have moved away from being discrete fields of knowledge and become 'intellectual technologies' that both explain and render conspicuous certain facets of our behaviours and our relations with others (1998: 10–11). These 'psy' technologies, albeit bowdlerised and misrepresented, have infused social and media space via the popularisation of trauma as mass entertainment. Steve and Dianne's claims are understood by viewers within this matrix of popularised 'psy' discourses which, as we have discussed, also occupy the public arenas of chat shows and radio confessionals. The first-person singular mode also has a disarming directness which seems to validate the perceived intimacy of the small screen. And whereas literary autobiography, for example, offers an essentially private and intimate encounter, on television the encounter muddies the boundaries of private and public spheres.

In doing so, it also confuses moments of personal revelation with the revelatory imperative of effective filmmaking or storytelling, and such moments run on parallel and sometimes connecting tracks. For example, Steve takes the filmmaker to his childhood home (not the house in which his father is later confronted). Standing in his bedroom, this is the point when Steve, for the first and only occasion, openly acknowledges the abuse he suffered at the hands of his father and recalls his childhood fear that he would never leave that room alive. If revelation and truth-telling are the objectives of documentary, then this should be the climax of the film – it seems to be the one moment when he acknowledges the centrality of his own abuse in the *private* family to his *public* story of serial killing. But the room is bare, clean and whitewashed. There is no visible sign of trauma and no apparent hope of a movement towards resolution, it does not have the *overt* uncanniness of a 'crime' scene and there is no scope for confrontation. It is at this point that the absence of the signs of Steve's trauma, while perfectly comprehensible in analytic and temporal terms, is incomprehensible filmically (see Elsaesser 2001: 199–200). As Bill Nichols notes, 'Witness and testimony, deposition and refutation, accusation and denial – all depend on direct encounter and physical presence' (1991: 232–3) which never happens between Steve and his father in this film. So too, all the other real crimes that are invoked by the film (such as the boy found dead at the river's edge) remain unsolved. But the imperative of the documentary investigation means that we, as audience, cannot be left here with matters unresolved. In a sense, Steve is left behind at this point because he has finally led the filmmaker to a dead end and Edginton takes on the lone role of pursuer, seeking to provide viewers with a more revelatory, more filmic but also ultimately more ersatz moment of resolution. The encounter in the whitewashed room presages the filmmaker's later encounter in the darker recesses of Griggs Sr's cellar.

In other words, the drive within the narrative for a public resolution cannot be accommodated in this more private scenario of Griggs facing up to his past in the whitewashed room. The story turns out to be much more about the filmmaker's drive to resolve the social trauma of a random killer than the personal trauma of the film's subjects. An account of intimate injury it is also, in keeping with this style of documentary, a process of accusation: of naming the abuser as part of publicly reclaiming the self. In this (as with other documentaries, such as those by Errol Morris discussed below and *Men in the Woods*) the documentary presents the pathology of its subjects in a form that lurches between the terribly intimate and the broader public myths that shape our collective stories of dangerous spaces where we encounter strangers in the woods, roadside dangers and the holes and cellars where we might find vanishing children.

In this example the film becomes the space in which viewers confront not only the subjects' personal family ordeal but our own broader anxieties about unprovoked violence as embodied in the mythology of the serial killer. In her study entitled *Speak of the Devil* (1998) Jean La Fontaine explains how experiences of child abuse by adult survivors become transformed into broader stories of satanic abuse in contemporary Britain and the US. She explains how bizarre allegations mask or explain away the fact that familial and community structures did not intervene to help the victim. The invocation of conspiracies and networks of ritual abusers ensure that there is always an irrefutable explanation for the lack of corroborative evidence. The enculturation of horror stories and the religious iconography and discourses of good and evil provide a ready-made lexicon for survivors to draw on that listeners will also recognise. This, together with the dominance of a therapeutic culture which encourages the telling and re-telling of trauma in every detail, ensures a fertile reception for these interpretations of individual trauma. These stories, like the Griggs' story, provide comprehensible explanations for familiar childhood suffering and its invisibility.

Crucially, these stories are the locus where therapeutic knowledge, personal trauma and media-driven popular knowledge interlock to produce something else: the intersubjective social/media space which Mark Seltzer, in his book *Serial Killers,* calls 'wound culture'. For Seltzer the continuing public fascination with stories of atrocity and serial murder reveals an erosion of distinctions between the body and the mind, the inside and the outside, the private and the public. He notes that 'the uncertain relays between private desire and public space in wound culture are nowhere clearer than in the … resurgence, of the category of "the trauma" … on the contemporary scene' (1998: 254). Personalised documentaries together with other vehicles for confession, autobiography, the display of psychic and corporeal trauma and so on are arguably symptomatic of the ongoing transformation in public culture; of the erosion of distinction between public and private. But this programme shows that this erosion – operating as it is through public entertainment-based forms of factual television – is complicated and conflicted – twisting together, as it does, the documentary subject's personal story with the generic imperative to produce narrative-fuelled entertainment.

Errol Morris: documentary as psychic drama

'REALITY? You mean this is the real world? I never thought of that!'
(First words heard in *Vernon, Florida,* dir. Errol Morris, 1981, USA)

Two broad themes run through the oeuvre of Errol Morris. Firstly he interrogates television documentary and developments in its form and prompts analysis of how the filmmaker might use formal innovation to think through the perilous and value-laden relationship between – crudely put – the 'aesthetic' and the 'popular' in contemporary television documentary. His work melds the innovation of experimental practice with the populist imperatives of tabloid culture. And secondly, Morris' work clearly exemplifies the move within recent documentary to examine interior states, memory and psychic trauma. These two characteristics locate these documentaries within a broader move within television, signified by the popular forms and new documentaries already discussed. This broader move can be loosely defined as a relatively open process of 'working through', in which contemporary television provides 'a forum of contending definitions with no final result' (Ellis 2000: 84).

As signalled earlier, in the early 1970s Stuart Hall usefully described the 'technics of television' as a one of relay, proximity and intimacy. These aspects had been obscured in the important but overly weighted concern with political and cultural economy in television studies to the detriment sometimes of 'the aesthetic' (see Hall 1996: 3–10). The notion of the aesthetic has had a convoluted and contested history in the debates about the form and nature of television in general and documentary in particular. There has been a tendency both popularly and within televisual critique to regard television as an 'aesthetically impoverished medium' primarily concerned with regular predictable output and enmeshed in the culture and concerns of everyday life (Goode 2003: 93). This has resulted in an overdetermination of its realist concerns, its access to the immediate factual realm and the imbrication of those representations in the everyday/domestic sphere. Often linked to this has been an emphasis on the popular address – an important emphasis – but one that again often negates the aesthetically challenging as the proper realm of independent cinema rather than the demotic space of television.

Similarly, documentary both in production and in critique has exhibited ambivalence towards the self-consciously stylised or foregrounded aesthetics of works that originate from its founding moments. Here, for example, if we focus on British documentary for one moment, we can acknowledge the ambivalence at the very heart of Grierson's critique of documentary. This ambivalence is clearly evident in the classic 1930s texts in which poetic depiction of social reality (in *Coalface*, *Nightmail* and so on) meshed with social observation and also clashed with the imperatives of an overtly more observational record of the British working class' everyday life (such as *Housing Problems*). As we have seen, the use of associative imagery and sound has been described as 'hallucinatory realism' – a self-conscious stylisation that has haunted the British and American documentary movements, signifying an 'inescapable tension' between documentary's status as discourse and as record (Corner 1996: 123). Bill Nichols has similarly claimed of innovative documentary practice: 'the paradoxical status of realism as a mode of representation that attests to knowledge and to aesthetic pleasure remains acute'. He adds that 'to resolve this paradox in either direction so that a text is made transparent to the world, as unmediated knowledge, or rendered opaque, as a realm of aesthetic signification, is to dull the very edge that gives realism its power and continuing use value' (1996: 57–8).

Errol Morris, in keeping with this paradoxical status of representational realism, has positioned himself against documentary practice that prioritises the historical world over imaginary ones. He has suggested that *cinéma vérité* in the sense of fly-on-the-wall realism, for example, 'set back documentary filmmaking twenty to thirty years' by presenting it 'as a sub-species of journalism' (in Bruzzi 2000: 5–6). He claims there is 'no reason why documentaries can't be as personal as fiction filmmaking and bear the imprint of those who made them.' For Morris, a rigorous adherence to observational style or expression 'doesn't guarantee truth' (ibid).[6]

We have seen, since the mid-1990s, a pervasive shift in comprehension of the word 'documentary'. Morris' work could be located within the new-style 'poetic' documentary which permits an engagement with fantasy and illusion by organising its material to produce emotional affect and even a dialogue with the 'collective consciousness' (Kilborn & Izod 1997: 83). Importantly to understand the therapeutic encounter in Morris' work we need to think about the traces it bears of earlier televisual innovations, in particular the first-person accounts in video diaries and chat shows. It shares with these an emphasis on confession and the to-camera addresses of the main subject or subjects. It also prioritises a notion of 'incompleteness and uncertainty, recollection and impression, images of personal worlds and their subjective reconstruction' (Nichols 1991: 1).

Morris' documentaries work hard with the twin aims of destabilising the sober discourses of documentary and with challenging conventional modes of filming recollections of real, often traumatic past events. He focuses frequently on individual memories and places these within a tapestry of archival, poetic and reconstructed scenes that prioritise the strange and often highly repetitive or ritualistic aspects of human behaviour. *Gates of Heaven* (1978), for example, explores the world of pet cemeteries whilst *Vernon, Florida* (1981) focuses on a community of bizarre swamp dwellers. The film *Fast Cheap and Out of Control* (1997) is an exploration of a topiary gardener, a robot scientist, a lion tamer and a mole rat researcher. His documentaries frequently focus on bizarre individuals and their stories. He describes his films as 'mental landscapes' that combine the journalistic and the 'bold created image'.[7] They share with tabloid culture a love of the perverse or the 'exceptionally remarkable' ordinary person. His documentaries can be seen as artful, intelligent representations of offbeat characters that allow them a dignity that extends beyond Morris' claim that: 'I've always thought of my portraits as my own version of the Museum of Natural History ... these very odd diorama where you're trying to create some foreign exotic environment and put it on display.'[8]

Morris' work has been located within broader interrogations of the role of documentary in representing history within the context of reality TV programming and 'the current post MTV generation of spectator-consumers' (Conomos 2000: 1). *The Thin Blue Line* (1988) investigates the case of Randall Adams, an out-of-town worker, who is seemingly wrongly accused of murder of a Dallas policeman and is sentenced to death partly through the police and judiciary's reluctance to indict a local teenager, Dan Harris who was also present at the scene of the crime. This film has been identified as a 'reflexive' documentary in that, like many of Morris' texts, it draws attention to both the form of the documentary, foregrounding the problem of presenting representations that are adequate to an event to which there can be no direct access (Nichols 1991: 57-8). *The Thin Blue Line* relies on the conventions of interview but also highlights the difficulty of ascertaining the truth as police officers, prosecution and defence, witnesses and friends produce statements that contradict one another. Morris emphasises the contradictions rather than turning research material and visual imagery into an evidential account of guilt and innocence. Just as testimony becomes mutual recrimination, evasion and self-vindication in *The Thin Blue Line*, so Morris detaches his imagery from historical reference. His reconstructions or staged scenes often rely on emblematic images – the iconic drawing of a handgun against a stark background, the slow motion of a milkshake sailing through the air to splatter on the tarmac, a camera shot lingering on police officers' feet. In these ways he rejects a conviction in events and the documentary maker's hold on the power of visual imagery to consolidate his or her version of the truth. Morris has placed such fabrications of the frequently traumatic and often newsworthy real event within his critique of documentary's claim to objectivity stating that:

> Often we like to reduce documentary to journalism and we like to feel secure about journalism – that we're not being tricked or betrayed or swindled or lied to. But no one really worries about it that much as long as it's being presented in the right idiom. As long as it looks real, people are delighted. But what the reenactments do in, say, The Thin Blue Line is provide this wealth of visual contradiction. They're never illustrations of what I think the world is. They're illustrations of lies. They're all ironic. They, hopefully, teach you how images can't embody truth. (In O'Hehir 2000: 1)

These images refuse any direct correlation between documentary reconstruction and truth, realism and fact (see Nichols 1991: 57–8; 99–101). But by allowing the various interpretations of the murder to have a space and his 'witnesses' to reveal their own hidden motives and assumptions, Morris suggests that some versions of an event are more plausible than others:

> Morris dramatises the quest for evidence and underlines the uncertainty of what evidence there is. He reminds us of how every documentary constructs the evidentiary reference points it requires by returning us, again and again, to the scene of the crime by means of a re-enactment that highlights suggestive, evocative, but also completely inconclusive aspects of the event. (Nichols 1991: 58)

This questions the 'reality' captured by film and the nature of spectatorship in interpreting the traces of the violent and traumatic past as it is relived in the present. As Linda Williams has claimed of The Thin Blue Line:

> The preferred technique is to set up a situation in which the action will come to [Morris]. In this privileged moment of verité (for there are finally moments of relative verité) the past repeats. We thus see the power of the past not simply by dramatising it, or re-enacting it, or talking about it obsessively (though these films do all this) but finally by finding its traces, in repetitions and resistances, in the present. (In Rosenheim 1996: 230)

Similarly, Morris' Mr Death: The Rise and Fall of Fred A. Leuchter, Jr. (1999) depicts the eccentric Fred A. Leuchter, an engineer from Massachusetts who repairs gas chambers and designs electric chairs, gallows and lethal injection systems. Leuchter's proficiency at such death technology leads to his naïve implication in the neo-Nazi Ernst Zundel's Holocaust denial movement and he is commissioned by Zundel to travel to Auschwitz to take forensic samples of the site to prove that the Holocaust did not occur. Possessing no knowledge of Holocaust history or of World War Two, Leuchter believed he could spend a single afternoon stealing rock samples from decaying fifty-year-old buildings and denounce the existence of the Holocaust with his conclusions. Morris leaves no doubt that Leuchter's forensic 'evidence' that the bricks at Auschwitz contain no traces of cyanide gas was amateur claptrap without scientific or historical merit. His lack of historical insight and depth of response to his journey to Auschwitz is revealed in the film in a mode that can be read as deeply ironic as well as deeply offensive. As Andrew O'Hehir notes: 'His impressions of the time he spent in a place where perhaps half a million people died are those of a teenager after a visit to the town cemetery: "It was cold, it was wet, it was kind of spooky"' (2000: 1).

Nonetheless Morris refuses to plumb the depths of Leuchter's psyche, to announce him as pathological, anti-Semitic, or evil and claims his search, whilst it is a search of 'personality' is also 'a fractured fairy tale' (in O'Hehir 2000: 1). Leuchter's childhood is evoked in a montage of archival footage of prisons, death rows, executions and prison guards. Through this iconographic collage the spectator is invited 'to appreciate the particular law-and-order ethos that Leuchter was raised in and which shaped his life-long interest in creating and perfecting execution technology' (Conomos 2000: 4). Morris locates his documentary within the personalised when he declares *Mr Death* as 'the story of a man who, hoping for the best, created the worst' (in O'Hehir 2000: 1). He adds that, 'there is something chameleon-like, something almost evanescent, ephemeral' about Leuchter that evades the documentarist's question: '"Who is this man?"' (ibid.).

Morris' *Interrotron Series* (1995) mixed high-tech studio interviews, dramatic recon-structions and news footage to tap into and unsettle the conventions of reality TV. The series used Morris' modified series of teleprompters 'the Interrotron', a device that enabled him to interview his subjects without being in the same room. Via a projected video image of Morris on a glass plate, the interviewee interacts with him but appears to be speaking directly to-camera without apparent intervention. Such apparent direct contact, intensifies the sense of intimacy of the interview and filmed close-up, the expressively lit faces of Morris' subjects become fascinating texts to be read for each slight modulation of expression or voice. The Interrotron enables Morris to be virtually eclipsed by the filming apparatus in a model that has been compared to the therapeutic process: 'The device intensifies the psychoanalytic valence of the film camera, operating as the equivalent of the impassive analyst in classical Freudianism' (Rosenheim 1996: 222). Developed during commercial advertising shooting, the Interrotron enabled Morris to succeed in the illusion of closeness to his subject whilst appearing to be absent from the filmic process. As he has acknowledged, the Interrotron

> enabled interviews to be edited in a way I've never seen anything edited before. I could essentially put together a seamless piece of interview that might have a hundred cuts in it. Obviously the cuts are there, but because everything is dutched with respect to everything else, you don't notice them. You have the benefit of montage without having to interrupt what someone's saying, or resorting to jump cuts. (In Rosenheim 1996: 223).

The artifice of Morris' work has been described as 'if not *cinéma vérité*, then the psychological *vérité* of cinema' (ibid.). Many of the stories in this series focus on the re-telling of murder stories and first-person recollection in montage with news footage, talk show excerpts, reconstructions, location footage, ironic extra-diegetic music and so on, compounding the overall sense of not one truth but a series of partial perspectives. For example, in *Digging up the Past*, the story of a posthumous confession fuels the bizarre but historically resonant account of a 1963 racial murder. Henry Alexander was one of four Klansmen who forced black truck driver Willie Edwards to plunge to his death from a bridge. Diane Alexander, prime focus of Morris' documentary, dug up a chest on her husband's instructions, after his death. The chest contained incriminating Klan memorabilia and newspaper cuttings of the murder which strongly suggested a resolution to the perpetration the murder. The documentary includes overtly tabloid-style reconstructions of the plunge of Edwards to his death and includes an excerpt borrowed from *The Donohue Show* in which Diane Alexander tearfully embraces Willie Edwards' widow.[9] Morris, however, confronts such over wrought conclusions revealing through Diane's interview that she was willing to absolve her husband. As Morris notes, 'the whole thing is really dreamlike. It's the ultimate faux-redemptive ending – the search for some overarching principle of justice or God' (in Rosenheim 1996: 230). In this sense there is no clear dividing line between tabloid and avant garde culture, factual representation and fictional embellishment. For, whilst Morris' work can be clearly aligned with a modernist technique in its use of montage, the self-reflexive play with technology and perspective and the juxtaposition of factual and symbolic material, it is also emblematic of contemporary popular news coverage – from talk shows to tabloid papers – for its use of the bizarre individual, the prioritisation of human interest emotion and scandalous story over fact and objectivity.

As is clear from the films discussed above, Morris is drawn to stories of death and of murder because they represent the limits of historical narration and factual reconstruction. To conclude our discussion of trauma documentary we will concentrate on recent examples of Morris' work, particularly *Stairway to Heaven* (1998), which depicts a female subject whose revelation of her personal belief system is charged with her visceral encounters with death in a slaughterhouse. These experiences underpin her coping with and making sense of her autism. Here, Morris complements the woman's estrangement and her unique visual perception through expressive formal techniques.

Stairway to Heaven was part of the *First Person* series of eleven half-hour television documentaries broadcast on Bravo from May 2000 and in the UK on Channel 4 in 2001. The first-person accounts in the films are stories of traumatic aspects of his subject's lives told to-camera in the first person, by each individual. The bizarre characters featured in the series include the cryogenic expert who stole his dead mother's head (*I Dismember Mama*); a woman who, while writing a book about falling in love with a serial killer, falls in love with a second one (*The Killer Inside Me*); the 'Unabomber's' pen pal (*Gary Greenberg, Unabomber Pen Pal*); the parrot who may have witnessed a murder (*The Parrot*); the director of a museum of medical oddities (*Gretchen Worden, Director of the Mutter Müseum*); and the woman who, after her son's messy suicide, became a cleaner at crime scenes (*Joan Dougherty, Crime Scene Cleaner*).

Morris' subjects, their address to camera, the half-hour format and their tabloid titles – for example, *The Killer Inside Me*, *The Stalker* – foreground their allegiance with tabloid culture. Psychoanalysis and its popularisation are again crucial here, for it provides the documentary subjects with a ready language for addressing personal dilemmas. The assumption here (like the popular television talk show) is that what is spoken about provides the route to what is deeply felt. The documentary becomes one more stage in the coping, facing and working through of an individual distress. As indicated by the title of Morris' *The Killer Inside Me*, the personal trauma functions as an anchoring point for the documentary narrative. It functions at the centre of how the subjects experience their relationship between the past and the present, between their private self and the public self. And most importantly, trauma functions as the enigma revealed – a bit like classical film narrative or, more appositely, film melodrama that proceeds via a flashback structure – the subject's story functions around telling how bits of the past patch together to cause present distress or present strategies of survival. The documentary then adds another layer to this imaginary capacity for self-representation and self-construction. The self-reflexivity here is twofold: at the level of the documentary subject who shares her or his personal story of their self-understanding with the audience. And, on a formal level, the self-reflexivity of the filmmaker, who sometimes attempts to undermine the power relations of the documentary process and foreground their own filmic control.

Morris' subjects are treated as articulate monologists, engaging with the spectator through direct, close-up to-camera accounts. Temple Grandin, the subject of *Stairway to Heaven*, stares into the 'Interrotron'. As discussed above, the teleprompter enables the interviewee to maintain eye contact with Morris while gazing directly down the camera lens. Therefore the interviewee speaks in the first person and appears to directly address the audience without directorial intervention. Sharing perhaps a technological desire to capture the multi-perspectival 'reality' of recent Reality TV, as the *First Person* series developed, Morris moved to a modified Interrotron device with '20 cameras rolled into one' – which provided multiple unusual angles on his subject – a process of attempting to re-present states of mind, error and self-deception.[10] In keeping with the technique of the video diary, the self presented here to-camera becomes a marker of integrity; the interviewee is primary guarantor of experience and knowledge. Here, again the conventional concerns of documentary segue with 'trash TV' and are given shape through the discourses of the personal trauma. Morris' work then exemplifies a broader popular script in which subjects try to 're-inscribe themselves into different kinds of media-memory' (Elsaesser 2001: 199).

In all these documentaries, the subject often interprets the events – fear, abuse, extreme grief, and so forth – through a ragbag of discourses – popularised psychoanalytic language, medical discourse, language of human rights, legal discourse. Importantly, the documentaries also emphasise and expand upon those fictional or symbolic discourses the subjects use that add emotional tone fairy tale and urban myth, horror and crime story, religious imagery. Both the self-conscious performance of Morris' protagonists and the role of popular and media culture in clothing those performances are emphasised. Morris' editing brackets Sondra London's accounts of her love affairs with two serial killers in *The Killer Inside Me* with her recollection of a romantic masochistic childhood fantasy of being swept up by a dark stranger bogeyman. The documentary includes video footage of London being serenaded by her second serial killer lover in a courtroom as he disrupts his hearing to perform to the court and to camera. London herself, in a home video, clad in a bizarre part-vampire, part-dominatrix leather costume, performs one of her poems on serial killers as 'fallen angels of death'. Referring to her current affair with a sadistic death-row rapist and murderer she concurs with Morris that her childhood fantasies have come true: 'Well I'm riding on the back of that grim reaper's horse, that's for sure.' London explains her lover's evil nature through the mythic character Gemini – a figure of pure evil that possesses human beings. She invokes his self-description as 'a possessed puppet of flesh'. 'Evil is real', London warns the viewer, 'evil walks this Earth like a natural man'. This is the material of the talk show but Morris goes one step further in revealing the self-consciously performative element of some of his subjects, implicitly suggesting this as motivation for both their individual behaviour and their consent to appear in his films. At the end of *The Killer Inside Me*, in extreme close-up, London acknowledges that she 'never wanted to be a repeatable person' and she is certainly presented as unique and remarkable as the subject of this film.

In the *First Person* series, the accounts of trauma involve intellectualisation of the real or imagined shocks or frights the subject has experienced. In *Stairway to Heaven*, Temple Grandin recounts two crisis points which constitute the trauma of her narrative: the sensory overload of autism and a subsequent encounter with the enigma of death. Firstly, she recollects her childhood experience of autism before diagnosis. The sensory overload she experienced was of such an unbearable intensity and, in recollection, was so beyond her childhood sense of meaning that her response was one of horrified incomprehensible alien-ation from the surrounding world. She painstakingly explains symptoms of her autism, the experiences of a world populated by 'an overwhelming tidal-wave of stimulation'. Everyday experiences trigger acute anxiety or fear: scratching petticoats feel like sandpaper 'rubbing off raw nerve endings', a bell sounds like a jackhammer in her ear. As with many autistic subjects, Grandin thinks more clearly through visual imagery than language. The documentary opens with Grandin's claim: 'I think in pictures. Pictures is [sic] my first language and English is my second.' The documentary then attempts to replicate this way of negotiating the world, capturing Grandin's sense that she has a video camera plugged into her forehead. One device that gives this exploration structure is the sense of a journey, of slow, hallucinogenic movement accompanied by Caleb Sampson's impressionistic soundtrack and extracts from Aphex Twin's haunting ambient sound collection. For example, in a section titled 'Diagnosed Autistic', Grandin describes her autism as being like a ball in a pinball machine. Over her account we see slow motion black and white images of a pinball ricocheting, accompanied by the click and whirr of the machine. As she compares the cattle's passage through the slaughterhouse system to people on a moving escalator at an airport, we see low-shot imagery of people moving swiftly along the ramp, one behind the other, like the cattle accompanied by slightly frenetic music.

This skill with visual imagery is shown as the key to Grandin's alleged ability to empathise with a cow's mindset. After experimentation, she finds that by being strapped into a cattle-inoculating squeeze chute, held for 45 minutes and rhythmically squeezed by the soft leather-padded sides, her nerves are calmed, by what she calls her 'neurotransmitter adjustment'. When she wants to find out about death, she enters a slaughterhouse – an experience that she renders spiritual: 'I wanted to find out what happens when you die. Regular religion was too abstract, it was just meaningless, the slaughterhouse was real.' This chain of associations led to Grandin's current occupation as designer of humane slaughterhouses – her 'stairway to heaven' is a spiral ramp which uses optical illusions to lead livestock calmly from the pen to the bolt gun and is used by one third of all slaughterhouses in the US. Temple Grandin here, like the talk-show confessor, invokes an origin or absent cause for her particular graphic and visual skills and for her present self-identity and motivation.

Morris uses devices throughout the documentary including intertitles, found footage, music, dramatised sequences, photo stills and ambient sounds to render Grandin's belief system. These stylistic traits give an affective dimension to her monologue. They sometimes elude clear comprehension but still succeed in avoiding turning her into raw material for poetic expression alone. Grandin's personal experience is also a metaphor for the filmic process. For just as the cattle are led trustingly to their slaughter by a series of optical tricks, so the spectator is led through the film through a visual pattern of passages: dream imagery of opening doorways from Hitchcock's *Spellbound*, slow-spinning graphics of a window frame, slow motion car journeys, detailed close-ups of slaughterhouse plans, canted camera views of cattle in pens, of suburbia, black and white stills of Grandin amidst the cattle.

Furthermore, the self-exposure of Morris' subjects – as in reality TV, talk shows or other forms of confessional culture operates as a kind of 'prosthetic trauma' for the community of viewers vicariously experiencing the cathartic re-living of the traumatic event. Of relevance here is the role of television in constructing the viewer as 'witness' through its repetitious playing out of traumatic events. As trauma demands a witness to note the validity of recovered events and that witness then bears the weight of consolidating the 'truth' of the 'victim'; so 'trauma TV' demands the viewer bear the weight of knowing responsibility. As John Ellis has claimed of television's relentless cataloguing of individual and collective horror – as we watch the unfolding of these events readily accessible in our living rooms 'we cannot say we did not know' (2000: 11). At once distanced and involving, mediated and yet compelling in their intimacy the audience is invited to judge through tears, shock, disbelief, laughter or changing channels – the authenticity or relevance for them of the re-told event (see Elssaesser 2001: 197). Witnessing foregrounds the importance but also the impotence of the viewer's experience – as judge of the ontological status of a traumatic event he or she can never fully know as 'real'.[11]

In Morris' documentaries, the sense of intimacy between viewer and subject is partly undermined by his infrequent directions and questions to his subjects. Morris' screen persona is often revealed towards the end of the documentary when he breaks the illusion of the to-camera address to ask the subject from off-screen a leading question. At the end of *The Killer Inside Me,* Morris intervenes to ask London, 'Why this attraction to serial killers?' She retorts, 'What a lame question, you can do better than that.' Which he does, rephrasing the question until she answers. In *Stairway to Heaven* he asks Grandin to recite a poem written by her blind roommate. Grandin asks the off-screen Morris how she should pose whilst reciting the poem, should she lean back, would this make her look strange, should she recite now? This interchange and the starkly down-lit face of Grandin looking up, as though to heaven, as she recites to Morris' instructions – reminds us of the power of the until now concealed filmmaker.[12] It also undercuts our status as witness or confessor – the absent third party to whom all Morris' subjects appear to speak directly. Such revelations of the filmmaker's controlling subjectivity and the undermining of that control deliberately reveal the documentary as a dynamic intersubjective process. Morris' work is self-consciously expressive and conceals, then reveals, authorship.

Death

Death is the absent presence at the core of many of Morris' documentaries. His subjects haunt the slaughterhouse, they clean up after violent crime and they steal the head from their mother's corpse. Here the logic and rationality of science segues with the 'unnameable dread' of our collective tales of horror. Death here is immensely practical but also powerfully enigmatic. It is central to Morris' short films and is also in keeping with longer works such as *The Thin Blue Line* and *Mr Death*. In the *First Person* series Joan Dougherty, the crime scene cleaner, literally scrubs up the detritus of violent death once the forensics experts have departed. In her story she recalls the messy aftermath of her son's suicide. Sondra London's story is littered with death – John Schaefer, her first lover, killed two women and was linked to 28 to 30 other missing women. In Morris' film, press headlines – 'Man imprisoned in sex slayings seeks new trial' – and news footage of two women found decapitated and mutilated by Schaefer jostle with printed extracts from his horrific written confessions to London. The thin line between the real of gratuitous murder and the sadistic fantasies of Schaefer are highlighted in London's claim to 'publish his murder fantasies as they came closer and closer to reality'. She adds, 'I find he's a good writer, he's also a serial killer as well.'

More broadly, Morris' work highlights an intrinsic relationship between trauma and death; individuals' traumas as they are retold for television camera conceal a more general psycho-cultural anxiety about death. Here, the status of Morris' work as personalised documentary is notable. Death is a fetishised object for many documentary filmmakers. Documentary seeks the defining fact – the assassinated President, the war or murder victim – whose ultimate moment and the story leading to that moment are retroactively sought. These moments are not always retrievable; a bit like the 'traceless traces' of the trauma story (Elssaesser 2001: 194). In terms of documentary desire to capture the real whether in objective or subjective form, death can both 'powerfully convey a sense of reality [but] it is also the place where the real ends' (Fetveit 1999: 798). Death then represents a conundrum for documentary as Vivian Sobchack has argued: 'while death is generally experienced in fiction films as representable and often excessively visible, in documentary films it is experienced as confounding representation, as exceeding visibility' (in Nichols 1994: 48).

Morris' work, unlike many conventional documentaries, does not rely on an authoritative historical or social referent to anchor the absent presence of death that is frequently the backdrop to his subject's bizarre post-traumatic stories. Instead death is offered as the catalyst for extravagant, sometimes absurd, personal responses shot through with pathos.

Death works on many levels in Morris' work. Most simply, he has partly aestheticised the stuff of tabloid culture: death, violence, sex interwoven with the bizarre. But we suggest that his work also knowingly begs psychoanalytical interpretation and borrows from a contemporary popularised therapeutic culture. Violence, sex, murder, death: this is also the meat of psychoanalysis, the intellectual tabloid of our culture. More broadly, Morris' work highlights the intrinsic relationship between trauma and death; individuals' traumas as they are retold for the television camera conceal a more general psycho-cultural anxiety about death. Here, the status of Morris' work as personalised documentary is notable because it comes up against an elusive absence in its attempt to capture the real. As Bill Nichols notes: 'at death's door we find documentary endlessly, and anxiously, waiting. It hovers, fascinated by a borderzone it cannot ever fully represent. (1994: 48).

Since the 1990s survival has become a prominent theme in the public narratives subjects tell to the media. As these confessing subjects of factual programming compete for singularity and for redress in an increasingly crowded media forum, and as the programmes themselves compete for status and resources, the stories of trauma become more bizarre. The personal stories of trauma, violence and death, then, could be viewed as both a record of individual psychopathology but also as a cultural trope – 'a strategic fiction that a complex, stressful competitive world is using to account for a world that seems threateningly out of control' (Farrell 1998: 2). As will be seen in the next chapter, the narrativisation of personal trauma is present not only in complex auteur-driven documentary but in a diffuse range of popular factual programming.

chapter 5
Therapeutic culture: narcissism and self-revelation

'Welcome to the Hotel California': TV narcissism and the real

> Mirrors on the ceiling
> Pink champagne on ice
> And she said
> We are all just prisoners here
> Of our own device
>   – The Eagles, 'Hotel California'

> The media have … become the last authority for self-perception, the 'reality test' of the social persona: I am seen, therefore I am. (Frohne 2002: 262)

In recent analyses of television culture a number of critics have provocatively outlined the congruence between TV as a mass media form and the public narrativisation of traumatic events or experiences. In Jon Dovey's account of contemporary first-person factual media, *Freakshow*, he locates the transformation and consolidation of factual genres in the 1990s within the context of a neo-liberal political economy in which commodification and capitalisation have reconstituted the public service in the shape of a market-led ethos. This ethos has altered the shape of public service broadcasting and whilst the focus may not now be on widening access, Dovey acknowledges that 'new domains for the expression of identity' have nonetheless been secured (2000: 4). These televisual spaces are, according to Dovey, 'filled by voices proclaiming and celebrating their own "freakishness", articulating their most intimate fears and secrets' (ibid.).[1]

The public disclosure and narrativisation of personal identity is a crucial ingredient of a revitalised (and economically viable) factual TV market. Entertainment media appropriate the 'real' feelings and emotions of 'real' people to signify credibility and 'unfiltered immediacy' (Frohne 2002: 259). A sense of self-staging, of the constructedness of reality and of the artificial realism of media worlds are commonplaces of contemporary culture. For those theorists locating reality TV within a postmodern society of the image, media spectacle has displaced real-life experience. However, the excess and expanse of the media world on offer cannot conceal a sense of impoverishment or loss of the material grit of the real. Slavoj Žižek has characterised the twentieth century as the century in which the 'passion for the Real' erupts in the face of the postmodern immersion in semblance (2002: 3). Ironically the search for the authentic amidst media spectacle has resulted in compensatory media representations:

> The authentic twentieth-century passion for penetrating the Real Thing (ultimately the destructive void) through the cobweb of semblances which constitutes our reality thus culminates in the thrill of the Real as the ultimate effect, sought after from digitalised special effects, through reality TV and amateur pornography, up to snuff movies. (2002: 12)

Žižek cites Peter Weir's *The Truman Show* (1998) and its antecedent, Philip K. Dick's novel *Time Out of Joint* (1959), as notable examples of the American paranoiac fantasy that the world around them, a consumerist affluent Western capitalist paradise, is actually a fake. This is a theme also followed in the popular blockbuster film directed by the Wachowski Brothers, *The Matrix* (1999). In all these fictions, the hero gradually awakens to the discovery that the world around him is a fiction designed to keep him happy and productive. Žižek reads these fictions as a comment on a dematerialised social imaginary: 'The underlying experience of *Time Out of Joint* and of *The Truman Show* is that the late capitalist consumerist Californian paradise is, in its very hyperreality, in a way *unreal*, substanceless, deprived of material inertia' (2002: 13). As such the protagonists proceed to discover the real behind the insubstantial everyday.

Real life appears devoid of substance in late capitalist society. Our neighbours and workmates and friends, immersed as they are in consumer culture, appear as real-life actors and extras: 'the ultimate truth of capitalist utilitarian despiritualised universe is the dematerialisation of "real" life, its reversal into a spectral show' (Žižek 2002: 14). This awareness of the false divide between the real world and the staged contained world of media life is encapsulated by one contestant of *Big Brother 4* (2003). John, previously ejected from the house, was re-introduced in a gimmick to revive the inter-dynamics of the rapidly diminishing number of housemates. He had been one of the most explicit commentators on the theatrical nature of the house and its inhabitants; speaking to the diary room about strategies to appeal to the public and about the performance of authenticity by some of the other contestants. By the time of his return, the other housemates had been isolated for weeks without any contact or news from outside apart from their highly constrained exchanges with Big Brother in the diary room. Commenting on the experience of being out and then back in the spotlight, John undercuts any notion of freedom that the housemates have connected to the outside when he sings to them the lines from the Eagles' popular song 'Hotel California'. The song tells of a dangerously willing entrapment as a visitor is lured off the highway to the enchanting delights of a hotel from which there is no escape:

> Welcome to the Hotel California
> Such a lovely place.
> Such a lovely place…
> Last thing I remember
> I was running for the door
> I had to find the passage back to the place I was before
> Relax said the nightman
> We are programmed to receive
> You can check out any time you like
> But you can never leave.

Housemates themselves forecast the inability to leave behind the experience of the *Big Brother* house by anticipating their future absorption into celebrity culture as a result of their 24/7 TV/web existence. As noted in chapter 1, other reality TV participants have commented on the problems, too, of extricating oneself from their own stereotyped media image.

Aside from the hours of self-absorbed confession and revelation that entrapment in the house promotes, eviction from the house is one of the key constructed 'traumas' that shape the housemates' weeks in captivity. To be evicted signifies a rejection by the public and by their companions who select those to be expelled. In the penultimate week of *Big Brother 4*, Nush, one of the two housemates selected to go up for public vote for eviction, explains her response to Big Brother in the diary room. She speaks hesitantly about her attachment to the house, claiming that it may be silly because she knows that the house is not real but nonetheless the place feels 'a bit like home'. She anticipates her nostalgia once outside, and looking tearful adds that the difficulty is in knowing that the experience of the house can never be recaptured, that one can never return. The stage-set of the house is clearly unreal but also extremely comfortable/comforting. *Big Brother 4*'s set-up has a heated outside pool, a large deck with huge bean bags in a seating area. The living area again has huge brightly-coloured sofas, cushions and soft rugs. The effect is modern but also infantile – resembling a child's playroom with bright colours and simple curved shapes. Isolation in the house is a key factor in the forced close interpersonal relationships that develop for public observation. A number of the contestants speak of their anxiety at leaving and possibly entering a hostile outside world as they have no sense of the kind of public reception they will receive. Whenever a housemate is voted out, those remaining huddle by the closed door to listen for cheers or jeers from an invisible public – an enigmatic sign of outside judgement. The house then is experienced as hostile at times, protective at others and the public become an unreal invisible but powerful other.

Kevin Robins argues that many discourses on the benefits of new media offer an escape from mundane reality into a new simulated reality. He suggests that such idealisation of the simulated worlds, made possible by new media technology, are 'powerful expressions of fantasy and desire ... articulated through the discourse of science and rationality' (1996: 39). The various new realities of reality TV offer artificially-constructed domains that hold real people. They are plainly simulations but contain characters that lay claim to an existence outside of media space. Some critics have aligned these programmes with game shows in their pitting of ordinary people against each other in an artificial environment. In reality shows like *Big Brother*, *Castaway*, *Temptation Island* and *Survivor* rules and regulations similarly structure the microworld. In one sense then to enter these worlds is to engage in a constrained world of reason and of order.[2] Danger and conflict are highly regulated: the crocodile or snake one encounters is likely to be placed there by the film crew; the risks of food deprivation or heat exhaustion are carefully monitored. Yet reality TV also offers the unscripted event that occurs when individuals are thrown together: structured through matrices of jealousy, rivalry, distrust, erotic attraction and so on. Robins' description of the 'microworld' of virtual reality seems analogous here:

> To enter the microworld is apparently to enter a world of logic and reason. But it is more than this. The microworld is also responding to deeper needs and drives than those of reason. This image space is also a container and a scene for unconscious and pre-rational dramas: getting 'into' the image is also about acting out certain primitive desires and fantasies or about coming to terms with fears and anxieties. (1996: 49)

The charge of identification with characters alongside the predictability of a managed environment and regularised life segues with the unpredictability of 'the real' – the event that may erupt beneath the surface of order at any moment. Reality TV offers contradictory pleasures, broadcast as a highly edited and condensed event (a single episode) *and* as 24-hour spectacle (as webcam footage), displaying an orchestrated microworld replete with the possibility of volatile agents and relationships. It offers the new 'fullness' of a mediated reality and hence, whilst very much part of the new media environment, it draws on the embodied human encounter to signify emotional and existential realism: the stuff that happens when real people encounter one another. Consequently, this type of programming 'could be understood as an euphoric effort to reclaim what seems lost after digitalisation' (Fetveit 1999: 798).

The rituals of the outside world are borrowed to structure the *Big Brother* routine. In the final week of *Big Brother 4*, the housemates are rewarded on their final evening with a mock Christmas Day. Completely isolated from the outside world for weeks, the Christmas treat serves almost like a homeopathic remedy as Scott, Steph, Ray, Cameron and John are all separately called into a room to receive a small inoculation of the reality that awaits them outside. The room is bare save for a giant throne-like chair and the floor is strewn with white mock snowflakes. Each housemate sits waiting and then receives a Christmas card posted in to them with messages from friends or relatives. The poignancy is in the deliberate insertion of a real message in an overtly fantastic fairytale-like *mise-en-scène*. This small dose of the outside world is continued later in the Christmas celebrations when the housemates each unwrap a package from outside, containing a special object from home. These are all intimate objects – a toy car, a walnut used as a gift each Christmas and so on – whose meaning is private, arcane and enmeshed in a personal history prior to the house. The effect is uncanny – as the housemates voluntarily stripped of their intimacy and privacy for weeks have a 'real' emblem of their unscrutinised lives brought in and unwrapped before the camera's gaze.

This uncanniness extends to the final day in the house. As each of the extremely nervous housemates anticipates the order in which they may be voted out, Cameron declares that he could not bear to be in the final two left in the house, he would be 'terrified'. As the eventual winner of *Big Brother 4*, he is in fact the last to remain, and as runner-up Ray departs, he begs him not to go. Left alone, Cameron talks to himself, looks agitated, snacks distractedly on food, reads out loud the opening sentences from the book of rules for the House: 'Welcome to the Big Brother House…' Intermittently, Cameron calls out to the invisible controller of the house to let him out, not to drag out the exit. After his departure, the camera continues filming. The house then takes on an ominous state. The viewer is offered shots of each empty room, echoing voiceovers of the housemates declaring themselves 'guinea pigs', imagining others watching and so on, accompany these shots. These ghostlike traces imbue the final images of the house with an uncanny quality. It is as if the fantasmatic support of the reality of the house has been stripped away, the house only means something if there are inhabitants there to watch and others outside to watch them. The images evoke emptiness but also imbue the house with a hallucinatory quality returning reality TV to 'virtual reality' now that the housemates have moved beyond the camera's range.

Contestants on shows like *Big Brother* or *Survivor* or *The Mole* often speak of their voluntary self-imprisonment in a media-created community as a challenge but also a way of confronting or finding themselves. Often the desire is also to find a quick route to a new media career. This blurring of real self and media personality points up the narcissistic nature of reality TV and of the role of the media as the new horizon of contemporary self-realisation. In an episode of *Judge Judy*, the US television court show, Judge Judy confronted a father and his teenage son who was an alleged dangerous driver, having sped through a suburb with his rowdy friends threatening the life of pedestrians. They in turn were suing their male neighbour, who, enraged at their refusal to stop driving and concerned for his children, had hit the side of the car with a baseball bat. Father and son had already had the verdict found against them in seven separate court cases and yet had still submitted themselves to television trial. Judge Judy, shaking her head in mock amazement, asked them why they had bothered to come on television – did they think this verdict would be any different as they were clearly at fault? Frequently on *Judge Judy*, defendants and prosecutors who have previously lost their case in a court of law submit themselves to the televised humiliation of appearing before the Judge. Their submission to the television gaze is symptomatic of a belief in the integrity of one's performance before camera to direct and rectify a false image of the self and to verify one's status as the *victim*.

Trying to understand the crisis in self-image a number of contemporary critics have latched onto the idea of contemporary society as 'a culture of narcissism'. In particular, Christopher Lasch indicates that narcissism is now a general condition of being in late capitalism; it signifies a detachment from a world seemingly without value. In contemporary late capitalist cultures such as Britain and the United States, cultural pluralism, lifestyle diversity and niche marketing arguably produce fragmented and self-reflexive selves. Older forms of authority and security – the law, democratic government, judiciary, medical experts and so forth – have been critiqued and displaced by an increasing public political cynicism and a turn to the self as the only possible marker of integrity (Frosch 1991). The politics of the self is a phenomenon arriving out of the 1980s and signals the rise of a narcissistic and self-reflexive culture in which individual crises, family histories and personal complexities provide an anchor for contemporary insecurities in the affluent cultures of advanced technocratic society.

To understand narcissism, as a contemporary malaise rather than pathology, is to understand the desire to consolidate a sense of one's self in a culture seemingly devoid of meaning and of objects and relations providing self-affirmation. Consequently, identity is affirmed through the luxury of a consolatory mirror image afforded by the ubiquitous presence of the media in our lives. It is worth quoting Lasch at some length here:

> We live in a world of images and echoes that arrest experience and play it back in slow motion. Cameras and recording machines not only transcribe experience but alter its quality, giving to much modern life the character of an enormous echo chamber, a hall of mirrors … Modern life is so thoroughly mediated by electronic images that we cannot help responding to others as if their actions – and our own – were being recorded and simultaneously transmitted to an unseen audience or stored up for close scrutiny at some later time … This intrusion into everyday life of this all-seeing eye no longer takes us by surprise or catches us with our defences down. We need no reminder to smile. A smile is permanently graven on our features, and we already know from which of several angles it photographs to best advantage. (1978: 47)

The apparent omnipresence of media observation is internalised as a sort of self-scrutiny. But also the self becomes dependent on the consumption of media images. So paradoxically the media image becomes both the de-realisation of reality and – through reality TV, game shows, talk shows, social experiments, CCTV footage and so on – the source for unhindered observation and detailed monitoring of real people like ourselves. In this 'new economy of attention' to appear on television is to assume cultural capital. Social distinction becomes dependent on media performance and even simply on media presence:

> Andy Warhol's promise that everyone could be a star for fifteen minutes has become the component of collective self-confidence and the standard for personal self-esteem, which postmodern individuals openly pay homage to in their technological self-marketing whether as contestants on *Face 2000*, or as participants in the 'community of shared destiny' in *Big Brother*'s container, or as criminals on death row fighting for the right to have their executions broadcast. (Frohne 2002: 261)

The desire to rid oneself of intimacy and to capture media attention demands the deliberate insertion of oneself into media space. To stand out demands that one share one's intimate secrets on camera, participate in the game show or talk show, submit one's legal wrangle to televised jurisdiction or sell one's home video moments for the fleeting recognition of canned laughter.

Whoever desires to be prominent or notable requires the mass visibility of media recognition, albeit for a moment. On the one hand, as we have argued, this yearning to speak oneself to camera suggests a desire for the mark of authenticity, for the social legitimisation of one's existence. In this sense, the process of revelation is partly shaped by a self-conscious absorption in the emotions, desires, needs, pains and memories that the contemporary individual, attuned to a popularised psychoanalytic discourse, uses to understand his or her location in the world. As Lasch argues: 'the emergence of a thera-peutic ideology that upholds a normative schedule of psychosocial development … thus gives further encouragement to anxious self-scrutiny' (1978: 48). The therapeutic discourses that pervade contemporary society reinforce notions of psychic and physical health, physical attractiveness, social integration and development, and interpersonal and career success as factors attendant on 'an eternal watchfulness' (ibid.). Consequently, subjects look for symptoms of malfunction or trauma. The individual polices his or herself for signs of ageing, ill health, psychic stress or social/relationship/career flaws and everything can be fixed by career or lifestyle coaches. Emotion and self-monitoring of internal responses are a core element of one's private and public persona. In response to whatever social dilemma the British talk show host Robert Kilroy-Silk is covering – whether ageing, drunk driving, unemployment or sexual abuse – he asks his participants 'How do you feel?'

On the other hand, the desire to be watched, to be witnessed by others uncovering one's intimate identity and even everyday rituals of cooking, eating, conversing, com-peting or sleeping reveals the craving for an observer to witness the minutiae of one's social performance. Recently the internet has been flooded by webcam sites which enable the viewer to continuously follow an event or place – a scene on a street or at an institution or the life of someone in their home, their fridge contents, their bedrooms. This indicates the importance with which the media has now become associated with social identification.

The current baring of the self to camera for reality TV displays two elemental truths: firstly, that our 'real' selves are only ever the performance of a role. In *Big Brother*, the participants step outside of 'real' life to 'play themselves in their screen-roles' but divided from us and framed by the television or computer screen their real selves can be more easily interpreted as culturally coded acts (Žižek 2002: 226). Secondly, reality TV lays bare the truth about integral fantasmatic structures of subjectivity caught up with illicit forms of observation. For example, Žižek notes that in the common fantasy of being caught/ observed while in sexual activity, the fantasy proper is centred not on the imagined sexual act but on the imagined other who watches us. Crucially, our sense of self is guaranteed by the fantasy of an 'other' who observes us and whose gaze confirms the solidity and worth of our existence. Therefore, rather than fearing the omnipresent surveying gaze we embrace it. Thus it could be argued that the dynamics of multi-platform observation replicate the imaginary possible characters watching us in a complex fantasy *mise-en-scène*. The media now has moved beyond offering the pleasure of pre-fabricated scenes to offer the pleasure of supposedly un-fabricated scenes. Here, the urgent need for another's observation extends beyond the masochistic desire to submit to another's gaze or the exhibitionist's desire to display. Žižek maintains that our current fascination with image-mediated reality indicates a desire for the eye of the camera to verify and validate one's existence: 'the subject needs the camera's gaze as a kind of ontological guarantee of his/her being' (2002: 225).

Therapeutic culture and new media economies of realism

Reality TV, then, arguably promotes and caters for the desire to be observed and to have one's existence validated through observation. It extends and plays upon the notion that daily existence is in some senses inauthentic or hyperreal or simulated or performative. It foregrounds the ways in which subjectivity more broadly is formed through a matrix of looks, of processes of seeing, being seen and of our self-conscious knowledge of being seen. It suggests that within media culture being publicly regarded can constitute an affirmation of the self.

Reality TV has contributed to the establishment of a *new realism* in the digital age which is founded on the individual subject's self-revelation and their interactions with others as the marker and touchstone of authenticity. This revelation is declamatory and must take place in a public forum. It must attract viewers through processes of both identification and voyeurism. On reality TV and with multi-platform programming we can watch the multi-perspectival aspects of one person or groups' interaction in all their minutiae; perspectives which seem to substantiate reality TV as a privileged mode of access to the personal. The most illuminating critical work on the multiple spectator positions offered by television has been undertaken in relation to soap opera. Soap opera's structure (multiple storylines and characters, open-endedness and patterns of time that echo real life) and its emphasis on the personal and the quotidian make it an important precursor of reality TV. Sandy Flitterman-Lewis, illustrating the merit of using psychoanalysis to address the specificity of fictional televisual experiences, pointed to the multiple and partial identifications of soap opera which stand in stark contrast to the much more anchored identifications of classical film narrative. She suggested that the 'constant plurality of secondary identifications intensifies the viewer's imaginary activity, enabling the slide from fictive to real in order to solidify the connections between the characters' world and ours' (1992: 237). Tania Modleski suggests that television soaps present us with a cast of varied personalities, these 'numerous limited egos' allowing for a transitory but highly engaging set of identifications (in Flitterman-Lewis 1992: 237).

This ability to interact imaginatively with a number of 'realistic' personas and their experiences on screen certainly seems to correspond with some of the structural characteristics of reality TV. Reality TV shows which offer a temporary community of individuals, for example, enable the viewer to occupy a range of roles, shifting, changing and doubling up on a variety of subject positions. Appealing to the mobile positions and scenarios offered in fantasy, the viewer can identify with individuals, yet also feel disconnected or frustrated as television participants' plans, deceits, motivations and deceptions are never fully disclosed. The ability to slide from fictive to 'real', or in the case of reality TV to slide from generic 'reality' programme to 'real' comes easily and smoothes the path into an acceptance of the new realism.

In the mass-media market, as the conventional political commitment of non-fiction television producers has been marginalised and fiscal considerations are prioritised new, more personal and more cost effective forms of non-fiction television have come to the fore. The multi-channelled conglomerated television arena demands cheaper programming and niche marketing. 'Trauma TV' – as a variant of the reality TV formats – has developed out of television innovations such as the video diary and the talk show to air social and personal issues to a mass audience and, in terms of production values, to do so economically.[3] Television confessionals and the therapy culture within which they are embedded are the cultural backdrop here. Therapy culture, infused with psychoanalytic discourse, has informed the popular imagination through mass media images. Psychoanalysis provides a shared discourse with which to economically transmit ideas about emotional conflict and desire. The common tropes of psychoanalysis – Oedipal rivalry, primal desires, taboos, anxiety about death, loss and survival, group identification, repression, dreams as ciphers of the unconscious – have filtered in simplified form into mainstream film, television shows, radio dramas and magazine advice columns.

Talk shows, some documentaries and a range of confessional light programming draw upon psychoanalytical registers to underpin the display of emotion and memory on the small screen, affording them a sense of emotional realism and analytical worth. They provide representations of the active witness; the ordinary person on screen as the 'privileged possessor and *producer* of knowledge in an extraordinary, often forensic setting, in which speech and truth are policed in multiple ways' (Peters 2001: 709). In doing so, some critics have laid claim to such programmes as a democratisation of the public sphere. For despite such policing, these programmes have been styled as both democratic and demotic; their ordinary filmic subjects *appearing* to address the viewing public in a less mediated and uninhibited form. Increasingly, the discursive gap between televisual subject and the viewer seems to have diminished as the ordinary individual is given the chance to speak directly to audiences via talk shows, video diaries and so on. And, more importantly still, the viewer gains the sense that they too could be on television, that they might also be on the threshold of media visibility.

It has been argued that such televised confession is a secular service that supplants or supplements religion and taps into a current desire to unburden the self of its anguish. In the mid-1990s, an incredibly popular phone-in line in the United States underlined the cultural need for an outlet for personal guilt or anxiety: the *Apology Line*. Thousands of callers phoned the elaborate computerised answer machine set in a Manhattan apartment and funded by an anonymous individual whose voice, as 'Mr Apology', welcomed callers and invited them to confess and to indulge in self-revelation. Originally set up in 1980 as an art project, by the mid-1990s the service, promoted by stickers and leaflets around New York, had around a hundred calls a day of which about a dozen left a message. The remainder of callers phoned to listen into a diverse range of confessions ranging from the banal to the criminal. Callers confessed to not crying enough at a grandmother's funeral, to spitting in hamburgers served to police officers, committing incest with adult siblings, adultery, drug peddling, arson and even murder. The answer service used voicemail technology to divide confessions into categories: sex, romance, humour, child abuse, the Church of the Apologetic Predator (for religious or spiritual problems), and addiction, as well as Apology Pet Corner. The Apology Line's slogan was 'Call, Listen, Perhaps Share'. Listeners called in sometimes to leave a message responding to others' confessions. The creator described the line as part 'vicarious thrill' in listening to others' violations and obsessions, part group therapy, a 'peer-advice thing ... People get an idea of where they stand in the community' (Freedland 1994: 27).[4]

In attempting to understand the need for such self-revelation, cultural critics have noted that mass forms of popular culture provide ways of confronting and managing the basic psychic tensions of contemporary urban life (Richards 1994; Elliott 1996). Furthermore, that negotiation of the self within contemporary collective living is arguably infused with therapeutic discourse: a process in which ultimately personal identity, location in the world, self-development, recovery and fulfilment often narrow to the small circle of the individual and those closest to him or her (Parker 1997). Popularised therapeutic discourse provides a language for acknowledging the intensities of subjective experience in a world where power structures and decision-making processes appear to alienate and exclude the everyday individual and the quotidian life. Some analysts of the late modern/postmodern age have argued that, from the end of the twentieth century onwards, 'risk' is an attendant factor of existence. As techno-economic development is equated with a sense of the possibility of wide-scale peril and insecurity on a global scale, individuals increasingly factor the imagined future dangers and merits of risky existence into their everyday sense of local, national and global events. For contemporary individuals this promotes a sense of scepticism about institutionalised knowledge and power and a heightened self-awareness that we are living with risk management in our personal daily lives (Beck 1992; Giddens 1990). Consequently, the *zeitgeist* of the affluent late capitalist social universe is of an intensified reflexivity in which 'people reflect upon the consequences of their action, in both the personal and social domains' (Elliott 1996: 68). This development of intensified reflexive rationality is linked to a heightening of individualisation, so that as broader social and institutional structures become subject to interrogation, the subject turns increasingly to seek an ontological security through calculations and assessments about personal life and life-style options.[5]

Therapeutic discourse can offer a route to the complexity of psychic life but it can, in highly simplified form, also be drawn upon to conjure up consoling fantasies of mastery over risk and over the self. Notions of a recoverable self and a re-armoured ego abound in women and men's magazines, daytime talk shows, life-style programmes and makeover shows. The route through personal dilemmas and individual dissatisfaction is located in the pathologised individual. Self-understanding is offered through pop-psychological analysis combined with a therapeutic scan over family history and personal relationships. For example, Alvin Hall, the host of a popular financial makeover show *Your Money or Your Life* (BBC1), is described as 'psychologist' and 'money guru' in the accompanying BBC paperback (Hall 2002: front cover). The paperback offers individuals or couples with financial problems 'a practical guide to solving your financial problems and affording a life you'll love'. The first chapter, 'Money or Your Mind', follows the standard formula of his half-hour television programme by locating the root of financial problems in emotional problems – the 'demons' which control excessive spending and ultimately loss of personal control. The self-help text is littered with psycho-speak: 'the psychology of the credit card', 'practise tough self-love', and 'the talking cure'. The television show features people who are in significant debt – through hefty mortgages, bank and credit card debts and overspending. Their behaviour is analysed as one of personal irresponsibility rooted partly in underlying psychological patterns of behaviour. To remedy their self-destructive conduct, Hall probes the inner psychological tics of his profligate subjects: what empty space inside or anxieties are they trying to remedy by overspending? Rather than, for example, analyse the broader economic structures that produce and encourage such consumption, the men and women on his show are excavated for emotional weaknesses and underlying traumas that trigger detrimental financial behaviour. The route to personal equilibrium, happiness and financial stability is through re-modelling the inner self via its connection to the consuming self.

The limits of subjectivity and the fantasy of remodelling a dysfunctional self are explored in lifestyle coaching programmes such as *Life Laundry* (C4). Participants are invited to submit their cluttered house to a coach who will teach them to rethink their relationship to personal belongings and to their domestic space. Participants are invited to explore different facets of their identity and to speak about their emotional investment in the detritus that is hoarded in their disordered houses; indeed, the programme is advertised as helping participants let go of material and emotional clutter. Both the home and the piles of belongings that are sifted through are acknowledged as libidinally invested objects. Homeowners often break down as they divest themselves of years of hoarded belongings and are encouraged to talk through the memories and feelings attached to toys, photos, collections, clothing and so on, as they emerge from the piles of clutter to a new streamlined identity. Gay Hawkins, speaking about lifestyle programmes, has commented: 'At stake here is a way of thinking about the role of television, not simply in making subjects ... but in *un*making subjects, in cultivating new sensibilities and engagements, in enabling different micropolitics of the self' (2001: 414).

BBC's dating lifestyle programme *Would Like To Meet* offers the opportunity to reflect on self-conduct, interpersonal relations, different personas adopted in different environments and how others react to oneself. The programme takes single men and women who feel that they have been unsuccessful with their love life and coaches them into new social behaviour to attract a partner. It offers advice and asks the participant to reflect upon their self-image and public image in different scenarios. In the final week of the third series (BBC3, 17 August 2003), Helen Thorogood, a 35-year-old career woman from Southampton, puts herself at the mercy of the programme's three resident 'coaches'. Her behaviour is subjected to the modification of the programme's body coach, celebrity stylist and confidence coach who suggest changes to her dress, conversation, social drinking, life goals, expectations of a partner and so on.

Helen's behaviour and her dress in bars, on dates and at work is subjected to a variety of filmic techniques that signal the mood and tone of the viewing experience. The wobbling tracking shots of a hand-held camera follow Helen and body expert Tracy Cox into nightclubs and bars where they meet and chat-up potential dates. The feel is voyeuristic but also mobile, like a night 'on the pull'. Video footage of Helen walking into work or to meetings is interspersed with footage of the coaches scrutinising video replays as they comment on her dress or note her attempts at behaviour modification. Filmed in medium to long shot, viewers see Helen within her surroundings. She is a component part of different spaces: a situated self, whose judgement about dress, image and appropriate levels of formality is modified according to setting of home, office or nightclub. In contrast, the to-camera intimacy of the video diary sections, with its amateur aesthetic of out-of-focus images, close-up direct address, Helen's hushed exchange and the rustling background noises signify a personal dialogue beyond the reach of the coaches' surveillance. Helen presents herself and her problems through therapeutic language. Speaking to camera, with tears streaming down her face, she explains her string of one-night stands as a search for (temporary) fulfilment followed by self-dislike. In these video diary sessions she links her sexual behaviour to her childhood bereavement following her father's premature death and a desire to fill a gap in her life. She locates her binge drinking in a lack of confidence and inability to approach the opposite sex without feeling inadequate. The result of the television life-coaching is pursued on the programme's web pages in which each participant updates readers on their personal progress and identity since filming stopped. The website has links to dating, parenting, relationship, health and lifestyle information.

All these programmes differ from, for example, the didactic quality of news or current affairs in that 'their performance of expertise is informal and authoritative rather than authoritarian' (Hawkins 2001: 418). Furthermore, they offer spaces for confession and self-interrogation and advice to the individual seeking 'to maximise quality of life through acts of choice rather than through relations of obligation and dependency' (ibid.). The would-be datable participants of *Would Like to Meet* are firmly positioned within therapeutic and lifestyle consumer discourses that locate them as bodies and psyches open to self-regulation and self-analysis. As with most lifestyle programmes, the ordinary people filmed are taken to be fully cognisant of the plethora of identities that they could possibly perform. Arguably such programmes also tap into the contemporary distrust of institutions mentioned above, and instead offer small-scale authorities; 'everyday experts of subjectivity' (ibid.). In this sense they are a populist response to widespread popular frustration about social institutions alongside a sense of individual emptiness or lack of fulfilment and offer instead new ways of mapping and re-fashioning the self in social space and interaction.

Numerous critics have situated the contemporary cultural experience of emptiness, dislocation or disconnection from society as symptomatic of postmodern experience. The search for personal meanings is linked to an age of globalised media images, in which everything appears as a copy, a simulacrum of something else – where authenticity and originality are endlessly deferred in the relay of communication. As Anthony Elliott argues: 'Some of the most provocative elements in recent discussions of postmodernity have been in those areas of social and cultural theory, which explore the splintering, surface facets of contemporary selfhood' (1996: 23). Elliott connects reflexive subjectivity with the fantasy processes through which subjects constitute, through imagery, both themselves and also others. He links this to an emotional receptivity in which the contemporary subject searches for and attains a sense of relatedness to others, generated through the postmodern circuits of technology, inter-linked computer systems and mass-media simulation (1996: 28–30). Media imagery offers a 'fantasy zone' for generating rolling identifications which enable the subject to think through their relationship with self and links with others. We could think of Trauma TV then, in its varied formats, as 'an affective, representational space in which to think through the limit of subjectivity: the struggle of placing the "subject" in question' (1996: 31).

To follow this line of thinking is to accept that, alongside the imaginary search for wholeness and plenitude never sated by the plethora of self-help media texts, the subject's discontent is frequently coupled with a nostalgic yearning for a sense of authentic community. Media imagery can offer pseudo communities of ordinary people temporarily bonding in competition, experiencing alternative ways of living as a group, or united in a studio discussing shared problems, dilemmas, answers and successes that suggest an affinity with others. Trauma TV – in its guise as confession, survival, quest, mock community – answers a desire to see on screen others who, through their particular stories, echo broader hopes for and anxieties about contemporary life and whose public self-exposure provides a form of social legitimisation of that yearning. It creates simulated communities who battle with simulated trials whilst reflecting upon their personal motivation and allegiances with those thrown together in the pseudo-world of the house, jungle, school or prison. In talk shows, where the interpersonal relations of host and guests are watched by a studio community, the viewer is also provided with a privileged proximity to individual pain, desire, horror, survival and memory, but paradoxically it does so in the very public and distant space of the television screen.

chapter 6
Trauma as popular cultural script: from talk show to lifestyle programming

> I want to raise the possibility that trauma may have become a 'popular cultural script' in need of contextualisation and analysis in its own right – a symptom, the cause of which needs to be sought elsewhere. (Radstone 2001: 189)

The public expression of traumatic memories can be considered as an important ingredient of the reality TV format. Thomas Elsaesser (2001) signals the raft of personal experiences and memories of trauma – personal memoirs, testimony, family history – currently in the mass media market. Whereas earlier periods tended to concentrate on publicly legitimated memories of trauma informed by grand narratives – war, ethnic cleansing, disaster – towards the end of the twentieth century private stories began entering the public domain. Correspondingly, the range of possible genres for dealing with the extreme experiences of trauma has also expanded as new, seemingly less formal genres accommodate personal accounts. Importantly, alongside that expansion has come the call for cultural critics to acknowledge the role of popular media texts in articulating trauma and for theoreticians to move beyond the individual subjective analysis to think through the cultural scene of such traumatic expression and its popularity (Radstone 2001).

In his analysis of 'post-traumatic culture', Kirby Farrell convincingly argues that trauma can be seen as both 'a clinical concept and a cultural trope' (2002: 14). He regards it as a contemporary medium for the expression of unease about a world in which power structures and forms of authority are beyond everyday influence and where individual responsibility and impotence seem all pervading. Trauma, seen as a trope, 'may be a veiled or explicit criticism of society's defects, a cry of distress and a tool grasped in the hopes of some redress, but also a justification for aggression' (ibid.). In the current 'post-traumatic culture' of Britain and the United States, which is attuned to the widespread damage of advanced industrialisation, the acute injury and internal damage to individuals and communities caused by war, plane or train disasters, sexual abuse or terrorism have all gained statutory recognition. In the post-Vietnam US, trauma has been part of courtroom exchange in claims for military-induced damage; a practice continued in the aftermath of the Gulf Wars both sides of the Atlantic. The women's movements have drawn upon trauma to politicise the private sphere and it has been cited to lend credence to arguments about domestic violence and sexual abuse. To this we can add that trauma can be used ideologically; the aftermath of civil war or state torture, starvation or rape is rendered invisible for cultural groups seen as outsiders intruding on 'our' national and emotional resources. Trauma can be used as a counter-claim to evict traumatised refugee-strangers from our land or to scapegoat outsiders. It has functioned at the centre of ideologically and ethically loaded debates about abortion and 'false-memory syndrome' and is now embedded in many areas of public policy and criminal law (Farrell 2002: 24). In all respects, what is certain is that 'trauma' is common currency. And the media function as a vehicle for the expression of violent cultural events and their aftermath as well as 'a register of dissonance', the jolt of cultural recognition of the individual and collective capacity for violence and atrocity.

Since the 1990s trauma has shaped some of the central media narratives and its popular expression has proliferated in Hollywood movies such as the account of survival and subsequent psychic crisis in Peter Weir's *Fearless* (1993) and Mike Nichols' *Regarding Henry* (1991). Alongside such fictions, diverse factual narratives explore 'post-traumatic stress disorder' from the war stories of 'berserking' Vietnam veterans to the celebrity profiles in *Vanity Fair* which locate driving ambition in the survival impulses arising from childhood psychological injury. Whilst trauma has become both an explanatory tool for cultural distress and an enabling fiction, Farrell suggests that a corollary of such cultural overexposure is the need for the traumatised subject and the media to find a reinvigorated discourse that can compel an audience numbed into compassion fatigue:[1]

> Efforts to objectify and express distress require the renewal or even the escalation of narrative conventions, because over-familiarity may dull the perception – and reception – of an injury, even though its pain persists. As a result, imagination keeps trying to devise a more forceful and convincing vocabulary. Today's horror is tomorrow's cliché… (1998: 33)

Farrell locates this overdetermination of 'trauma' within the socio-political shift emergent in the 1990s (the era of Thatcher and Reagan; see Farrell 1998: 155–63), where 'survival' becomes a more prominent theme than 'nurture' and 'self-fulfilment':

> To put it starkly: although people had far less reason to struggle over subsistence than in earlier centuries, they faced far more comprehensive and acute competition for the

symbolic materials of subjectivity, the markers of status and autonomy that prevent social death. (1998: 30)

Trauma emerges as a concept to connect disparate forms of distress and claims for redress in 'an increasingly wider-ranging competition for status and resources' (ibid.). Similarly, Thomas Elsaesser has argued for the centrality of popular television formats in circulating traumatic narratives to a mass-media audience who look to the media within the social context of diminished support systems:

> It is here that the media, and in particular television, have played an especially out-standing but controversial role. In the format of the talk show, television has shaped an entire culture of confession and witnessing, of exposure and self-exposure, which in many ways – good and bad – seems to have taken over from both religion and the welfare state. (2001: 196)

In this light, psychoanalytic discourse and popular media texts meld and are validated as the necessary democratisation of the public sphere. The televisual 'culture of confession and witnessing [has] made trauma theory the recto, and therapeutic television (also disparagingly called trash TV) the verso of democracy's failure to "represent" its citizens' personal concern in the public sphere' (ibid.).

As we have already argued, crucial to this popularisation of trauma is the diffusion of psychoanalytic discourses in contemporary culture and in particular the concept of the recoverable self.[2] Reality TV can be analysed for its popularisation of psychoanalytic discourse from the 'ego psychology' prevalent in American-style confessional chat shows to the increasingly popular survival show in which a series of combatants overcome personal inhibition and physical limitation to attempt to achieve a higher and often financially lucrative status. The immediacy of the 'real event' is established through images of determination, failure, personal strength and inner conflict. In talk shows such as *Oprah* or *Sally Jessy Raphael* (NBC) video footage of 'survivors' in their hometown or amidst family, work colleagues or friends, sometimes provide an everyday 'authentic' backdrop to the studio confession. In survival shows, technology provides some signification of auth-enticity. Sweeping overhead shots capture the action and the location of competitors or mobile tracking shots of camcorders follow them, footsore but determined, over rough jungle terrain. Close-ups or night-vision shots of competitors show them in highly dangerous but also highly monitored circumstances: balancing on wires over ravines, perched on a pole in the sea for hours under a blistering sun, burrowing underground in pitch-dark passages echoing with disorientating sounds. In shows like *Survivor* or *The Mole*, or historical reconstructions like *The Trench* or *The 1940s House*, participants speak to video camera of their tiredness, fear or pain. Whilst such footage acknowledges the visceral effects of intense competition or physical deprivation, the hidden 'damage' or psychological barriers to success have to be verbalised and are often couched in therapeutic discourse either by host, commentator/expert or frequently by the subjects themselves.

The conventions of talk shows are crucial, as precursors of the reality TV format as they familiarised audiences with therapeutic discourse and valorised the televising of raw emotion as a marker of a previously undisclosed emotional reality. Sigmund Freud (1925) makes a distinction between ideational elements (interpretative discourses) and affect (raw psychic experience). The rendering of the unconscious into words and representations can be understood as both cathartic and healing but also as a defence mechanism in which intellectual discourses smooth over disturbing violent emotions. Talk shows provide forums for public confessional that appear open and direct, but also substantiate the idea that talk conceals as well as unveils the latent traumatic event. Shows such as *Oprah*, *Trisha*, *Ricki Lake* or *The John Walsh Show* (NBC) convey the idea that some experiences are too 'real' to be expressed by words alone and rely on guests breaking down in tears, showing signs of distress, wringing their hands or visibly trembling as physical registers of hidden damage. Popularised psychoanalytic notions of trauma, working-through and recovery are embedded in the presentation of these programmes. In fly-on-the-wall documentaries such as *Cutting Edge: The Wedding* (C4) and British reality TV series such as *Nurse* (BBC2), *Lakesiders* (BBC) (the filming of the 'community' of workers and shoppers at an Essex shopping mall) and *Airport* several participants break down at different moments in the narrative as they reveal marriage break-ups, emotional worries or family troubles. These moments are constructed as those nearest to real communication, outside of language when the person filmed bares their soul to the camera.

In an episode of *The John Walsh Show*, Walsh carefully interviews a young woman who has been set alight and badly scarred by her ex-partner. Two men, hearing her screams, had saved her when she was only seconds from death. Her memory of events is hazy and has been pieced together with the evidence of her rescuers (who also appear on the show) and police accounts. Her story of recovery is articulated through a mix of religious and therapeutic references. Invited to recount the experience, the camera lingers on her face, deeply damaged, particularly at the moment when her voice trembles and falters, she fidgets with her hands, and tears start in her eyes as she tries to recall the previously traumatic void of burning alive. In this, perhaps rather too obvious example, we can see the broader talk show convention of valorising the body and the voice as markers of an invisible reality to which only the interviewee has recourse. Geoffrey Hartmann has located this desire to animate the transient or ungraspable as part of visual culture's 'illusion not of making absent things present but present things more present (than they are or can be)' (2000: 112). He claims that television, even when presenting factual information rather than fiction, 'emits a hyperbolic form of visuality' as a means to assure truthfulness and to justify the audience's credence' (ibid.).[3]

Some talk shows – *Jenny Jones*, *Jerry Springer*, *Ricki Lake* – have embraced hyperbole and increasingly orchestrated physical conflict or violent responses between former partners, betrayed children, rival lovers or angry neighbours to ensure the camera shot of explosive behaviour or 'raw emotion' and to exploit the audience's response – the cat calls, boos and cheers, sharp collective gasps and gusts of incredulous laughter (Grindstaff 1997: 168). Those shows that do not revert to carnivalesque displays of extreme behaviour, but present themselves as mannered confessionals, face the technical problem of how to represent the traces of a traumatic experience which by its very definition *as trauma* is absent, perhaps even to the speaker themselves. And secondly, how to represent this in a way that counters the cold, objectifying status of the 'imperturbable camera' and its intrusive gaze when dealing with human vulnerability and exposure (1997: 118).

In his analysis of different modes of witnessing, John Durham Peters has suggested that public testimonies of private pain are always inadequate. Inadequate in the sense that the spoken account deals with a 'universe of reference' (2001: 711) always divergent from the audience no matter how much the type of trauma may be similar to that experienced by others. The media representation of trauma then is in a double-bind, for words are inadequate to the mind-blowing experience of trauma but words are the main public means of conveying such events. The close-up of the person uttering, bearing witness to the trauma of survival is evident in *The John Walsh Show* as the guest shields her mouth with her hands at points of most discomfort. She falters over words, gives a fragmentary account of the experience of burning, dissolves into brief silences, or speaks articulately about her process of recovery. The primacy of her voice at these points signifies that the camera, host and audience have privileged proximate access to the woman's reclamation of her self. Hartmann suggests that in such audio-visual testimony: 'What is essential is the mental space such minimal visuality ("I see a voice") allows' (2000: 118).

Watching in close-up the talk show guest being compelled to speak includes the television viewer in the provisional community of studio guests, host and friends or relatives who are privileged to hear this account first-hand. When questioned by Walsh about her current feelings for her attacker, the woman (like many talk show guests) resorts to the commonplace: 'I cannot put what I feel into words.' Her experience, like many that are aired on talk shows are particular to her, inexpressible, yet through the conventions of the show intended to represent the universal – the common experience of pain, horror, rage, anger, grief, betrayal or distress. Here reality TV produces the intimate revelation, the moment when the viewer shares the innermost secrets of those filmed, a moment beyond language and part of human interconnection. The reality constructed is as much about a tapping into popular knowledge of psychoanalytic therapeutic processes as it is about viewing them, thereby addressing a knowledgeable analytic viewer.

In shows such as Britain's *Kilroy* or America's *The Donahue Show* such confessional television talk is structured as an opposition between the representative intellectual experts and the distressed individual. The public sphere of health care or legal expertise and the private sphere meet and often clash with the individual sufferer providing the marker of authenticity. In the context of broader debates about popular television forms as either a new demotic space or a post-democratic space emptied of political power for the individual citizen, such shows have been presented as spaces where the individual ordinary suffering citizen is celebrated. He or she is represented as the touchstone of experience who taps into but also exceeds the discourse of self-help groups and experts (Livingstone & Lunt 1994; Scott 1996).

One episode of *The John Walsh Show* exemplifies the typical playing out of the above characteristics. John Walsh talks to men who have turned in a relative to the police for murder. Bill Babbit is one of the guests. He surrendered his brother Manny, a Vietnam veteran, for the murder of a 78-year-old woman. Babbit recalls this traumatic event in the first person to a studio audience. The witnessing of his brother's mental deterioration after military service in Vietnam and the discovery of his crime are recounted in a measured voice interspersed with sympathetic prompts from Walsh. Babbit quietly narrates his numbed realisation of his brother's crime, the horror of acknowledging the murder, the ethical crisis of informing on him and the stages of coming to terms with the loss of a loved one who was markedly changed following service in the Vietnam conflict. His personal crisis culminated in the blow of the law reneging on its promise that his brother would be spared execution but would be given therapeutic treatment instead.

Unlike confrontational talk shows, which rely on the spectacle of conflict (for example the American 'child' brides, husbands and parents who clashed on an episode of *Jerry Springer* screened on ITV2 in the same month) – *The John Walsh Show* is constructed as strongly therapeutic and highly supportive of the victim. The programme is situated in reviews and NBC publicity as supported confession on the part of the courageous ordinary person who has surmounted an exceptional distress that has distorted the contours of their everyday life. It is both confessional and public address. Walsh shifts between different models of popularly inflected therapeutic discourse: self-help, psychoanalytic, self-esteem and community advocacy. He extols the virtues of lawful citizenry even alongside painful familial betrayal and defines Babbit's disclosure to the police as a role model to others to 'do the right thing'; 'make the right phone call'. Babbit is presented as a traumatic hero – doing what any good American citizen would do but reaping the psychological and personal damage.

In keeping with talk show conventions, *The John Walsh Show* is 'not a balance of viewpoints but a serial association of testimonials' and, in a now-ritualised process, family members or friends are often called upon to add their personal account (Carpagnino *et al.* in Livingstone & Lunt 1994: 63). In this episode for example, Manny Babbit's adult children are called up alongside their uncle. They have not spoken to their uncle for over three years since he turned their father in to the police. Walsh switches to a mix of therapeutic, religious and counselling discourses. Continuing the role of therapist, he uses a lowered voice, maintains eye contact with the guests, asks questions, reinterprets accounts in psychoanalytic terms and confronts their emotions or responses to events.[4] He asks the uncle to 'get past the anger' that the children feel. He asks the children if they have come to terms with their uncle's actions and their father's execution whilst suggesting that Manny Babbit has now 'gone to a better place'. He talks of 'healing', pain and loss. Of the murder victim's family, Walsh speaks to camera, stating that 'I pray they have found the closure they sought'. In *The John Walsh Show*, as in many talk shows, therapy turns into media-friendly fireside homily.

As images of trauma are increasingly embedded in popular formats the difficulty of freshly inspiring empathy arises for the programme makers and the corresponding pressure to respond with empathy occurs for the viewer. To accentuate the horror and distress, the talk show draws on a number of filmic and narrative devices. In *The John Walsh Show*, a number of representational tropes accentuated the strength and integrity of Babbit's emotional distress whilst he himself appeared calm and measured. John Walsh used repetition to reinforce the immensity of events – for example when told that Manny Babbit was on death row for 18 years, he incredulously turned to audience and camera to repeat '18 years' several times. Babbit was shot in medium close-up to accentuate the minutiae of his emotional facial expressions. News headlines – 'war hero ends his life in death chamber' – complemented the account of Manny's exemplary military service and consequent psychological disintegration. The audience in particular registered a personal identification through their tears or hands clasped to face or breast as the tale unfolded.

John Langer has located such techniques within the culture of popular journalism.[5] He suggests that news stories of everyday men or women who are suddenly ensnared in a state of crisis also draw on the physical presence of witnesses who provide testimony on behalf of the victim; adding a veracity not available to media professionals and offering an image of emotional engagement. In response to key moments, the camera frequently cut to the shocked or anguished or sympathetic response of one or two of the audience who compensated for Babbit's composure. Manny Babbit's children and their story provided another level of identification for viewers; they suggested that trauma, even when it did not affect the subject directly, could occur to someone close to them. Walsh's interventions offered a slightly more detached identification with the victim: 'safe yet still concerned, sympathetic without getting overwhelmed, engaged but at a distance' (1992: 121).

As with many talk shows, Walsh is positioned on the side of lay people rather than experts (Livingstone & Lunt 1994: 36–70). In keeping with his former hosting of *America's Most Wanted: America Fights Back* he is constructed in NBC publicity as an advocate of the victim with a highly credible reputation. The publicity claims that, following the 11 September 2001 attacks on the World Trade Center twin towers, the White House called on him 'to help the American people come to terms and better understand the war on terrorism.'[6] Walsh himself declares himself an *ordinary* man who also shares an *exceptional* allegiance with victims. His own personal tragedy frequently enters public discourse as evidence of a special knowledge of pain, suffering and a lack of closure, which his television shows allegedly provide for others.

In July 1981 Walsh's six-year-old son Adam was abducted and later found murdered.[7] The suspected perpetrator was never charged with the crime and later died in prison serving life for other felonies. In the Babbit interview, Walsh presents himself as a survivor of the emotional destruction that crime can cause: 'Heartbreak and anguish can consume you for years, like it consumed me for years and take you to places you don't want to go.' As an ordinary individual he situates himself outside the state institutions and represents a candid despair at statutory punishment, colluding with Babbit's anger at a judicial system that deprived a war veteran of therapy and enforced a death row sentence. Walsh speaks of the 'criminal *injustice* system I've lived with for 21 years'. In an interview about his work on *America's Most Wanted* tracking the 11 September terrorists, Walsh describes his horrific encounter with Ground Zero and conjures up images of traumatised families searching for missing relatives in the rubble of the twin towers. In this and numerous other crime scenes, Walsh links others' anguish to his own search for his missing son. He is representative of the media celebrity as privileged possessor of psychic crisis. His personal pain constitutes justification for his media role of articulating the trauma of the ordinary person: 'We are going to tell those stories of the people that are waiting because I have been there. I walked in their shoes when I was searching for my son.'[8]

In this respect, such talk shows have in common with television and film 'trauma drama' a readiness to communicate popular scepticism about social institutions. Jane

Feuer (1995) has suggested that the trauma dramas, popular on US television in the 1980s, pitched official against individual action in narratives that uncovered hypocrisy and official cover-ups to the detriment of the ordinary individual and family. Her first example is ABC's *Friendly Fire* (1979), in which 'ordinary' American parents are driven to investigate their son's 'accidental' death at the hands of his own side in Vietnam. Describing Feuer's analysis, Derek Paget concludes: 'The very title of the film throws back at the military its own ghastly newspeak euphemism, the product of a war of "body counts" and "pacification programmes"' (1998: 170). Trauma drama and US talk shows often share the self-help individualism endorsed in the Reagan years and showcase the actions of individuals forced to pursue the truth in the face of official incompetence or suspected cover-ups. They both proclaim a heightened realism underscored by the narratives of personal battle and triumph over institutional failure or irresponsibility. Paget claims, that in this respect, trauma drama 'opens up documentary space' and 'thereby mimics the actual experience of individuals forced to act on their own behalf' (1998: 171).

Arguably, therefore, Walsh's persona represents a broader move within popular realist formats to challenge the 'expert' and their specialist knowledge and to hold them accountable to ordinary people (Livingstone & Lunt 1994: 98–9). Authorities and experts are given second ranking in a hierarchy of credibility behind ordinary people, whose suffering ranks highest. Additionally, in talk shows, experts are increasingly exhorted to adopt both a conversational or self-help discourse and to claim personal experience to legitimate their advice to a media/studio audience. This was illustrated in an episode of *Kilroy* (BBC1, June 2003) on experiences of child abuse. When the expert was called upon to provide the closing message of the programme, Robert Kilroy questioned him in personal terms, disclosing that the expert had formerly been the victim of child abuse. Whilst this may have been a strategic move by Kilroy to humanise expert *impersonal* advice with his *personal* story, the speaker angrily rejected this positioning. In a distinct clash between host and expert the latter refused to embellish his advice with intimate personal details and rebutted – 'I've not come here to speak about that.' He alleged that his appearance on *Kilroy* was solely to promote his charity and help-line for abuse survivors to which Kilroy retorted that at least he had been given the final few minutes of television speaking time. In contrast, at the end of his confession on *The John Walsh Show*, Bill Babbit spoke explicitly about his personal experience claiming it as the backdrop to his formation of a charity: Murder Victims' Families For Reconciliation. However, despite the different emphases, in both cases, the ordinary anecdotal account of trauma was prioritised over the expert abstraction illustrating that, in talk shows, experts are most valued if they appear on a level footing with the disenfranchised. Furthermore, in talk shows, trauma is rightly defined as an experience of continuing impact; in which a past wounding event continues to return and to influence the present life.[9]

To their credit, many talk shows gesture towards moral integrity and claim to use the ordinary person's trauma and survival to (try to) motivate their viewers towards an ethical life. Again, the role of trauma as cultural trope seems apposite, for television disclosure of personal trauma energises public narratives of right and wrong, good and evil, and marks the ordinary subject for their ethical decision to speak out. These stories of severe trauma represent one end of a spectrum of televisual representations that attempt to shape our ethical sensibilities. For, as Gay Hawkins argues, new popular formats – from programmes on changing personal dress, garden or house styles, to cookery and diet shows, talk shows and morning news-chat – 'involve examinations of *ways to live*'. They divest 'information about the care and management of the self, explorations of the tensions between collective versus self-interest, audience participation in quests for the truth of the self' (2001: 412). In early June 2003, television reviewers noted a swathe of new reality life-style programmes hitting the British TV screens. A sub-genre of factual programming on lifestyle coaching was in full swing and in the US, journalists also commented on the mounting success of 'makeover' reality TV. In the second week of June, a number of programmes competed with more conventional documentary programming for audience numbers. These shows appeared to be a development of popular makeover programmes such as *Changing Rooms* (BBC1) and *What Not to Wear* (BBC2) and of talk show confessional mixed with the voyeuristic observation of ordinary people beloved by reality TV.[10] Dubbed by reviewer Jason Deans as 'car crash lifestyle TV', he commented on the propensity of such programmes to invite viewers to voyeuristically observe ordinary people and to 'share in the humiliation of participants who have aspects of their personal lives ripped to shreds'.[11] In contrast, editorial director Daisy Goodwin of Talkback Productions (maker of numerous 'self-improvement TV' shows),[12] argued that: 'Everyone wants to know how to improve their life … these shows both give you hope – you think, "If she could find a date, so could I" – and make you feel better about yourself, because you think, "I'm not as bad as that"' (in Lyall 2003: 2).

Talkback Productions' *The Dinner Party Inspectors* explored dinner party decorum by visiting a private party set by an ordinary group of friends or relatives each week. The inspectors, a slightly parodic upper-middle-class duo, Victoria Mather and Meredith Etherington-Smith, swilled white wine while watching the party via a surveillance video and the television audience's own surveillance of the party was cross-cut with the inspectors' withering comments on dress sense, culinary disasters, appropriate behaviour and conversation. Through much of the series, therapeutic discourse infused dinner table talk. In one episode, the hostess spoke of her search for psychological wholeness, drawing on pop-therapy solutions from feng shui to a magazine-style checklist of positive and negative life points. In another excruciating episode, a hostess pushed her guest (who was clearly uncomfortable with the self-analysis of some of his fellow diners) into revealing that his brother was stabbed to death. The first episode (10 June 2003) – in which Jamie, a gay cellist from Islington, North London threw a party to introduce his long-lost straight sister to musical friends – was followed by *The Reality Check* (C4) which continued the therapeutic theme. Acting coach Kate Marlow played therapist as she descended on a group of professional female footballers and asked them to play out their childhood traumas to rapidly establish an unresolved sexual tension between the male coach and players that was wrecking pre-match preparation.

While such lifestyle programmes are concerned with observing the everyday rituals of social interaction and how they throw up social embarrassment, awkward behaviour and minor clashes; they share with talk shows a concern to shape and govern the messier aspects of collective life. The experts' guidance on rules to live by and to succeed is bolted onto the subjects' own self-help diagnosis. In contrast, talk shows reveal a current cultural fascination which events, which exceed everyday experience and which demand a different mode of experiencing their 'reality effect'. Trauma is a disorder of time and of memory yet the television show demands that events, which should unfold according to their own dynamic for any therapeutic purpose, must be marshalled into the constraints of a half-hour slot in which a number of guests may vie for disclosure time. Programmes like *The John Walsh Show*, *Kilroy* and *Judge Judy* offer ethical dilemmas and solutions that range from individual choices to the privileging of categorical legal and moral imperatives to fashion one's life. For example, Judge Judy Sheindlin cuts through the ambiguity of any traumatic encounter to locate moral responsibility in either the defendant or accused stood before her. *Judge Judy* replicates the legal system's prioritisation of live testimony, which is construed as a carefully regulated performance of memory-retrieval. The Judge's presiding over a 'live' televised event is underlined by her monitoring of the defendants' and witnesses' facial expressions, body movements and verbal tics. Her pronouncements on blame and cause are expressed in plain speech: 'you were a lunatic', 'you were drunk as a skunk', 'he picks on you because you're a pigeon', 'Paul ... She put you through school. You'll reap the benefits of her hard work for the rest of your life, and you felt no moral obligation to reimburse her? If that's the case, she's well rid of you.' Here, everyday dilemmas are the source of personal conflict and discontent. Judge Judy offers a set of judgements, practical rules and strategies for managing the self and for anticipating the problem of living with and accommodating others. Similarly, Jane Shattuc notes the frequent move from the personal to large-group identification in talk shows like *Oprah* which are ultimately fuelled by the dictates of mass entertainment:

> The host generalises the particular experience into a larger social frame to capture the interest of a larger audience. For all their individualised narratives, the shows speak in generalities, but not about changing specific social and political institutions. (1997: 96)

The 'danger' of such generalisation and ethical absolutism lies in the slide into an 'ontology, a self-contained worldview, or value system' which, it is assumed, can be overlaid onto any account of social and/or psychic injury. As Bill Nichols argues:

> Ethical actions then appear to be driven by timeless values rather than deriving from a code by which those with power police themselves and others as they opt for regulations of conscience and social responsibility as an alternative to coercion. (1991: 102)

While John Walsh, for example, may celebrate the surviving victim over 'the criminal injustice system' he nonetheless situates that survival within other religious and therapeutic frameworks. Systems like Christianity, self-recovery therapy, the legal system, or indeed 'soft' journalism become 'the boundary or frame that supplies the repertoire of values and the means to apply them to a given situation' (ibid.). Talk shows then may offer a misleading sense of assurance whilst enabling the temporary representation of the ordinary person's survival and empowerment for they demand a certainty of memory and solution not readily available to the traumatised individual in everyday life.

chapter 7
Video justice: reality crime television

Wild footage from a wild world

Television and other screen cultures have always exhibited a preoccupation with law-breaking and the powerful tensions that it engenders. Both their fictional and factual productions offer audiences innumerable variants of crime: its operation, its protagonists and its effects. During the 1980s and 1990s in Britain, true crime television programming such as *In Suspicious Circumstances*, *Michael Winner's True Crimes* and *Expert Witness* (all ITV) offered dramatised reconstructions of crimes of violence and murder whose representational charge resided in the extra-textual knowledge that these events *really did happen* and that the criminals were caught. Their authority as crime programmes rested in their commitment to the infallibility of the law. All three programmes presented cases that had been solved and part of the viewing pleasure lay in the alliance between presenter, police and audience in the reconstructed narrative of the detection, pursuit and capture of the criminal. None of these programmes represented the aftermath of the arrest; trial and punishment are both rendered invisible, and the voice of the criminal subject remains silenced. So even where non-fiction television allows for the use of reconstructions which can re-play events usually obscured from cameras, the emphasis is on the crime not the punishment.

Other programmes perhaps more properly described as 'law and order' programming follow this emphasis, working in conjunction with police and deploying both reconstructions and real footage of criminal acts and criminals to piece together stories of crime (see

Biressi 2001: 203). UK programmes such as *Crimewatch UK, Crime Monthly, Crimestoppers* (ITV) and in the US *America's Most Wanted*, which promote themselves as extensions of the law by inviting viewers to help solve crime, provide dramatic reconstructions which allow viewers to 'see' a real crime take place, offering an experience unavailable to consumers of either news programming or crime fiction (see Schlesinger & Tumber 1996). They allow viewers to encounter the traumatic moment of criminality either by re-playing CCTV and police camera footage or through dramatisation.

As with the observational documentaries and docusoaps discussed in chapter 3, true crime and law and order programmes occupy a controversial place in the industry's value-laden hierarchy. Nick Ross, one of the presenters of *Crimewatch UK*, is keen to distance himself from true crime, saying, '*Crimewatch* and its sister programmes are in the public interest. *True Crimes* by contrast, for all its skilful use of television arts, could only be of interest to the public' (in Hill 2000a: 219). The distinction made by Ross is revealing. It is plain that the show needs to demonstrate a public service role through the resolution of crime but this cannot be effected in isolation from the requirement to entertain its audience. After all, only a handful of the people viewing the programme could have personal knowledge that might help solve the crime; everyone else will need to form connections of an entirely different nature in order to sustain their interest in the programme. On an earlier occasion Ross and co-presenter Sue Cook described how the makers of *Crimewatch* have a very shrewd idea of what is wanted in the show: 'with a quarter of a million crimes recorded every month you would think *Crimewatch* would be spoilt for choice. In fact it is remarkably difficult regularly to find three crimes worthy of reconstruction' (Ross & Cook 1987: 29). What constitutes 'worthiness' is not elaborated on but it must be the case that the crime chosen has to be 'reconstructable' and of interest to a broad audience. But there is an awkward paradox in that a programme that seeks to solve cases with the aid of the public is also a 'show', an entertainment whose success is reflected in viewing figures of up to twelve million. It is dependent upon the very crimes that it seeks to solve for its success. By the time it is ready for broadcasting this paradox is painfully apparent: 'Frankly, at this stage, with all this investment in time and effort, not to say the BBC's resources, we pray that the crimes are not solved just before we go on air' (Ross & Cook 1987: 34).

As reality footage focuses on the criminal act and sometimes its resolution, it is far less common for viewers to be able to follow the criminal beyond his/her arrest to trial and imprisonment. Plainly there are practical reasons why cameras are unable to penetrate court and prison boundaries. Consequently, where the criminal on trial can be viewed in media culture this spectacle has taken on huge cultural significance. The classic example is the televised trial of Nazi war criminal Adolf Eichmann in 1961, which represented a major landmark in US television history (see Shandler 2000). Only much more recently, with the advent of *Court TV* in the US, have television arbiters such as Judge Judy and filmed trials such as the serialised O. J. Simpson hearings of 1994 been able to go further in revealing the processes of the law without recourse to any dramatic reconstructions. In the case of *Judge Judy*, the mundane domestic dispute, neighbourhood conflict or minor financial claim are all unpacked before a television audience. Viewers witness the fine detail of interpersonal clashes and legal debates, the petty wrangles of life brought to juridical arbitration and filmed subjects are made accountable to the judge's and the television audience's discerning scrutiny. Similarly, the O. J. Simpson case brought to mass audiences the processes and discursive practices of the courtroom, seemingly through the fixed, impartial eye of the camera but directed through extensive and detailed commentary.

Public fascination with the Simpson case, of course, began much earlier than the televised trial, with the filmed high-speed car chase in which the suspect took flight from the police. This scene, reminiscent of so many fictional crime thriller movies, is actually quite representative of reality crime footage: powerfully charged for viewers with the knowledge that this is real, charged with the 'here and now' immediacy which is the always potential technological precondition of television as a form (see Fiske 1996). Recent programming such as *Chopper Coppers*, *Cops* and *Shops, Robbers and Videotape* deploys the same kind of footage; presenting a spectacle apparently grounded in the *authentic* and the *immediate* moment that characterises both realism and television itself.

Since the 1990s, new reality genres of crime and emergency services programming have appeared. These rely even more heavily on amateur, CCTV or police footage to present a montage of criminality and emergency services drama and, unlike law and order programming, they make little claim to help prevent or solve crime. These shows made a real impact on American schedules and they soon went on to constitute a steady presence in Britain. Series such as *Blues and Twos* (Carlton, 1993), *Coppers* (Sky, 1994), *Police! Camera! Action!* (Carlton, 1996) and *999* (BBC, 1992) became popular family viewing and garnered high viewing figures.[1] These newer forms of reality crime entertainment have extended the arena of the preoccupation with crime and pursuit as display. They constitute a new spectacle of criminality in which it is not the punishment but the scene (seen) of the crime itself which is present and made highly visible in the public sphere. Criminality, which we would expect to be hidden from view, is made visible and frequently seen to be dramatic, apparently random and unprovoked. Yet it can be re-wound, re-played and slowed down for viewers to appreciate just like a sports programme. Reality crime footage also constitutes a form of exchangeable currency within media networks. Current reality programming consists of hybrid genres that are recombinants of earlier forms, including dramadoc, straight to camera interviews, news and police footage, CCTV, expert opinion and spectacular set-piece scenes of criminal behaviour, pursuit and capture. Each component: video clip, interview, still image etc., variously sourced and infinitely reproducible, has been extracted from its cultural context to become a unit of exchange, a small piece of an electronic televisual assemblage.

Unlike news, contemporaneity is not important here, and programmes will often present a mixture of footage and stories up to a decade old. This combination of footage can be understood partly as a popular archive, a new, more populist extension of the established disciplinary archives of the law such as the forensic, medical and prison or reform photography that historically captured and categorised the criminal subject (see Tagg 1988). But unlike previous archives, whose authority was dependent on their status as 'documents', these films, while shot through with the televisual and filmic codes of realism, are also infused with the extra-diegetic props of fictional or tabloid crime stories. They represent a fusion of the objectifying and disciplinary photographic imperative with the tabloid journalism agenda of entertainment and diversion. The aesthetics of realism (badly framed images, poorly lit shots, images caught against bright light) underpin and authenticate the immediate realism and documentary posture of the footage. But added to the mix is music to accentuate action, dramatic editing, emotional to-camera speeches and the juxtaposition of similar events (street muggings, car chases and so on) to build up the drama and enhance the seamless pleasures of a flow of criminal scenes unfolding before the spectator's eyes. This combination constitutes the sense of 'wild footage from a wild world' (Ellis 2000: 98) – reality with an entertaining inflection.

These programmes, aimed at a family audience, have attracted extensive criticism from media critics and some viewers (see Hill 2000a: 219–20 and 2000b: 133–7). As a form of 'tabloid television' they represent all that is generally condemned in popular culture; tending towards the reactionary and the retributive, exciting, exploitative, voyeuristic and entertaining. They are also considered to be symptomatic of the tabloidisation of news and current affairs where the 'discourse of sobriety' has been forsaken for 'infotainment'. As such they blur the boundaries between the public and private sphere, amalgamating the primary aims to inform and to entertain into one unique package. And the informational content, such as it is, is expressed within 'common sense' discourses about justice and law and order that produce a knowledge about victimhood and criminality which is usually retributive and highly conservative.

These programmes also play a significant role in the more general contemplation of crime event as mass media entertainment. For as soon as a notable or exceptional crime hits the headlines it becomes circulated within media formats with astonishing speed to become a media spectacle. As Kevin Glynn notes in his account of American tabloid television:

> The vortex of representation swirling around the crime events, the characters involved in the events, the characters involved in the fictionalisation of events, and the characters involved in the reporting on the fictionalisation of events all become part of a single simulacrum, within which it becomes virtually impossible to neatly disentangle the various levels of reality and representationality involved. (2000: 46)

The pleasures of watching reality crime TV have been subject to much speculation. As a result of her research into American audiences S. Elizabeth Bird suggests, for example, that far from viewing these dramas with an ironic or amused detachment or with a carnivalesque enjoyment viewers approach these forms as they would any other kind of factual television (2000: 215). They ask themselves, 'How does this story apply to my life and why should I pay attention?' This kind of question points to the likely connection made by viewers to crime narratives through processes of identification, such as 'Could I too become the victim of crime?' or 'What would I do in that situation?' British audience studies corroborate this. Researcher Annette Hill quotes a woman who declares, 'These true life stories are great. If I had more time … I would watch as many of these types of programmes as I could. They make you appreciate life' (2000: 131).

These kinds of identifications also beg the question of to what extent the fascination with these programmes is rooted in the ways in which they generate a more general fearfulness and caution. Richard Sparks has observed that the expansion of television and related industries has coincided with long-term and sometimes acute anxiety about crime (1992: 16). It becomes impossible therefore to unravel the relationship between television as an instigator of fearfulness and the broader cultural preoccupation with crime, risk and endangerment. Moreover, as television brings a putatively public sphere issue into the private domain of the home the demarcations between external events and personal experience, between objective fact and subjective knowledge become ever more muddied. Nonetheless, it can be argued that the narrativisation of crime in both fact and fictional forms provides a secure container for fear and those things that incite fear – the other, the alien and so on, shaping it and directing it into manageable formations.

Moreover, it is a complex business, with crime genres as with horror genres, to understand where fear ends and pleasure begins. Many reality crime programmes show dramatic footage of criminals abandoning moral and legal codes in spectacular fashion and some younger viewers especially find this stimulating.[2] But where the pleasures of witnessing crime, disaster and other life-threatening occurrences are somewhat vicarious, these are at least partially offset by the moral discourses of criminal justice, the address to the responsible citizen and overt support for the emergency services employed in many of these shows (Goodwin 1993; Biressi 2001: 77–88). Such discourses of reassurance and moral authority also act as a counterweight or palliative to the viewer's possible sense of helplessness in the face of apparent criminal mayhem. An ideological framework is provided by the programmes' dramatic structure that demonstrates that either the camera's evidence or police intervention will lead to the arrest of the criminal and the arrival of a 'guilty' verdict. This is reinforced by the 'reputable', usually male, television presenter whose commentary works hard to preclude an easy identification with the criminal rather than with the victim and society more generally. Consequently, while the visual image is emphasised as the primary hook in attracting viewers (signalled in programme titles *Police! Camera! Action!*, *Shooting the Crime*, *Crime Caught on Tape*) there is also an attempt to subordinate the multiple potential interpretations of this imagery to a single indisputable reading of the events. So although there may be some pleasures to be had in witnessing the many challenges to the law and social norms evident in these shows there is no way that these programmes can be said to present a *thorough-going* critique of the law. In fact, the programmes work hard to provide a cultural prop for the law's authority and much of the footage is provided by law enforcement agencies. If the law is challenged in these programmes, it is only through the depiction of a relentless catalogue of criminality that suggests that the law's job is never done, that complete lawfulness is always an unfinished project – but even then, of course, its very incompleteness is a further justification for the law.

The use of surveillance technology and the dissemination of film footage on reality TV have produced new ethical dilemmas and new inflections of the citizen's imaginary relationship with the law. Firstly, reality programmes expand the membership of law enforcement to include supposedly vigilant and supportive televisual citizens whose active interest and 'assistance' validates the filming and screening of criminal spectacles. Secondly, programmes invite the viewer to collude in the entrapment of the 'criminal' and the closing down of this violently chaotic world. Thirdly, they provide access to the vicarious pleasures and dangers of the criminality but do so *under the cover* of a 'responsible' factual programming agenda. In these ways they interpolate the individual viewer as a crucial co-producer of the new realism of reality crime television, highlighting the complex operations of viewer engagement with these forms.

Crimes can even be actively produced in order to feed a programme. Programmes such as *Rat Trap* (Carlton, 2000) actually set up a potential crime scene in order to film the ensuing thievery and mayhem before asking viewers to identify the criminals being filmed. On some occasions the scenes were without any potential legal outcome at all as the protagonists were too young to have their faces shown on screen. Executive producer Sarah Caplin, who was called upon to defend the programme, argued, 'We are not creating the crime, nor are we inviting people to steal … We are replicating normal activities … and using cameras to see what happens next.'[3] This 'replication' of 'normal activities', neither wholly an *authentic* crime in real social space nor wholly a *fictional* crime in media space, constitutes a new social/media public forum and with it an invitation to think through the ethics and etiquette of its inhabitation. As viewers, we know the preconditions of the crime, that it is a 'sting' or 'lure' established to catch criminals in the act and to open up the scene (usually of necessity hidden) to public view. These activities may not be unusual, but despite Caplin's assertion, neither are they 'normal' because they are outside of the acceptable bounds of civic behaviour; indeed it is the aberrance of crime that invites such avid curiosity.

The law and media culture

The ethical complexities of these new forums of social/media space shift, depending upon the relationship between the individual subject of film footage and the uses made of the film within its local context. For example, in 1995 media debate arose over the case of Geoff Peck, a resident of Brentwood in the English County of Essex, who walked into the street and cut his wrists in an abortive suicide attempt. His actions were caught on camera and the police were soon on the scene. The footage, however, was sent out by the council in a press pack to promote its surveillance system ('cameras save lives'), sold to the BBC and ITV and finally circulated in forums such as local and national papers and a reality crime show. Peck turned on his TV set only to see himself trailing a true crime programme. The title of one of many newspaper articles expressing doubts about this and other cases 'the all-seeing eye that understands nothing' (Conrad 2000) summarises the disquiet over this seemingly impartial but actually highly invasive technology. Media journalists and alternative media groups such as Undercurrents (1997) have asked, for example, at what personal cost is this footage released into the public sphere.

Media culture's relation to the law underpins anything that might be learned about the inhabitation of the new social/media space of CCTV-dependent reality programming. Michel Foucault's reflection on the strategies of power may be useful here. He notes:

Law is neither the truth of power nor its alibi. It is an instrument of power which is at once complex and partial. The form of law with its effects of prohibition needs to be resituated among a number of other, non-juridical mechanisms. (1972: 141)

In Britain, the law's self-image is of a practice that is neither partial nor instrumental but rather as one that has arisen organically from 'natural' justice, developed through precedent and argument and which sustains social order. In its ideal-typical form it is regarded as unpolluted, necessarily avoiding complicity with pragmatic politics or populist agendas. In fact, the media and media technologies are co-extensive with the law and operate in dialogue with it as supportive non-juridical mechanisms. The success of tabloid newspaper campaigns alone in gaining the rapt attention of British Home Secretaries past and present attests to the media's role in the formation of law-making and criminal justice policy.

But more complexly, the conditions of public intelligibility and acceptance of the law and policing as prohibition resides in the law's relation to media culture more generally. The media is one of the central mechanisms through which our knowledge of the law and law breaking is produced, circulated and naturalised into common sense. The examples of Peck's attempted suicide on film, of the boys captured in a pseudo-crime for *Rat Trap* or of a presenter reassuring viewers that the thieves were caught at the end of the car chase scene in *Police! Camera! Action!* all point to the complex interactions between law and media. The law has merged with the broader disciplinary apparatuses of contemporary society from privatised corporate CCTV to entertainment-based reality TV and is arguably no less powerful for this incorporation. Geoff Peck's case foregrounds this problematic, begging the question of whether by taking a personal, but 'antisocial', action in a surveyed public space he forfeited any right of media privacy.

The near omni-presence (in Britain at least) of the camera creates a new power relation between subject, action and space in the course of everyday life; a relation that always potentially posits a new dimension through the possible presence of mediated witnesses.[4] The subject becomes an object in the field of vision captured by the camera and his/her actions may be thrown open to public view. When footage is sold on, it is extracted, organised and acted upon so that it is endowed with meaning and re-situated in contexts that purport to present a critical ontology and regulation of ourselves: we have been warned that should we undertake these anti-social actions we will not only be penalised but specularised. The viewing subject needs to decide how to ethically engage with and understand this footage in the context of the programme package. It may be justified within critical discourses of freedom and empowerment (i.e. the public's right to know, to be reassured and to *witness* the effective operations of the law). But it should also provoke debate and a censure of power for its instrumental colonisation of public space and the dangers of incorporating such ambiguous images into 'infotainment' packages.

Questions of media ethics need to be examined in the light of the new complexities of the relationship between law and media and through a scrutiny of the media technology that functions as part of a general social disciplinary network. Joost van Loon has argued, for example, that technology needs to be understood *ethically* not simply as an enabling tool but as an instrumental way of revealing, ordering and 'enframing' the world. Thus technology itself, most explicitly with the example of *Rat Trap* cited above, has to be regarded as *constituting* the violent event at the threshold of visibility:

> For example, in the videotaped beating of Rodney King it is quite clear that what the case was actually about was not the beating as such but its meaning in the light of the videotape which allegedly captured it. Without the tape, there would never have been a case to begin with. (2000: 62)

This does not mean, of course, that Rodney King was not 'taken down' by law enforcement officers but rather that the amateur footage renders the event 'something else'. For van Loon video technology functioned with what he calls the 'media-ensemble' or technologies of police brutality (cars, lights, helicopters and so on) to produce a hybrid media form, a 'revelation via shock therapy' (2000: 64–5) which had real consequences in the social world. In cases such as this the 'ethical sensibilities of enframing' need to be understood and taken on board by media workers. This will not eliminate 'distortion', which is in any case impossible, but work to engage audiences in the processes of mediation and prevent televisual technologies being dismissed as purely instrumental, as simply the 'all seeing eye that understands nothing'.

These ethical issues are also embedded in broader civic questions about the demarcation of public/private space within a heavily mediated modern social sphere. New technologies have extended the field of vision within public space, creating a new psycho-geography of lived space. Broader global issues of media technology and image exchange are crosscut with the local and national issues of politico-economic-legal investment in surveillance technology and the specific fantasies as well as realities of crime that fuel this. Britain, for example, boasts at least a million security cameras – the greatest number in Europe and CCTV has arguably attained the 'status of icon of the emergent post-social zeitgeist' (Hughes *et al.* 2000: 332).[5]

In Britain the spread of cameras arguably police the divisions between the 'the good citizen' and its criminal 'other' through highly subjective visual social clues. For example, surveillance control room operators may focus on individuals who are either in the 'wrong' place or the 'wrong' time, or who belong to certain (i.e. 'wrong') social groupings (see Norris & Armstrong 1997a and 1997b). Cameras are often situated in areas where property and corporate interests are given priority over community affairs and they are often operated by private security organisations which further muddy the boundaries between the public and the private. Does the 'good citizen' register the presence of the surveillance camera on urban streets? Do 'innocent' citizens regard themselves as invisible, thinking the camera merely marks and captures the criminal subject and leave them at the edge of the frame? The public's understanding of surveillance camera presence is seriously under-researched but where it has been it seems that in Britain, at least, filmed subjects seem unconcerned (see Honess & Shandler 1992).

It is unsurprising in the light of the encroachment of scopic technologies in everyday life that two of the crime cases which became most prominent through the attention of the British media, the murders of James Bulger in 1993 and Damilola Taylor in 2001, featured film footage. The last public scenes of the boys' lives were captured in Bulger's case on CCTV from a shopping precinct, a construction company camera and Taylor's case in the civic space of the library and social housing estate. For understandable reasons, of the more than thirty people who witnessed James Bulger being pushed and dragged to his death by two older boys, only one person tried to intervene. What was more perplexing perhaps was the sense, voiced both in Bootle where James lived and more broadly, that because the abduction had been filmed it should have been prevented.

There was, as Sarah Kember describes it, frustration and confusion about the role and efficacy of video surveillance as policing. She notes, 'We become angry at a technology which failed to police our own boundaries between who in society is responsible and who is not; who is to be protected and who is one to be protected from' (1995: 121). There was a growing realisation too that cameras are actually installed to protect property and facilitate commerce rather than to prevent unforeseen inter-personal crime.[6] In addition, the importance of the camera as a *symbolic* presence is often overlooked. Just as life-sized cardboard cut-outs of a uniformed police officer situated at the entrances of shops deter shoplifters so too dummy cameras act as totems of the law's omniscience. Their very presence is an injunction towards self-policing which, when it fails, increases the public's sense of fearfulness. Thus the scandal of the murder of Stephen Lawrence in South London was heightened by the knowledge that the cameras that witnessed his attack by a group of men were dummies.

The cases cited here all demonstrate – albeit with different emphases – that the alliance of television technologies with governmentality (local government, police, privatised security) produces a scopic colonisation of public space which, in turn, may then go on to appear in reality TV formats. These depictions in turn help form the imaginary relationship between policing and the public. In factual programming the police have become ever more strongly allied with televisual technology. The mythologisation in crime fictions of the police as possessing supernatural powers of observation, deduction and detection is further extended in reality forms so that the police, like television itself, seem to be ubiquitous, always present whether visible or not.[7]

Crime television and the modality of witness

John Ellis has argued that it is the distinctive experience of 'witness' which has been one of the abiding characteristics of twentieth-century media culture. He is speaking essentially about the increasing importance of the mechanical technology of photography and then audio-visual technologies of representation – cinema and television, and the ways in which they posit new relations between text and audience. The modality of witnessing as described by Ellis goes some way to explaining the experience of television. Features such as direct address, the technology of transmission, sound, live performance, the rhetoric of liveness, the promise of the immediate and the presence of TV audiences constitute, when taken together, the particularity of television. And it could be argued that more especially the spectacles of news, live media events, reality TV and other non-fiction forms, which purport to speak about the world, are the most typical – i.e. archetypal – forms of television. Twentieth-century technologies have put forward evidence of historical events, visually documenting war, genocide, famine, assassination and the lives of famous people and ordinary people to a degree that is unprecedented. He notes:

> The feeling of witness … is one of separation and powerlessness; the events unfold, like it or not. They unfold elsewhere … So for the viewer, powerlessness and safety go hand in hand. In another sense, of course, the act of witness is nevertheless powerful. It enables viewers to overlook events … Yet at the same time … individuals … become accomplices in the events they see. Events on screen make a mute appeal: 'you cannot say you did not know.' (2000: 11)

This points to the shifting field of involvement and distanciation, activity and passivity that others have described in relation to television viewing at large (Ang 1982: 96–102; Fiske 1987: 173–6; Silverstone 1994: 152–3). The 'complicity', the sense of being somehow an accomplice of televised events, becomes more pointed when these events are violent, traumatic and 'real'.

Video Justice: Crime Caught on Tape (Fox, 1997) is one of the more controversial American reality crime programmes which has also been broadcast in the UK (2001). Like a number of British as well as American series on crime, policing and the emergency services *Video Justice* consists of a patchwork of shaky film footage sourced from CCTV and private security cameras, police cameras and home-video tapes. This is edited in with interviews with medico-legal experts, law enforcement agents and members of the public who have become the victims of crime. Extra-diegetic music is used to build suspense and cue emotional responses to the material shown.

The programme's twin warning and invitation to viewers cautions that what they are about to see is 'graphic, troubling and real'. It begins with a sequence of violent monochrome images anchored with a voiceover that notes, 'There's a war going on in America, a hidden war, between citizens and criminals. There's a new weapon in that war – the video camera.' Just as its relentless depiction of crime verges on the hyperbolic so too does its commentary which constantly asserts either that the criminal was caught or that 'this film might be the only way to catch him'. The metaphor of a 'war against crime', commonly deployed by citizens, journalists and politicians alike, is given extra meaning when located in the US, whose mythological history is bound up with gun culture. Moreover, the condition of fearfulness embodied in the language of embattlement is arguably symptomatic of broader social anxiety. Christopher Lasch, in his ground-breaking work on the growing culture of privatisation and the increasing narcissism of American culture, explains the national condition of solipsistic self-regard as a response to the 'warlike conditions which pervade American society, from the danger and uncertainty that surrounds us, from the loss of confidence in the future' (1978: 27).

The programme illustrates many of the issues raised so far. Its hour-long assemblage of video clips spliced together as an entertainment package presents the viewer with spectacles that, for British viewers at least, provoke both a sense of powerlessness and also of security. The events are located in an 'other' place, a country strongly associated in British television and Hollywood popular mythology with crime, widespread possession of firearms and urban danger. In contrast, for the American viewer, the programme's direct address signals a world that is both frighteningly alien but also perilously close and unpredictable.

At the same time, the footage also accentuates the volatile moment, the *excitement* and, sometimes, the near-death experience of crime. Footage of speeding cars, teenagers smashing up immaculate showcase homes and street fights, arguably offer the viewer some of the transgressive pleasures of the accomplice looking on. The depiction of varied criminal acts – speeding drivers, property desecration, theft, beatings and robbery with violence – all heavily de-contextualised, tend to reduce all crime to the level of spectacle. The programme barely bothers, if at all, to differentiate between the degrees of seriousness of the different acts, comically juxtaposing drunks falling down in the streets with armed robberies. Across this wide spectrum of engagement with the various events of the text the way the footage is reconstituted and presented allows no discussion or contemplation of context: the emphasis is on the incoherence, plenitude and simultaneity of 'the real'.

Video Justice also interestingly foregrounds the role of the camera as an accepted part of everyday life. Both victims and perpetrators frequently know the camera is present and sometimes interact with it. It can even be a provocateur and stimulant to action. Signs of performance provide evidence of this awareness of the camera. On Video Justice we see the corner store robber shielding his face from the camera as the store owner attempts to fight back; young men filming their violent attack on a passer-by and teenagers filming their rampant destruction of the show home. Most often though the photographer as controlling subject is, of course, non-existent in the case of much CCTV footage: the imagery replayed for a television audience after the criminal act seals its significance within the framing programme and invites the viewer to validate its status as evidence.

Taken as a whole the sixty-minute show, edited to present a 'rollercoaster' experience of speed and a variety of registers and illegal acts and misdemeanours, offers a 'carnival of crime' which is clearly entertaining as well as disturbing.[8] Besides the highly controversial scenes of shootings and beatings viewers are also offered scenes of social inversion, which temporarily test the bonds of ordered society. One section of the programme offers the spectacle of a group of exhilarated teenagers, male and female, demolishing immaculate new show homes with hammers, fists, paint and anything else they can lay their hands on. They filmed themselves in the act, arguably constructing an alternative home video that challenged the conventions of family photography and the ideal of domesticity. In another scene youths filmed themselves firing paint guns in a parody of drive-by shootings. Viewers are drawn into the game as they travel with the boys through the town at night and watch with glee the shocked faces of pedestrians, cyclists and homeless street people as they fall to the ground, hit with exploding paint balls.

A theatrical display of youthful transgression and the colonisation of public night-time space is replayed in mediated form. It is difficult not to read this textual strategy as one imbricated with the pleasures of voyeurism and the forbidden gaze. The programme works hard to justify the broadcasting of footage that was originally shot by the criminal protagonists themselves. The voiceover reassures us that films such as these also often turn out quite fortuitously to constitute the incriminating evidence – that they were in fact scopic law enforcement technologies in disguise. But this reasoning of film as evidence can be subverted or at least challenged in disconcerting ways. For example, the boys who were prosecuted for paint-balling were indicted through their own camerawork which showed not only the shock of passers-by as they were hit but the gleeful pleasure of the offenders. It was stated that it was this visual and aural evidence of their pleasure in the act that inspired calls for a heavy sentence. In response the boys were advised by their defence team to be filmed as they apologised and were pelted with paintballs.

Appositely, Ariella Azoulay has discussed the role of the camera in constructing the 'subject-hostage' who wields the camera as apparently an autonomous agent capturing his or her actions and documenting the space of the act as fact. She suggests that the possession of the camera also constrains and perhaps provokes the action of the photographer who 'becomes a captive to the camera's activity' (2001: 92). This process complicates the network of power relations between subject and object conventionally associated with the role of the camera as provider of evidence:

> When a person assumes the position of the viewer who commands the field of vision and suddenly is viewed by others and also is activated like an object – like a camera or pistol, something else that attracts, tempts or repulses – the power relations between subject and object are reversed. (2001: 62)

In the case of the paintball snipers, a video narrative of their own gleeful shootings became a video narrative of their guilt and was then counterpoised with a video of their contrition. As an act of counter-discourse it produced a new story about the boys which implied that the first video could not be regarded as a summate and final interpretation of events. *Video Justice* (together with the court), however, interpreted this film as suspect: its constructedness or artifice was simply more evidence of their guilt within the framework of the programme. Clearly then, in the social/media space of crime film footage, only film that *appears* to be spontaneous (the boys must, after all have *planned* to take a camera along with them) constitutes evidence for both court of law and law and order programming.

Similarly, their submission to the camera's scrutiny did not bear the same evidential weight as the footage of their distressed victims. Such use and re-use of video footage prompts careful analysis of reality TV for the multiple potential constellations of power-knowledge that the vantage point of the victim, perpetrator, camera, camera operator, editor, lawyer, police officer and jury may throw up against one another. And of course raises the enduring question of the defining features of realism and the camera image.

Inevitably perhaps, since very few of the cases shown on these programmes remain unsolved, these and other law-breakers are *seen* to be brought to justice. The viewing pleasures of carnivalesque criminality are consequently fleeting, framed as they are by generic codes that demand that the law's sovereignty remains paramount. One comic scene confirms this, reinforcing the implacability of the law in the face of a challenge of the most everyday kind. A speeding driver is pulled over by a highway patrol cop and given a ticket. The driver responds by completely losing his temper, shouting and shaking with rage to such an extent that his truck rocks. In the face of the driver's near apoplectic fury the cop remains laconic and imperturbable; even making the driver get out of the vehicle to pick up some litter that he has dropped. Eventually the driver, having lost a decidedly one-sided argument, drives away deflated. We watch the whole scene via the camera installed in the patrol car parked behind the truck. Consequently we never see the face of the cop and the driver's face is deliberately blurred. The exchange is between the driver – the 'unknown citizen' who is utterly humiliated and the cop who is an emblematic implacable figure of the law. The scopic technology seems to confirm the law's status as paramount, irrefutable and adamant. The driver is anonymous, we are denied any visual evidence of the speeding offence for which he was stopped and we do not hear whether he challenged the fine in court. The story of the citizen and the law is truncated so that the law's power is incontestable.

While the potential pleasures here are as various as the scenarios depicted they are all arguably rooted in the intersection between three things: that the events depicted are 'real', that they focus on the transgression of legal limits and that the law is seen generally to be re-established. These are scenarios of power; its illegal adoption and its legal reassertion in social/media space. And as with the mediated events cited above, an imaginary relationship between public and police is formulated and sustained through the privileging of visual technology in which little seems to escape the eye of the law.

Finally, reality TV unites the public sphere of law enforcement with screen entertainment via a highly attractive and ubiquitous trope in media culture – dramatic criminality. While the primary function of the police is to maintain social order these stories and programmes of legal/media pursuit underwrite the more popular misconception of the law as highly interventionist against dramatically violent crime. The ultimate justification for the public deployment of cameras is founded upon the notion that they can protect the public and diminish fearfulness and fearfulness can be a unifying modality in contemporary culture.

> Our belonging comes not from the fact that we are all criminals but rather from the shared fact of victimisation. It is through our victimage that we come to belong to the social body. To be a victim is to be a citizen. (Young 1996: 55)

The reassurance that 'justice' has been done in the majority of cases recounted in *Video Justice* does not obviate the threat of personal vulnerability that weaves through the narrative. The 'war' going on in America needs victims, and as Alison Young suggests in the quotation above, it is the collective victimage of viewers, that posits them as citizens allied with the police in the battle against crime. The apparent fascination with the seemingly relentless catalogue of crime on reality TV is arguably predicated upon personal fear of injury and victimhood. This is seen most graphically and most movingly in the scenes where the victims of crime speak directly to camera, their voiceovers used to direct viewers' understanding of visual material and inviting empathetic identification.

The status of the reality recorded by surveillance technology and replayed for television audiences prompts the important ethical and political questions signalled in this chapter. One of the structuring principles of broadcasting has been the division between fact and fiction; the former's status resting on the accumulation of evidence, legitimated sources, documents, professional journalistic practices of objectivity, aesthetic and generic practices of camerawork, authorial voice and so on. The omnipresence of video cameras and the proliferation of surveillance footage as the medium of the real event further complicate the divisions between generalised surveillance and reality entertainment. With reality TV a hybrid artefact is produced in which the boundaries between evidence and entertainment, media and social space are transgressed. Ultimately reassurance is afforded only to the domestic viewer who chooses to view the apparent 'successes' of 'video justice' without questioning the practices, protocols and limitations of surveillance cameras in our public spaces and the circulation of their footage in media space.

chapter 8
Man in a glass box

> This dissolution of the boundary between inside and outside gives rise to a fourth aspect of the felt experience of physical pain, an almost obscene conflation of private and public. It brings with it all the solitude of absolute privacy with none of its safety, all the self-exposure of the utterly public with none of its possibility for camaraderie or shared experience. Artistic objectifications of pain often concentrate on this combination of isolation and exposure. (Scarry 1985: 53)

As noted throughout, the exposure and, more particularly, self-exposure of psychological and bodily trauma has become the central feature of our 'post-documentary' culture. Television talk shows, observational documentary, life-style programming and reality TV all facilitate the exhibition and consumption of personal pain and suffering (as well as joy and individual success). Generally speaking, this showcasing of personal trauma is a gendered one; with many of the established and newer formats dismissed as feminised media culture; with few, if any, intellectual pretensions. This is partly the case because the domain of emotional suffering, at least, has been conventionally designated a 'feminine' one, with women especially licensed to speak about bodily or psychological insecurity, vulnerability or damage. When 'masculine' damage or trauma is at stake, its presentation and articulation in media culture takes on quite different forms and meanings. Bearing in mind this context, this chapter examines an example of the new hybrid of reality TV and performance piece: the David Blaine event entitled 'Above the Below'. It does so in order to explore the meanings, symbolics and ethics of the current specularisation of bodily trauma in social and media space; revealing the multiple ways in which an ethics of the self and of becoming is articulated in a popular form. Ultimately, the aim is to make more complex our understanding of 'the apparently oxymoronic "popularity" of trauma' as cultural text (Radstone 2001: 189).

In early September 2003 illusionist David Blaine was sealed within a plexi-glass box and suspended above Tower Bridge in the centre of London with the intention of starving himself for 44 days. His exploit was clearly a media spectacle and was designed to generate 'event television'.[1] As noted in chapter 1 event television is 'high concept', aiming at reaching a critical mass of viewers through extensive visibility and multimedia choice. As such, it is often stripped across a television channel everyday for a number of weeks and is supported by multi-platform media such as interactive TV or the Internet. The commercial aim is to attract huge audiences and become part of the popular discourse of everyday life. Like soap opera serials, the action is contextualised and amplified by hyperbolic media commentary including talk show interviews, tabloid newspaper coverage and the circulation of participants' images as celebrities, a process which prompts conversation among audiences about the characters and their behaviour. But unlike soaps, the talk generated is not contingent, rather it is an essential part of the event's success. The promotion of talk produces the anticipation, elaborate ongoing evaluations and retrospective judgements upon which the commercial success of the venture depends (Couldry 2002: 272, see also Scannell 2002).

'Above the Below', devised by Blaine, fits this pattern of a commercial media enterprise whose success is predicated on the audience's interaction with events and their reportage. It was broadcast by Channel 4 and Sky 1, who presented it as a variation on reality TV. Special shows were devoted to it on 19 and 20 October 2003, the latter being the day when the illusionist exited from his self-imposed imprisonment. The event was streamed live on Channel 4 broadband 24/7 and filmed by Blaine's collaborator, the avant-garde filmmaker Harmony Korine, for a future documentary also entitled *Above the Below*. It was promoted as the pinnacle of Blaine's major productions since 1999 which had so far included interment under the streets – 'Buried Alive' (1999), encasement in a block of ice – 'Frozen in Time' (2000) and 'Vertigo' (2002), in which he stood atop a 100-foot pole, without any means of support or a safety net, for 36 hours. Many of Blaine's other acts have involved physical endurance or illusions that challenge physical taboos such as eating snakes or slicing off his own ear. Indeed Korine recalls his first, rather bizarre, introduction to Blaine in a pizza restaurant: 'he got into one of the ovens and turned the heat on. He stayed in there for hours' (Rose 2003).

British critics of 'Above the Below' tended to locate Blaine's exploits within the context of extreme forms of reality TV in which overt suffering or potential suffering formed a central feature of its appeal. Certainly, one of the reasons for situating the event in London was because reality formats have found great success with British audiences. Popular challenge game shows had already demonstrated that audiences have an appetite for watching physical suffering or psychological shocks. Also prominent during the Blaine period was the Channel 4 broadcast on Sunday 3 October 2003 of *Derren Brown Plays Russian Roulette Live*. The title is self-explanatory. With only a few seconds time delay, viewers watched illusionist Brown hold a Smith and Wesson snub-nosed revolver, randomly loaded with a single bullet by a member of the public who had been screened by a psychologist, to his head and pull the trigger. He pulled the trigger on three empty chambers before turning the gun away from his head and shooting the bullet. It seemed to audiences that Brown visibly shook when he reached the third chamber and was uncertain whether or not it was empty. Although this was eventually revealed to be an illusion, commentators had already included the show in the category of voyeuristic, extreme and unacceptable reality programming (Hattersley 2003).[2] The differences here, and they are important ones, is that 'Above the Below' was not revealed to be a deception, and it also numbered amongst its viewing constituencies those that came along to watch the event live on the ground over a sustained period of time. This seemed to be a genuine although highly planned 'happening' and it was an event evidentially in social space as well as media space.

'Above the Below' then was a live event and Blaine's exploits were multiply-mediated. As will be explained later on in more detail, Blaine's agenda was explicated and his suffering mediated through extensive commentary. The plexi-glass box both separated him from audiences and contained/framed him, as did the documentary footage, live television filming and web-streaming. These multimedia platforms reinforced the sense of immediacy that is so characteristic of the televisual experience. As already noted, John Ellis describes how television, above all entertainment technologies, has epitomised the process of 'witness' through its aesthetic promise of liveness and intimacy. In particular, the abundance of audio and visual information signifies the live event, helping to intensify the experience of witness: 'witness is underwritten by the presence of the entirely unremarkable within the image, and of the "atmosphere" of sound' (2000: 12). The spectacle and noise of the shifting, heaving crowds around Tower Bridge offered precisely this congruence of the contingent, unremarkable and ordinary together with the remarkable scene of Blaine's suspension above them. So too, the images of ordinary people beneath the box seem to condone the event as acceptable, if exceptional, entertainment. Finally, these senses of 'witnessing' are further accentuated when the event is of a traumatic or disturbing nature.

For those watching at home audio-visual technology clearly offers a different experience from that of being present at the pro-filmic event; offering a 'modality' of experience in which the viewer feels both powerful and disempowered, involved and helpless. There is a real contrast here between the ordinary and the domestic and the extraordinary and geographically distant. This contradictory positioning, argues Ellis, obliges a certain powerless complicity with the unfolding of events whether we agree with them or not – for even if we do not approve of the event we cannot undo or disavow our knowledge of it (2000: 11). Having said this, not only our knowledge, but our *understanding* of such events is also inevitably formed by their framing and contextualisation and, for the live event above all, commentary is needed to direct and orientate viewers. As will be seen in more detail, despite the extended reporting and press releases of 'Above the Below', Blaine and his supporters refused any simple explanations of the enterprise. Indeed their interviews and expositions only helped to perpetuate the confusion of distinctions between truth and illusion, art and entertainment, introspection and exhibitionism that came to characterise not only the event but the public's reaction to it.

Body time/television time

The presentation of 'Above the Below' as a countdown of 44 days also signalled the production's generic relationship to reality programming and, more particularly, to the peculiar (and contradictory) intimacy of this very public enterprise. As Misha Kavka and Amy West suggest, ordinary clock time is expunged by reality genres which operate within their own temporal logic. Instead of linear time featuring years and dates within a historical context they segment the time into days, hours and minutes as experienced by the programmes' participants; offering countdowns to dénouements such as house or lifestyle transformations, the achievement of personal challenges, feats of endurance or release from various forms of incarceration. In these ways reality entertainment collapses the time of production into the time of transmission, producing a 'single order that mobilises a community of viewers' and affords them the optimum sense of immediacy and intimacy or at least, that is the intention (Kavka & West 2004: 141). The live streaming of 'Above the Below' reinforced this collapse so that theoretically the 'liveness' and 'immediacy' of being able to view Blaine at all times (including the prolonged 'dead time' in which he does little or nothing) involved audiences in the enterprise. It established continuity between the external time of viewers and time as experienced by Blaine himself and which is marked upon his body through starvation.

Time in reality TV frequently begins on 'day one' and is measured by rituals of sleeping, eating, set activities and the graphics of the screen clock. This is the case with Blaine where the clock was set from the day of his incarceration and much of the debate was about how much 'time' he had and whether he could last out its duration. In Korine's film, a female spectator is overheard repeatedly asking in an awed and incredulous voice, '*how* long has he got left to go?'[3] On another occasion, Blaine is filmed discussing with his production manager the feasibility of his surviving for 44 days. His manager warns him that even if he survives he could go 'past the point of no return' into organ failure and asks what would be the point of surviving publicly 44 days only to die on the sixtieth when everyone else has gone home. Blaine himself compared the challenge with the protest carried out by the Irish hunger-striker Bobby Sands, who died in 1981 on the sixty-sixth day of his protest.

In interview with Korine he offered a variety of explanations for the enterprise, stating at one point that 'I'm doing it for myself.' But later he added, 'I love making people watch suffering 'cause I had to watch it my whole life … I saw everybody that I know, my mother, my real dad, drop dead in front of my face.'[4] He goes on to recall his mother's unfailing stoicism in the face of a long terminal illness. Blaine's project designer commented, 'David doesn't recognise limitations – he wants to go right to the edge and wants to do it in public to show how real it is' (Asthana 2003). Blaine seemed to be challenging not only himself but also 'time' and specifically time's erosion of corporeal strength, vitality and agency with these references to the political body (protestor) and the sick body (patient). As the days unfolded the public and media commentators became increasingly convinced that 'Above the Below' was not going to be a feat of illusion after all but a feat of 'real' endurance and a battle against the clock. The authenticity of the enterprise as both reality TV and endurance feat is marked out through the temporal logic of the project (44 days not 43 or 45) and by locating the body and its experience as the object of time passing.

As Blaine undertook his fast over Tower Bridge, sustained allegedly only by water unadulterated by supplements, the spectacle of his suffering attracted bizarre behaviour from the general public. Suspended near the Tower of London, his exhibition of suffering and public responses to it recalled the pre-modern spectacle of public punishment and humiliation which was to be replaced by far more insidious and occluded disciplinary mechanisms of bio-power and surveillance (Foucault 1975). In this case, however, the event was in fact a bizarre marriage of the pre-modern and the post-modern with Blaine's suffering transformed into multimedia spectacle. Police voiced concerns about scenes of public disorder including an attempt to sever Blaine's water supply, the appearance of air guns and the firing of paint balls and other projectiles at the box. Others taunted him by beating drums to prevent him from sleeping or by cooking food nearby so that the smell would torment him. Overall, while Blaine certainly had his fans, the early days at least attracted extensive criticism from the public with some website commentators observing that only his death would make interesting viewing and even then they would probably miss it as the media would not dare to show it.

Despite the 'expert' and documentary evidence, as well as the evidence of their own eyes, audiences were, at times, both unsympathetic and sceptical to the degree that Blaine's US public relations advisors were alleged to have wanted to pull him out. They were concerned about the 'near medieval barrage of abuse' which he initially attracted and which was potentially dangerous (Palmer 2003). British commentators observed that the event said more about the British public than it did about Blaine: 'Like the crowds outside the *Big Brother* house, conspicuously for or against the evictee, what we seem most at pains to do in all this is to have the self-contained individual made part of our crowd, to have him say something about us.'[5]

The analogy with *Big Brother* was an apt one as the success of the series was predicated on the participants winning a kind of public popularity contest. *Big Brother* contestants had to prove their skills in negotiating the social setting of the house and its inmates and, it soon emerged that anyone too smart or too media savvy, would be regarded with suspicion. In *Big Brother* it was the girl or boy 'next door' that tended to come out victorious after a series of evictions in which housemates often re-entered public life only to discover that they had been the subject of vitriolic media abuse while inside.[6] Blaine had none of the advantages of 'ordinariness' which so endeared reality contestants to the British public and, far less well known as a celebrity in Britain than in the US where he was already a star, neither did he have the public's more distanced admiration. Blaine himself commented, 'I expect most people not to understand, and be angered by it.'[7] It seemed he had set himself a near impossible task in that he attempted to be spectacle and reality, entertainer and ascetic and an elevated celebrity with popular appeal. He had to literally 'stage manage' the contradiction, in Korine's words, of 'public isolation'.[8]

The body in pain

Public scepticism about the degree of suffering underwent by Blaine was rooted partly in the impossibility of sharing an understanding of pain as it is experienced by the individual subject. As Elaine Scarry has argued in *The Body in Pain*, corporeal suffering necessarily involves a split or division between one's own sense of reality as a suffering subject and the reality of others who can only learn of one's pain at one remove. This splitting is essentially dangerous as, unless a feat of the imagination or creation spans this divide, others not only fail to empathise, they can in fact feel permitted to inflict pain themselves (1985: 4–12). This was graphically illustrated in the scene in *Above the Below* in which Blaine invites a member of the public to repeatedly punch him in the stomach. The well-muscled pugilist makes three convincing attempts to floor his challenger, prompted by an amused and jeering crowd. In the example of 'Above the Below' the crowd and its capacity for empathy are twice removed, through the 'splitting' described by Scarry and through spectacular display which, by definition almost, precludes dialogue.[9]

Media coverage made it very clear that Blaine's body and its decline was central to the narrative of the event. The Channel 4 website declared in the manner of a show-ground huckster 'THE FEAT: read the complete low down on why and how David Blaine is enduring 44 days of isolation, the dangers he faces and what will happen to his body.' Newspapers summarised 'what could go wrong'; noting 'after three weeks, hallucinations or dementia set in. After four weeks, bones begin to weaken and muscle tissue shows signs of damage … a person could face severe brain damage, damage or failure of internal organs. Death is possible at any time…' (Austin 2003). In his second week Blaine was quoted as saying, 'I have entered starvation mode, low energy … really low energy and a freak taste in my mouth … I believe this is starvation. I read it could happen after two weeks. I didn't believe it' (in Asthana 2003). It was in subsequent days that public opinion, on the ground at least, seemed to become more favourable and crowds became less negative in their attentions towards the man in the box. The longer Blaine remained in the box, the more he starved, the more approval he seemed to attract and crowds of up to 10,000 visitors in a day increasingly overwhelmed the sceptics.

Huge crowds gathered on the day of his release. Blaine, stripped to the waist, was weighed as he exited from the box and was shown to have lost four stones in weight. As he emerged screen captions made his suffering explicit; listing symptoms including dizziness, impaired vision, thinning of the organ walls, arrhythmia, muscle spasms, blood toxicity, loss of skin pigmentation and so on. He appeared to be frail, ill and close to emotional breakdown. He only managed to say a few words to the crowd, punctuated by sobs: 'This has been one of the most important experiences of my life … I've learned more in that little box than I have in years … I've learned how strong we all are as human beings.' With a backdrop of screaming crowds the scene became a parody of the moment when the star emerges from the movie theatre to greet his/her fans or evictees leave the *Big Brother* house. But instead of being guided by minders into a luxury car Blaine was pushed towards the waiting ambulance. The cameras following him as he was carried into the vehicle produced footage reminiscent of 'emergency services' reality TV as paramedics connected him up to drips and monitors and gave him an ECG. In this sense the depiction of this experience was part of a wider 'post-documentary' aesthetic; the 'continuing "colloquial turn" in the culture and a shift towards greater engagement with everyday terms of living and the varieties of ordinary "private" experience, both pleasant and traumatic' (Corner 2004: 291).

The continual monitoring and final weighing of Blaine's body marked it as the site of transformation and self-management; a spectacular rendition of the 'before and after' imagery used by advertising for charities and slimming clubs alike. His performance suggested a kind of 'technics of the self' in which individuals can through self-monitoring form and transform their bodies and, consequently, their souls, thoughts and conduct. As Baldwin *et al.* (2004: 186–7) suggest, the consumption of food and drink is a truly 'generic practice' which is understood as a necessity shared by all. But in developed nations, at least, 'accepted present-day standards of eating – what we eat, how quickly food is consumed, when we eat – involve a considerable degree of self-control' and this too is commonly understood. The tremendous success of the weight-reduction diet as commodity, lifestyle and regime forms the discursive backdrop to Blaine's stunt and its attendant fascination. The same period witnessed an overwhelming interest in, for example, the 'Atkins diet'; an interest which went far beyond its efficacy, entering into the morbid arena of detailed discussions of biological processes (fat breakdown, ketosis, constipation, urine analysis and so forth). The 'problem' of weight control was never far from public fascination with the stunt. In interview with Libby Brooks (2003) after the event Blaine comments:

> If I'd had food in front of me I couldn't have done it. I can't even control myself on an aeroplane. I need to eat, eat even though I don't want that food … I'm a binge eater, which is the worst thing you can do for your heart and your metabolism.

Brooks adds, 'for a moment one wonders whether the whole stunt was just the elaborate execution of an eating disorder'. The climate of the 1990s onwards has been one in which body management, in all its manifestations, has become a central preoccupation. Jason Jacobs suggests that the period represented 'an unprecedented intensification of the medicalisation of everyday life: regular health scares, the theorisation of the "risk society", the promotion of "healthy living" … as a moral as much as a medical imperative' (2003: 12) and all contributed to a popular engagement with medical fictions and their strange association of morbidity and glamour.[10]

These concerns are also articulated in reality 'emergency services' TV and in documentaries and lifestyle programming that attended to diet, plastic surgery and makeovers; these last arguably aiding self-disciplinarity in support of society's normalising mechanisms (see Goodwin 1993; Hawkins 2001; Palmer 2004: 177–80; Wheatley 2001). In this sense, critics were wrong to associate 'Above the Below' solely with the grossest exploitation reality programming, for the event also tapped into the prevailing 'ethical turn' in reality formats towards self-disciplinarity and the making and re-making of the subject. As Gay Hawkins explains, new programme formats have been promoting 'ethics', not in the sense of moral imperatives, but in the sense of 'becoming' and the technics of the self that this involves. This ethical turn (and the Foucaultian and Deleuzean theories that explicate them so effectively) involve not only 'bodies, actions and sensibilities' but also an 'ethics of existence' revealed in the 'practical and everyday terrain of making oneself a subject' (2001: 414). Blaine's exit from the box, then, while evidential of his re-fashioning of the body through starvation was also, in keeping with this broader cultural turn, an expression of a supposed psychical transformation.

As Blaine tried to express the depth of his experience crowds cheered in the festive manner common to many forms of public celebration or entertainment. Despite the 'emotional high' of the moment of his exit from the box he was unable to fully reveal his corporeal trauma or to 'show' his physical and psychic pain or the transformation these had effected. This would require some form of demonstration of the erosion of corporeal distinctions between inside and outside, mind and body. In reality lifestyle programming visible transformations are obviously the most legible: the tidy house, the newly slim or fit or fashionable body. Or, in talk shows and other 'confessional' forms, when subjects are in pain, this has to be expressed verbally and hyperbolically in order to connect with audiences. Blaine had no adequate language to express his experience, no wounds to show to his audience, no grotesque body as a signifier of damage;[11] a situation in complete contrast to several of his most dramatic magic tricks, which had worked exactly in this mode of overt wounding where he pretends to injure himself.

The problem with 'pain' is that it is essentially a private matter. Pain inhabits the body, which is 'the most contracted of spaces, the small circle of living matter' (Scarry 1985: 22) and that pain 'unmakes' the subject, reducing and objectifying him/her in the eyes of others; only the successful expression of pain can help span this divide.[12] From this perspective Blaine was disadvantaged from the outset in that the undoubted pain of gradual starvation has, from a distance, few external signs and his enclosure made communication nearly impossible. In any case, as Scarry observes, the expression of pain is itself always mediated, operating through proxies (those who speak on behalf of the subject such as doctors or PR advisors), analogies ('my pain feels like...'), legal document or art work (1985: 6–10). Within Scarry's terms, for Blaine to 'successfully' communicate and gain the 'correct' form of engagement with his audience he would need to transform spectacle into art, private pain into public expression.

Hunger artist

> The convening of the public around scenes of violence ... has come to make up *wound culture*: the public fascination with torn and open bodies and torn and open persons, a collective gathering around shock, trauma and the wound. (Seltzer 1998: 1)

As noted in chapter 1 the exhibitionism and concomitant voyeuristic distancing and objectification of the subject in pain has been identified as partly the inspiration for the new forms of observational programming now known as reality TV. A number of critics have pointed to reality TV's roots in psycho-social experiments such as the notorious Stanley Milgram (1961–62) and Stanford Prison Experiments (1971). The Stanford Experiment introduced volunteers into the hierarchical, anonymous world of the penal system where they adopted the roles of prisoner or guard for the duration. Isolated from the world, the experiment soon spun out of control as the prisoners rebelled and the regime became more hard-line. One 'inmate's' textbook symptoms of a nervous breakdown were even dismissed by the experiment's director Philip Zimbardo as fakery; a misconception made as he himself became overly immersed in his character of 'Prison Superintendent'. Critics of reality TV's exploitation of its participants note wryly: 'Zimbardo ... is sometimes spoken of as being a frustrated artist, and reality TV creatives can be equally viewed as industry versions of today's conceptual artists, creating templates for installation-worlds'; worlds which may be regarded as ethically problematic (Cohen & Brenton 2003: 91). 'Above the Below' is one such problematic environment. Whether understood as experiment, art installation or reality vehicle its attraction still depends upon its exhibition of preventable starvation. The debatable question then is whether the 'intentions' motivating the event, even if they could be fully apprehended, can ever be said to mitigate its exploitation of the subject.

The artistic imperative of 'Above the Below' was signalled in a number of ways. Korine's involvement in the film of the event already marked the enterprise as avant-garde project as well as populist crowd pleaser. So too did the overt references to writers and artists including Franz Kafka and Chris Burden. Blaine's reference to Kafka's short story 'A Hunger Artist' (1924), in particular, signalled the peculiar conjunction of populist performer, artist and misunderstood religious ascetic that Blaine's feat seemed to invoke. This story tells of a successful side-show star whose feat is to fast for forty days, sipping only water, for the entertainment of a paying audience. He sits in a cage, watched constantly to ensure that he does not cheat but, in fact, he is honourable and would do no such thing. This surveillance and the crowd's liberty to feel his wasted limbs overcome any scepticism. Eventually, however, as more spectacular circus acts render him redundant he starves to death, neglected in his cage. The allusion to Kafka and his work signals the ascetic, almost messianic, connotations of Blaine's act as well as the acknowledgement that the public may not 'understand' or appreciate it. Blaine's silence, his obvious contemplation (he claimed that he would leave his body and go 'astral zipping') and his overwhelming abstinence necessarily distance him from the crowd.

In contradiction to the idea of the body as a residence that can be vacated or a gross object that can be overcome Scarry claims that the suffering of the ascetic is precisely not about *denying* but about *emphasising* the body to the exclusion of the world and its concerns (1985: 34). Moreover, within a secular society in which the media frequently depicts deprivation as being 'elsewhere' and usually caused by economics, war or natural disaster, overt religiosity or introspection is often regarded with suspicion. As such, self-inflicted starvation, which is of course qualitatively different from disease, would be viewed by the sceptical as a peculiarly masochistic, even narcissistic activity. For if the body is a means or instrument of agency that permits engagement with the world then the refusal of engagement may be regarded as challenge; a challenge taken up by the audiences who aimed to gain Blaine's attention and 'make' him react to them.

Those visiting the site certainly commented on the carnivalesque atmosphere beneath the elevated form; a side-show mood involving adults and children, tourists and locals, hamburger vendors and committed fans. Together they constituted an unruly 'grotesque' body as outlined by Mikhail Bakhtin in *Rabelais and His World* (1968). Bakhtin describes how this body is *embodied* through the consumption of food and drink and how, in doing so, the body becomes worldly:

> The distinctive character of this body is its open, unfinished nature, its interaction with the world. These traits are most fully and concretely revealed in the act of eating … Here man tastes the world, introduces it into his body, makes it part of himself. (Bakhtin 1968: 281)

In contrast to their 'below', Blaine's suspension 'above' signalled the occupation of a different cultural sphere; or at the very least a different iconographic register – that of the classical body as figured in the form of the classical statue. Peter Stallybrass and Allon White note: 'the classical statue is the radiant centre of a transcendental individualism, "put on a pedestal", raised above the viewer and the commonality and anticipating passive admiration from below. We *gaze up* at the figure and wonder' (1986: 21). Unlike the multiple, teeming, mobile and 'split' body of the crowd, this classical body is figured as distant, isolated, sealed and contained. Several of Blaine's earlier exploits placed him in equally elevated positions, most notably 'Vertigo' (cited above) in which he stood atop a tall column for a day and a half precisely resembling a statue. Korine's *Above the Below* also shows Blaine standing on one of the London Eye's glass pods high above the Thames river; the shot is strongly reminiscent of the statue of Christ overlooking Rio de Janeiro. Not only Blaine's suspension but also his incarceration in the transparent box affirms this positioning as contained. It is also reinforced by careful and discrete administration of his bodily functions through both intense medical supervision and catheters. In order for Blaine to remain dignified and 'above', his bodily functions, their operation and even his physical deterioration require constant management. In a sense then, this is pain without the markers or indignity of pain, bodily trauma with its offensiveness heavily masked, suffering of an elevated kind.

Additional meanings are lent to this figuration of suffering as either Christic, self-indulgent or introspective through references to the work of performance artists such as Chris Burden, whose public and sometimes spectacular acts of self-harm have been read as implicitly (sometimes explicitly) political and worldly.[13] His most notorious works explored the psychological experience of danger and pain and involved shocking abuses of his own body. In 'Shoot' (1971) Burden was filmed at a gallery reception while a friend shot him in the arm and in his overtly Christic piece entitled 'Trans-fixed' (1974) he allowed himself to be nailed by his palms to the roof of a car. 'Five day locker piece' (1971) is the clearest antecedent of 'Above the Below'. In this work Burden was incarcerated in a locker measuring two feet high, two feet wide and three feet deep for five days. He had ceased eating several days earlier. The locker above him contained five gallons of water and the locker below contained an empty five-gallon bottle. These works occurred during the Vietnam War and have been read within this context. Kathy O'Dell (1998), for example, has argued that 'masochistic' performance artists such as Burden foregrounded significant ruptures in the social contract. They also explored the coupling of isolation and exposure signalled by Scarry in the opening quotation. The artist's encasement in locker, cage or plexi-glass box is a metaphor for the isolating experience of suffering even when it is made visible and on display. It highlights the potentially dangerous distance or chasm between those in pain and others and the political implications of the inevitable lack of empathy entailed by such distanciation.

Some commentators have chosen to understand Blaine's work (or its reception) in political as well as personal terms. 'Vertigo', for example, was read by admirers such as the late paraplegic actor Christopher Reeve as an assertion of the power of mind over body whereas others regarded it as a living tribute to those killed or damaged by the events of 11 September 2001. One fan commented that Blaine's presence was a declaration that 'we're still here – especially after what we went through'.[14] In the case of 'Above the Below' there was the suggestion that self-imposed suffering (and by a US citizen) was inappropriate and 'crass' in the light of the British public's opposition to the 'war against terror' launched against Iraq. Speculation also addressed Blaine's Jewish ancestry and whether his interest in the events of the Holocaust had influenced his work. When asked whether the suffering of the concentration camp inmates was connected with his exploits he only commented enigmatically, 'I think it was really difficult for them because they never knew whether they were going to get murdered or not. The only similarity I can come up with is hunger' (in Sigesmund 2003).

Performing gender/trauma

As in other ritual dramas, the action of gender requires a performance that is repeated. This repetition is at once a reenactiment and reexperiencing of a set of meanings already socially established; and it is the mundane and ritualised form of their legitimation. (Butler 1990: 140)

Having noted this conflation of meanings and roles arising from the public performance of personal suffering as spectacle (Christic, artistic, ascetic, political) there is one additional layering that merits consideration: the gendering of Blaine's body within this field of vision and within these contexts. Visual representations are especially important to the cultural process of differentiation between the genders and the surface and interiors of bodies are frequently looked to as evidence of biological sexual difference. Blaine's elevated body in 'Vertigo' and 'Above the Below' is essentially articulated as a 'masculine' performance of the classical body with all its associations with high culture, heroic and transcendental individualism. As Stallybrass and White (1986: 23–5) imply, and Mary Russo (1994) demonstrates at length, the opposition between classical and grotesque body can be a gendered one; with the sealed and elevated body as masculine and the grounded, open, split and grotesque body as feminine. Within culture, and indeed within art history, the classical statue has been understood as possessing the attributes of rational, intellectual authority. Anthea Callen has shown, for example, how the well-known Greek classical statue the 'Apollo Belvedere', was taken as an ideal of masculine authority and one used as the model inspiration for painted and sculpted portraits authorising the power of politicians, leaders and gentry (2002: 606–13). Images of the grotesque, then, are precisely those which are abjected from the bodily canons of classical aesthetics and the grotesque as a bodily category emerges as a 'deviation from the norm' with the female body (already a deviation from the norm) rendered doubly grotesque (Russo 1994: 8–12).

If Russo's grotesque female body is made doubly grotesque, Blaine's body is multiply-masculinised through its biological designation as 'male', through the positioning and policing of his body and its corporeal signs and through its masochistic display. It has already been noted how the outflow of Blaine's bodily functions were hidden and/or discretely removed. It was possible to watch his deterioration without witnessing the offensiveness of starvation or overhearing expressions of pain. And, again, in the example of Chris Burden's locker performance, the seclusion of enclosure meant that his bodily functions and his suffering also went unseen. From this perspective, and in Blaine's case in particular, these were performances of 'containment' in more than one sense of the word and signifiers of the masculine (almost macho) performance of suffering. The communication (such as it is) of Blaine's suffering is always delivered in a deadpan way, revealing very little in terms of any emotional or physical hurt. Aside from the moment of his exit Blaine always spoke of his impending suffering and risk-taking with dry humour or blunt pragmatism. When asked about his fear of falling from the column in 'Vertigo' he responded with the simple observation that the potential for instant death was enough to keep him standing. Again, Burden's dry and laconic presentations of his pieces enact a refusal to be regarded as physically weak or vulnerable. Blaine's stoicism, therefore, is one of the contradictions of his act as 'Above the Below' has to present a creditable picture of suffering while containing its signs and expressions. Ultimately, this stoicism has to be maintained as it is also a necessary accoutrement of masculinity; one whose importance has by no means diminished within the media culture of the twenty-first century.

Amelia Jones, in her illuminating analysis of gender and performance art (as defined by her as 'body art'), explores the complexities of the relationship between the artistic performance of suffering and shifting formations of gender and sexuality. Her analysis points to the tenacious survival of normative codes of masculine power and artistic sovereignty even as these were being challenged, superseded or ironised in the art world. Jones argues, for example, that performance work of the 1970s both ironised the heroic aspects of artistic predecessors (such as Jackson Pollock and his action painting) but also frequently maintained many of their legitimising elements (1998: 104). Importantly, she suggests that the prevalence of masochistic strategies, specifically in male performance, was rooted in the inability of the male artist to un-latch himself fully from the ineluctably gendered artistic myth of self-coherence and self-assertion (1998: 128–9). Reflecting on the work of Kathy O'Dell, already cited above, who argues that masochistic scenarios can be read as resistance or challenge to the modern social contract, Jones chooses to insist on the *gendered* and *sexualised* meanings of these scenarios and the masculine grounds of masochism itself. She notes:

> Such a wilful subjection of the masculine body to the violence of the other might seem in a direct and simple way to unhinge male subjectivity's normative link to the active wielding of power. And yet ... this 'perversion' of masculinity can also function as a means of ensuring the coherence and power of the masculine subject. (1998: 130)

In this context, Jones points to the mythologisation of the male artist martyr and romantic individual and his assertion of coherent self-hood through the overt display of his endurance and 'survivability'.

Like the hero of sequel action films, the masochistic performance artist continually sets himself new challenges that attest to his indestructibility, variations on a theme of the durability of the male body. The repetitious structure of these scenes is made more explicit when we consider other projects orchestrated by Blaine or by his most recent collaborator Korine. We have already noted the scene in *Above in Below* in which a young man continually punches Blaine. This seems to be a more controlled version of Korine's project 'Fight' (undated, with Blaine as camera operator) in which Korine deliberately picked fights on the streets of New York in order to get himself assaulted by different ethnic groups. In *Above in Below* the pugilist and his friends are black. The assertion of the self through the presentation and visual record of the impervious body as both 'masculine' and 'white' is almost too obvious here but nonetheless needs to be mentioned. These scenes can also be read in the light of David Fincher's controversial film *Fight Club* (1999) as ceremonies of masculine self-assertion and redemption through aggression and a rejection of feminised culture. With a nod towards Judith Butler as quoted above, therefore, spectacles of masculine suffering such as those of Burden, Korine and Blaine may be regarded as theatrical and hyperbolic repetitions of the more banal and everyday performance of gender; re-enactments that continue to legitimise and ritualise masculine power and ensure its display.

To conclude, it makes sense to understand the fascination, confusion and intermittent hostility surrounding 'Above the Below' as responses partly rooted in Blaine's performance of bodily trauma and masculinity *together* within the current moment of media culture. Put simply, Blaine's act does not seem to properly fit established models of performance and display. It may invoke spectacular performances of masculinity with antecedents in popular entertainment but not in any consistent ways. It may reference them through its codification of martyr, artist, survivor and so on, but far from explicitly. It may present itself as a reality programming 'event' but it ultimately fails to position itself clearly within this frame of reference. As already noted, the exposure and, more particularly, self-exposure of bodily and psychological trauma has become the central feature of our 'post-documentary' culture and the foundation of 'tabloid' and reality TV. But popular television's exhibition, revelation and consumption of personal pain and suffering has been consistently, although not wholly, marked (and frequently condemned) as 'feminine'. The emotional arena of talk shows, the domestic or leisure space of observational documentary, the sexualised space of reality TV more broadly, all permit the public articulation of the personal within the formerly masculinised space of the public sphere. While 'Above the Below' adopts the structuration of reality formats (webstreaming, liveness, temporal collapse and so forth) it did not adopt their discourse of emotional exhibitionism or easy-going sociality. As such it occupied a far more ambivalent space within media culture and arguably failed to provide the necessary illusion of uniting subject and viewer that reality programming requires.

conclusion
'Reach for the stars': celebrity, social mobility and the future of reality TV

Celebrity in the modern social realm

The commercial success of reality TV formats has coincided with a period in which formal politics has become increasingly media friendly and packaged for media consumption. In 1997, when New Labour finally defeated the long-established Conservative government to achieve power in the UK, arts and entertainment celebrities gained prominence as exemplars of a new meritocratic and essentially *modern* democratic social realm.[1] The administration at 10 Downing Street actively sought the endorsement of musicians, actors and movie stars in its attempts to deploy a new, more inclusive and populist lexicon as part of its electoral address and managerial style. As a consequence, it was those who had succeeded in entertainment, rather than say industry or finance, who were often held up as exemplary figures 'close to' New Labour. Such entertainers and sports people, some originally from very disadvantaged social backgrounds, came to the fore as people of influence and social standing.

In the same cultural moment, the notable success of several of the new television forms discussed earlier in this book, docusoaps such as *The Cruise*, hybrid 'reality' shows such as *Big Brother* and later *Pop Idol*, transformed the terrain of media culture, showcasing ordinary people as potential media stars. The modern social realm was, it seems, further expanded to accommodate a new brand of celebrities, of ordinary people rendered remarkable through their encounter with new hybrid media forms and by their absorption into the complex processes of identification and voyeurism that made them household names and characters with the familiar feel of our own families. These new media stars appeared to be able to 'make it big', to not only become wealthy but, more importantly, to sustain a transformation into celebrity stardom without overtly drawing on education, entrepreneurial skills or even any obvious talent.

Reality TV's development of new iconic personas and their projection into a media-driven social mobility was, of course, partly anticipated by longer-established media narratives of class mobility. Biographies and news coverage of celebrity British footballers, pop performers, comedians and film stars have been central to the mythologisation of working-class social mobility in media culture. So too, narratives of football pools wins, bullion heists and lottery jackpots have long provided fantasy avenues of escape that were independent of the cultural capital gained through education, birth, entry into the professions or even talent (aside from the talent, that is, to entertain).[2]

The successful launch of the television drama series *Footballers' Wives* is a good example of a public fascination with the transformation of ordinary people into a new media-ocracy through fame, personal achievement and stunning affluence. The focus of the series, which has its roots in tabloid women's magazines such as *Hello!* and *OK*, did not dwell on the skills of players but on the fame and fortune of the newly affluent and media savvy footballer and his wife as celebrities.[3] The depiction of Victoria and David Beckham and their family life as 'popular royals' (resident in 'Beckingham Palace') was one clear influence on the programme. Their lives are exemplary too of a doubled agenda which famous working-class celebrities need to negotiate if they are to remain in favour. They must maintain the much-mythologised 'down-to-earth' values of working-class family culture and authenticity while fulfilling the expectations of glamour and overt consumption that sustain their public personas. They operate as an important counterpoint to those born into celebrity during a period when, for example, the public no longer feels obliged to look to the monarchy or other elite persons for role models of exemplary domesticity or overt consumption.[4]

The popular impact of these and other celebrities seems to reside precisely in their very disconnection from traditional structures of influence (inheritance, education and so forth) together with their intimate connection with the media and the consumer lifestyle which the media privileges and foregrounds. Although celebrities have been described by some media critics as a 'powerless elite' they wield a form of power formerly unrecognised as such (Alberoni 1972). Graeme Turner *et al.* (2000) have argued, for example, that:

> the celebrity's ultimate power is to sell the commodity that is themselves. This fact has been thoroughly integrated into contemporary popular culture and the marketing of celebrity-as-commodity has been deployed as a major strategy in the commercial construction of social identity.

In this context, the *accoutrements* and *appearance* of celebrity is paramount. Although the celebrity is a figure of consumption writ large they must also retain the individualism that sets them apart and renders them remarkable and commercially marketable. What might be called 'classed cross-dressing' becomes one overt and instantly recognisable expression of both their agency and their success. The sartorial and material signifiers of class transformation mark both working-class origins and the move away from them; the pleasurable and playful excess of financial escape from those origins and sometimes too a rebuke or an offence against respectable 'taste' (Tasker 1998: 40). This move up is also problematised because class mobility seems superficially to be dependent on consumption or the unstable transformation of stardom. The dual dynamics of transformation and submerged 'real' classed identities that appear in many media representations of the socially mobile 'media-ocracy' are crucial. Representations of social mobility and celebrity in reality TV foreground and reveal the complex interdependence between class and performance, the freedom of taking on new identities and a popular conviction that there is some hidden essence or 'true' working-class identity concealed beneath the 'glitz'.

Critical responses: disgust, democratisation and desire

> Reality TV is not the end of civilisation as we know it: it is civilisation as we know it. It is popular culture at its most popular, soap opera come to life. (Greer 2001)

As we have already signalled in chapter 1, current responses to reality TV coalesce around several themes. One common strand is that of derision. This response is encapsulated in Germaine Greer's much cited quotation above. In her article on reality TV, Greer jeers at the mass audience of these shows and predictably situates them within a 'dumbed down' tabloid television arena in which, she claims, a mixture of banality, exhibitionism and character-play guarantee audience ratings and therefore their domination of the schedules.

In keeping with broader attacks on tabloid culture and of the 'feminisation' of factual programming, a number of cultural critics (often championing a lost cause which is implicitly 'high culture') decry those who produce, watch and perform for the cameras. The ethics of what is acceptable in mass media representation is linked to broader debates about the decline of more privileged objective factual reportage and programming. In Britain, this debate is specifically linked to the role of television in an arena in which the public service ethos has been diminished. Objectivity, fact and debate are bandied about as lost values of a formerly intellectually curious journalistic age.

The Reithian theme of self-improvement and a broadcasting service that strove to use television to take viewers outside their realm of immediate existence, to educate and inform, is lamented as a lost educative ideal in an increasingly commercially-pressured media environment. As noted in chapters 5 and 6, reality TV, it is claimed, replaces this intellectual adventure with the limited exhibitionist challenges of the game show or the emotional outpourings of confessional culture in which the biggest challenge is to get on with a small bunch of housemates/prisoners/competitors for a limited period. With reality TV the aim is not to take viewers outside of their own experience but to present them with a fully recognisable and familiar realm of the ordinary and the everyday. The ethic of self-improvement seems, for media sceptics, to be parodied; as those without the traditional markers of media role models are seen to succeed – if not in Reithian terms, then at least within the terms of the populist media.

The disdain for the entertainment-led audience is matched by distress about changes to televisual form and genre. Frequently, the documentary becomes the marker of quality filming based on rational investigation of historical or socio-cultural fact. The detached but committed observational gaze of the documentary maker of the past has, it is claimed, been replaced by a slow slide through the docu-soap of the 1990s to the current reality TV show. An anxiety about the decline of documentary proper is often articulated to an anxiety about reality TV's dependence on spectacle linked to a manipulative misuse of the camera. Here, for example, the prominence of the 'close-up' is highlighted. This fear of the seductive image is captured in language that stresses the distraction of the viewer from rational viewing: 'we *cannot think straight* ... if our *emotions* are being *jerked up and down* by ... zoom lenses' (Broder in Glynn 2000: 22). Underlying this anxiety about 'easy' pleasure is recognition of the destabilisation of the status of the distant and powerful documentary camera and the move towards televisual intimacy.

As noted, in contrast to the above criticism, others have celebrated this cultural phenomenon as part of the contemporary expansion and democratisation of public culture. It is argued that reality TV's popular expression of social concerns and everyday events, conflicts and traumas within a highly managed environment signal the opening up of the public sphere to ordinary concerns and ordinary people who, if they are popular enough and lucky enough, can become famous. Where celebrities are already a prerequisite of the show – for example in the recent adaptations of survival shows for celebrity participants – the authenticity of the show is marked by the supposed provision of insights into the hidden 'real' aspect of celebrity personality. Phil Edgar-Jones, the executive producer of *Big Brother*, described the second *Celebrity Big Brother* as a stripping away of celebrity personas: 'With normal *Big Brother* we're making ordinary people extraordinary. With this, we're making famous people very, very ordinary' (in Day 2002). In short, reality TV is celebrated as a democratisation of public culture and the deconstruction of the components of fame that partially constitute the celebrity media subject and the construction of social identity more broadly. It is this agenda, well accepted in Britain in particular, which potentially threatened the success of the David Blaine event discussed in the previous chapter. As a reality format Blaine the celebrity needed to connect with his audience and yet the nature of his enterprise could only fail to render him ordinary or accessible.

The process of constructing celebrity and stripping it away can be captured in John Langer's notion of 'the especially remarkable' (1998: 45–73). In his analysis of tabloid culture, he highlights the prominence in current media culture of the 'other news': a form of cultural discourse intimately connected with gossip, storytelling and the scrutiny of the newly famous as well as those with a longer-held celebrity persona. Langer situates the celebrity within a co-dependent media context in which celebrity status is both ratified by media presence but also operates as a privileged authority in media culture. Celebrities increasingly have taken on the role as 'primary definers' of news. The very force of representation of the celebrity gives their actions and statements a kind of privileged authority in a world increasingly characterised as divided by those who have access to image making and the rest (1998: 50–1). This other news does not represent elite persons within the context of their institutional backdrop and does not primarily consider their role as power brokers or decision makers – but rather values their informal activities, public rituals of display and consumption and their private lives.

This 'calculus of celebrity' then is flexible and focuses not only on celebrities but upon those who have achieved possibly fleeting public attention through specific personal achievements.[5] For example, the 'ordinary' stars of reality shows suddenly acquire massive media visibility but possess very little in the way of institutional power or control and, unless they obtain excellent PR management, can find it hard to deal with media spin. Reality TV both proves and extends the mythic belief that traditional versions of mobility and success, once closely associated with economic or social achievement, are increasingly implicated in and beholden to the mass media processes of publicity. Langer suggests:

> On the one hand ordinary people are constructed as especially remarkable for what they do. How they breach expectations, their remarkableness is lodged in the extraordinary acts they perform. This separates them from us, makes them different and transcendent; they start where we are but move beyond. On the other hand … The implication is that, although these people are assigned especially remarkable qualities based on what they do, such qualities and performances could just as easily be within our grasp. If those seemingly mundane occupations and enthusiasms … can become the springboard from which those ordinary people ascend into the realms of the especially remarkable it could just as easily happen to us as well. (1998: 72)

The appeal of reality programming lies partly in how seemingly ordinary people are suddenly 'especially remarkable' and how that celebrity status is endorsed by the spectacle of their widespread public presence. For example, *Pop Idol UK* (2002) screened countless auditions of would-be pop celebrities. The show attracted over 30 million viewers who watched and voted for those singers who would remain until the final contest between Gareth Gates and the ultimate winner Will Young.[6] These two contestants have both become chart-topping pop singers with massive media coverage.[7]

The 2002 spin-off *American Idol* warned potential contestants that their appearance on television may be 'disparaging, defamatory, embarrassing or of an otherwise unfavourable nature which may expose you to public ridicule, humiliation or condemnation'.[8] Nonetheless its popularity with would-be idols and audiences alike ensured a second series in 2003. *American Idol 2* appeared on Fox TV and concurrently in the UK on ITV2 in March 2003. It followed the structure of the UK predecessor and the final twelve contestants were introduced to their audience through pre-recorded video cameos that emphasised their 'ordinariness', their smalltown American homes and the support of their local schools, military barracks, church or family. These to-camera testimonies by family and friends and shots of the contestants feeding the ducks, visiting their old workplace at a hair salon or supermarket, or training with ordinary soldiers located them as 'no-one particularly special', as 'regular' or 'all American' young men and women. But, at the same time, the 'folks' that spoke of them and their singing skills, as a child amateur performer, in the church choir, in a local bar, served to elevate their status. These subsidiary characters, like the live audience for whom the contestants then perform, function textually as a sign of public acclamation: 'the especially remarkable are seen (by us) to be seen by others in the public domain' (Langer 1998: 63).

These short video narratives of personal triumph over ordinary obstacles and *over obscurity itself* anticipated their live stage performances held before music industry judges and the television audience. The appearance in front of cameras before a voting audience was constructed consequently as the tangible reward for their accomplishments *per se* despite the more obvious rewards and lure of winning the competition. In such competitions, the ordinary masses of viewers who follow the course of the contestant's path to fame are crucial. They serve a similar role to the subsidiary characters present at the edges of the frame in television camera or paparazzi shots of the star persona, for their presence 'watching, waiting, attending or serving' the ordinary celebrity endorses his or her status (Langer 1998: 72). Furthermore, this identification with the 'especially remarkable' individual allows for the possibility of a sense of activity for the television spectator, of a hand in the elevation of the ordinary person to celebrity status.

Correspondingly, Peter Balzagette (2001) argued that reality TV is 'diverse programming, and access to the airwaves for a more diverse spread of people'. He declared that this democratisation, also signalled by the audience's ability to contribute to the elevation or elimination of the stars, goes hand in hand with a change in social attitudes about television and identification. As signalled earlier, he characterises this as a desire for 'emotional investment' latched onto the appeal of interactivity and audience participation. For Balzagette, audience figures clarify this desire to participate in and determine a programme's conclusion; a motivation which ensured that over the first two series of *Big Brother* around 34 million phone votes were cast for who should stay and who should go in the *Big Brother* house.

This investment, articulated through constant media, especially tabloid press, coverage was prominent in the fourth production of *Big Brother* but was already crucial to the construction of the previous series as a media 'event'. *Big Brother 3*, which ran in the summer of 2002, followed the standard formula of isolating twelve voluntary participants in a house without media contact with the outside world for 64 days. These were gradually eliminated and ejected by telephone poll until the winner remained. In the final week of the programme, 8.5 million votes were cast, signalling for some media commentators that the series epitomised 'the model of participatory programming'.[9] The press measured the extent of its success by competing for exclusive interviews as the final four to emerge from the house were deluged with cash offers; the figures offered often dwarfed the £70,000 prize collected by the eventual winner, 22-year-old Kate Lawler.

But the issues we have raised throughout about the seemingly unremarkable subject of reality TV and their entry into the celebrity matrix are best exemplified by Jade Goody. Goody, a 21-year-old dental nurse from South London, fourth from last to be expelled from the house, received wildly fluctuating media coverage from the press whilst in the house and was the subject, halfway through the series, of vitriolic attacks from the tabloids. Goody was undoubtedly 'marked' negatively as working-class by her body, her voice and her supposed intellectual ignorance. She was loud, apparently uneducated, bibulous, excessive, overweight and getting fatter as the series progressed. The press revelled in quoting 'Jade-isms', the stupid things said by Goody in the course of the series. She displayed the bodily excesses that marked Roseanne Barr as a blatantly working-class woman but without the wisecracking wit that shielded Barr from the worst misogynistic criticisms (see Rowe 1995). Dominic Mohon, editor of the *Sun*'s showbiz column 'Bizarre' urged readers to evict Jade with the deeply misogynistic and class-based slogan, 'Vote out the pig.' He informed readers that 'Jade is one of the most hated women on British TV and life will be hard for her when she leaves the house.' She seemed to exemplify Annette Kuhn's observation that:

> Class is something beneath your clothes, under your skin, in your psyche, at the very core of your being. In the all-encompassing English class system, if you know you are in the 'wrong' class, you know that therefore you are a valueless person. (1995: 98)

However, tabloid attacks were upturned by positive viewer support for Goody resulting in tabloid battles for exclusive rights to her story when she emerged from the house. Ironically, Rupert Murdoch's *Sun* and *News of the World* outbid rival tabloids and paid £500,000 for exclusive interviews with her. Since then Goody has been re-branded as a 'national treasure'.

Goody's success fits the pattern highlighted for the 'especially remarkable' in that when the ordinary celebrity is prone to setbacks, these setbacks are played out before the public gaze. She won through only after a dialectic of ill-fortune and effort had been played out. And crucially her success was attributed to powers beyond her grasp: she was subject to the inexplicable hand of fate, the power of the television audience and the manipulations of the television production crew. When she exited from the house she appeared dressed in a glamorous evening gown three sizes too small and was soon confronted by *Big Brother* host Davina McCall with a montage of clips revealing her excessive behaviour and her apparent stupidity. Talk show comedian Graham Norton, who reclaimed her as a camp icon, was also there to meet her and went on to depict her in his shows as the plump, giggly and dense dental nurse reminiscent of a 1950s *Carry On* film.

Subsequent media coverage focused on the re-education of Miss Goody. The television programme *What Jade Did Next* (Channel 4, October 2002) followed her as she worked with a personal trainer, learned how to deal with the media, learned how to drive and was schooled in the very demanding work of public appearances. Her background with her single mother on a working-class social housing estate was contrasted with the opportunities on offer to her since her appearance on the reality show. She was a stark signifier of the possibility of self-transformation and social mobility in spite of class origins and limited social skills. Jade's narrative of desired transformation also revealed how class plays a central role in the production of femininity and the regulation of it. The escape which Jade articulates in *What Jade Did Next* reveals a knowledge on her part about the attainment of not just economic wealth but the cultural artefacts of taste and knowledge, of cultural capital. The possession of the 'right' car, of literacy, of designer clothes and private property are signifiers of social mobility hedged with the dangers of the disreputable: the trashy dress, the uninformed opinion, the too-loud laugh. In keeping with earlier fictional fantasies of achievement, reality TV offered Jade Goody a way to exhibit incipient talent for performance, 'rough at the edges but with the potential for learning' (McRobbie 1991: 215).

Celebrity hybridity and packaged demotic culture

The address to the reality audience varies depending on the format of the show. But across the board there is a shared assumption that the audience possesses the media literate capabilities to assess the contestants/participants of the reality TV show – even though the criteria of judgement are often un-formulated and unspoken. These criteria are grounded in vague notions of identification, appreciation and also crucially of dislike and disdain. Participants of *Big Brother* or *Pop Idol* or *The Club* (ITV2, 2003) knowingly present themselves to a judgemental audience. Their task is one of interaction and the overt immersion in the competitive structure of the show. As noted in chapter 1 participants are selected on the basis of contradictory criteria and are often stereotypes of the diverse identities that populate contemporary media culture – lesbian or gay, black, heterosexual bachelor, twenty-thirty something white 'Essex' girl or boy, stud, tart, shy loner. These types share (are presented as sharing) two features: an everyday commonality and a hunger for celebrity status. The winning group formula for a reality TV show appears to be a combination of the typecast, the banal and the exceptional.

Frequently, the participants are presented as classed subjects. Whilst the boundary between working class and lower-middle class is now often blurred in contemporary British culture and the very formations of classed hierarchies have radically altered, the participants generally are presented as residing somewhere in this region: they are clerical workers, mechanics, bar keepers, service industry workers and so on. Where, as in the UK *Big Brother 5*, they include university graduates and entrepreneurs this aspect of their cultural context is heavily muted in the edited broadcasts of the show. They are also frequently aspirant media celebrities. In many reality shows there is a submerged narrative about escape across classed boundaries. Also the production and editing of the show reveals a level of unacknowledged cultural capital at play. The taste and disposition of the contestants is under scrutiny; their clothes, banal conversation, interactions with other contestants, ambitions, everyday activities as related to the audience are markers of their position within the class hierarchy. As noted in our earlier discussions of the group dynamics of the UK version of *Survivor* and *Big Brother 1* it is important not to appear *too* wealthy, *too* cultured or *too* tasteful. Yet, as with Jade Goody, appearing too trashy, too sexual, too uncultured can also provoke media opprobrium and infamy. Contestants need to be distinctive but not too distinctive.

A strategy of 'violence' then is encouraged in the reality TV community. The judgement on which contestants should stay and which should go is structured as a demotic decision but it is a decision formed through division and exclusion. This is a system of judgement and classification. A vote determines who is unworthy of respect or esteem – for the contestant the outcome of the vote makes overt the fact that one's performance on the show is readable for others: the people watch you, observe you and decide upon your fate. Here, we would argue the seemingly more fluid opportunities of celebrity identity fuse with the traces of a class-based system. There is both a celebration of aspiration (and the desire for escape from the limitations of ordinary life) and a judgemental scrutiny of the participants' behaviour – to appear too ambitious, too outrageous, too performative is to invite audience disdain. Yet to appear too dull, too isolated, too introverted is to also invite banishment. Of course, the conventional markers of class identity alone are inadequate to predict who will survive and thrive in this media environment. Yet the reality competition often takes place around two axes rooted in economic and social capital – that of material goods (prize money, media contracts) and that of less tangible phenomena such as popularity.

Crucial to the possession of the celebrity status that comes with popularity is a particular form of distinction in which the contestant, as he or she appears before the media audience, can be outrageous, bold, greedy, bitchy or ruthless but they cannot appear pretentious. Pretentiousness is primarily a classed charge which calls aspirant working- or lower-middle-class identities to order: 'who does she think she is kidding?' or 'we can see right through him'. As Steph Lawler notes, 'pretentiousness is a charge levelled at people in whom what they *seem to be* is not (considered to be) what they are: in whom there is a gap between *being* and *seeming*' (2001: 121). One of the pleasures of reality TV for the audience then is trying to spot the gap, to see through the contestants' inauthenticity. Yet inauthenticity, the ability to put on a show, is at the same time part of the skill of the celebrity persona.

In this context 'classed cross-dressing' carries with it pleasures for both the aspirant celebrity subject and the media audience but also dangers. Arrogance, outrageous or overtly ruthless behaviour can be construed as part of older established narratives of transformation in which the working-class boy or girl who wants it badly enough eventually has it all. Consequently, such behaviour signifies a desire to escape limits, to 'be someone', to grab a status and power normally denied. Attendant on this performance is an inevitable lack of nuance or sophistication *within the terms of class by which the contestants are constrained*. To successfully adopt markers of 'cultured' identity *in their entirety* would be to underline too clearly that class and power can be vestments or trappings rather than some integral part of one's essential identity. Classed cross-dressing then involves always the danger of discovery, of passing as one of a 'higher order' and the attendant pleasure for the audience of unmasking someone's hubris.

Reality TV – the future?

The institutionalised cultural management that is at the core of celebrity culture was wedded to a new development of the reality show in the form of new series such as *The Club* and *The Salon*. In these, the distinction between the authentic celebrity and the would-be celebrity and between the reality of the game and of the game as a packaged show have been further muddied. In the 'fly-on-the-wall' series *The Salon* (C4) workers from a real salon are re-located with new recruits to run a salon undertaking hair and beauty treatments for both the ordinary public and for celebrities. Viewers can win the chance for an appointment. In a postmodern turn, both amusing and bizarre, the first series witnessed a visit from disgraced family variety-show presenter Michael Barrymore for a hair cut and the new series saw staff welcoming Brendan, a spectacularly bad candidate from *Pop Idol*, for a pedicure. In both cases the reality TV workers of *The Salon* were overheard indulging in celebrity gossip about their clients. The show pointed towards future forms that create a new social/media space in which 'real' people and celebrities co-exist side-by-side.

In early 2003 Carlton broadcast a new show called *The Club* which also provided this new social/media space. The show was staged in a real location, a retro-themed, two-floored bar called *Nylon,* in London's square mile. Each week for the duration of the six-week show, three celebrities took control of one of the bars at Nylon and their team of bartenders would battle it out to make theirs the coolest one. Each week the celebrity nominated a member of his or her team to get the sack; viewers were witnesses to the nomination and to the celebrity's frank appraisal of their staff. Television viewers were also asked to vote for the team member that they wanted to lose their job and the sacking took place live on TV. Open auditions were then held and those who voted *or who attended* the club could, if they chose, ask to be nominated to replace the sacked employee.

Chrysalis-owned Galaxy radio network teamed up with Carlton to promote the show and when it started, its presenters, celebrity bar managers and team members were featured on dance music stations; Galaxy DJ's even managed the decks at Nylon. The club had the capacity to pack in over 500 revellers (Day 2003). It was promoted using the now-common media practice of 'emotional branding' (Lull 2000: 170). In this case, the commodity was associated with the subjectivities of everyday working-class life. The three celebrities selected to run the bar were emblems of working-class culture made good. Samantha Fox, the former *Sun* 'page three girl' of the 1980s, who, as the official website profile stresses, started work on the *Sun* at sixteen years of age and has gone on to make a wide-ranging showbusiness career for herself. Fox had accrued an iconic status as a former tabloid star and still signifies a brash hedonism and visual excitement combined with a determined desire for celebrity success. She was presented throughout the programme as a tough achiever who combined glamour with tabloid's populist appeal. Her climb to success is marked by a significant gender and class realignment in which working-class women resist 'discourses of sobriety' through the unashamed use of their sexuality in the accrual of celebrity status; a positioning which sits easily with the personas and self-professed ambitions of reality TV's contestants.

The second bar manager was Dean Gaffney, who started work on the long running British TV soap opera *Eastenders*, again at the early age of fifteen. Gaffney is presented as a working-class success story, which melds real-life with his soap persona. The website states that he is 'no stranger to hard and unglamorous work, and he vividly remembers pounding the pavements on his paper round as a boy'. This is immediately juxtaposed with tales of his current penchant for fast cars and drinking sessions at *Stringfellows* night-club: 'the trials of celebrity lifestyle!' Gaffney's bar eventually won the £15,000 prize money. The third bar manager was Richard Blackwood, a former MTV presenter turned Channel 4 presenter then pop star. The web profile again presents Blackwood as a person who wants to be remembered as 'a real personality that came from nothing'. All three managers work extremely hard and there is a strange juxtaposition of discourses as 'celebrities' labour intensively in the maintenance of the celebrity status. The best thing about the series is that it reveals the 'hard work' behind the superficially effortless image of entertainers.

But of course, in this context the revelation of the real work of stardom is also part and parcel of the unique selling point of the show. All three bar managers reveal the use of celebrity to represent the emotion of the cultural product: they signify the importance of ambition, exceptional personality and a drive to achieve success even with a poor start in life. What is interesting is the elision between their celebrity personas and their real-life status. All three are presented as working-class without specific reference to these terms. Gaffney's soap persona is melded with his personal media achievement whilst Fox exemplifies how being a working celebrity means interpreting economics in sexual as well as financial terms.

There are a number of points to be made about the innovation and self-referential and often hybrid status of *The Club*. The contestants too are mainly from fairly mundane jobs as clerical workers, bar men or women, supermarket workers and so on. They share the common desire to succeed in media terms. *The Club* breaks down the division between would-be and successful celebrity that had heretofore been maintained in, for example, the *Big Brother* and *Survivor* shows. Celebrities work alongside ordinary contestants in the bar and are overtly constructed as cultural workers with shared ambitions. Whilst the division in power is maintained – through the hierarchy of the bar managed by the established celebrity – there are moments when this breaks down. At one point, Fox's crew chastises her in the appraisal session for drinking too much and jeopardising their chances – a scene in which Sam walks off camera twice and later apologises to her team. The contestants and celebrities challenge any easy notion of classed identity. Both groups in a sense occupy ersatz class positions – drawing too easily on narratives of gritty success that, in the case of the celebrities, obliterate the distinctions between their public and private personas. Both perform for camera whilst also baring their more 'authentic' anxieties about other team members in by-now well rehearsed confessional to-camera moments that supposedly characterise reality TV's glimpse of the authentic person.

But finally then, both *The Salon* and *The Club* are worthy of attention because their formats erode the divisions and distinctions between the audience and the performers in ways which point towards the future development of factual entertainment programming. Shows such as the USA-based *Survivor* have operated a no-fly zone over their island-competition space to exclude the danger/chaos of outsiders breaking into the reality of the mediated event. *Big Brother* shuts contestants away from the physical presence of ordinary others and opens them up only to the televisual/computer gaze. In contrast, *The Salon* allowed anyone to make an appointment and *The Club* was open to the public who could visit every night of the week including the televised nights. For a minimal fee they could join in the media event, buying drinks at the bar, talking with and assessing the contestants and celebrities and, if they were lucky, appear on the small screen itself. *The Club* especially was a provocative re-inscription of the local and particular experience of the neighbourhood bar into the global distanced voyeurism of television land. If you were young enough, had disposable income, dressed smartly and lived in London you too could inhabit a reality TV space. This constituted a marked extension of the viewers' exercise of their discrimination in voting and offered a fleeting few-seconds of media fame as the camera caught them at the bar or nearby amidst *Nylon*'s customers. Even Blaine's 'Above the Below' took place in a public space and many visitors noted that it was the experience of seeing him in the flesh and the sensation of being part of the crowd on the ground – that is, being part of the event – that won them round as fans. These new hybrid forms are reality TV writ large, allowing people to routinely select and weave mediated, publicly available symbolic representations and discourses into their everyday lives and starkly revealing how their participation can be packaged, commodified and sold back to them as audiences.

Concluding comments

As this book draws to a conclusion we have returned to the terrain where we began with a discussion of reality TV as a changing vehicle for the representation of ordinary (that is, non-elite) people and a platform for the projection of ordinary voices. We have charted quite extensively the ways in which realist genres, especially documentaries, broke new ground in the representation of ordinary people and everyday life and how they increasingly sought to provide a forum for the articulation of working-class experience. Our introduction also noted how ordinary people and the 'working classes' in particular have been deployed by filmmakers and read by audiences as being *in themselves* signs of the real and of the authentic. The presence of ordinary people and the provision of access for demotic voices are often taken to be markers of the realist credentials of factual and fact-based programming. And many films and programmes that preceded popular observational documentary and reality TV (and some of those that continue to be made today) were also motivated by explicitly radical political agendas rooted in a celebration of the contribution of ordinary people to the life of the nation and in demands for political action, social justice or a change in social attitudes.

As has been demonstrated, the 'politics' of the more popular factual programming and reality TV in particular is quite differently articulated. It can be overwhelmingly conservative, producing knowledges ('revelations') disguised as truths ('reality') about the criminal subject, the sexualised subject, the confessing subject, the consuming subject, the traumatised subject and so on that close down any collective impetus to effect change or to challenge the status quo. Although reality TV frequently dwells on issues of social difference and hierarchies of classed or cultural distinction and it is predicated on the importance of depicting ordinary people's experience (and arguably practising cultural politics in doing so) its trajectory is nonetheless quite different from its more overtly politicised generic antecedents. It is attentive to individual aspiration and competitive individualism within frequently fake or highly proscribed micro-communities and attends to social mobility within an increasingly mediated social/public realm. This emphasis on the individual, their ambitions, fears and interpersonal relations with fellow contestants, neighbours, family or workmates brings pressure to bear on the filmic subject to reveal all on television. The increasingly destabilised and permeable borders between the media and the social realm facilitates this and, in doing so, radically alters the cultural landscape within which we all have to abide. Moreover, as noted throughout, the increasing presence of cameras in our lives, their incursion into public spaces and their apparent widespread acceptability is in itself altering the ground of our self-presentation and self-fashioning. To borrow an observation from Jon Dovey, 'We are all learning to live in the freakshow, it is our new public space' (2000: 4). The question which should perhaps preoccupy us now is how we choose to navigate this space and make it our own.

Notes

introduction

1 www.bfi.org.uk/bookvid/books/handbook/overview2002.html, accessed 19 July 2002.

chapter 1

1 When citing programmes, the channel on which they first appeared will follow in brackets. Where a series or single programme is discussed at length the year of first broadcast will also be cited.
2 For a succinct account of the commercial development of reality formats and the formation of Endemol see the chapter 'Format Wars', in Brenton and Cohen (2003: 44–80).
3 On the format, critical reception and audience responses to *Big Brother* specifically see Mathijs and Jones (2004), the special edition of *Television and New Media*, 3, 3 (August 2002); Liesbet van Zoonen (2001); Douglas Allen (2003) and Janet Jones (2002). For a broad range of articles on reality TV, including those on *Big Brother*, also see the collection edited by Su Holmes and Deborah Jermyn (2003).
4 Paddy Scannell's (2002) definition of *Big Brother* as television event is congruent with Nick Couldry's in as much as he emphasises the non-contingent nature of the event

(as opposed, for example, to the 'happening') but he also suggests the temporality of television events, arguing that they have the same structure as stories (beginning, middle, end) and correspond to the structure of the human life-span. The suggestion of an ending or closure here is problematic as the life of talk and the celebrity life-span of the characters can be unpredictable, uneven and fairly open-ended. Scannell rightly observes that shows such as these, running over nine weeks, have a real challenge to sustain themselves as events.

5   *Pop Idol* won the prestigious Golden Rose of Montreux in 2002 and was described by the grand jury as 'perfect television'.

6   Peter Bazalgette, the Chairman of Endemol UK, in '*Big Brother* and beyond', Huw Weldon Memorial Lecture 2001.

7   There is a very good example, from the US, of a successful marketing strategy that really did turn a television series into event TV and whose finesse ensured that fans felt they had played a part in its formation. SONY courted fans of the teen-drama series *Dawson's Creek* and encouraged their involvement in the development of a media convergence project that interleaved the show with *Dawson's Desktop* in order to introduce transmedia storytelling. This convergence successfully combined marketing and entertainment. The *Deskstop* sustained fans' interest by filling in between episodes, providing email, chat, bookmarks and a backstory that provided in-depth character – knowledge that fostered a 'cult' engagement with the series. SONY worked so closely with the web scriptwriters that they could anticipate events, introducing tangential characters and events that would influence the show's television content. The co-option of the programme's pre-existing fans' groups into the promotion of the new online show was highly instructive and raised serious questions about the future autonomy of fan cultures (see *Media in Transition 2: Globalization and Convergence*, May 10-12, 2002 Massachusetts Institute of Technology, Cambridge, MA).

8   *Castaway 2000* relocated a carefully selected group of 28 men, women and children onto a storm-blasted island in the Outer Hebrides for 12 months. The series was to be a social and psychological experiment. A group representative of British society would have their physical and psychological stamina tested to the limit (Stuart 2000).

9   There is a small but growing body of research underway addressing the relationship between programmes such as *Survivor* and global imperialism. See, for example, Julia Lesage (2002) and Mike Hajimichael (2002).

10 *Fear* was filmed in a style resembling the 'reality' fiction horror-film shocker *The Blair Witch Project* (1998) and *Fear Factor* is a game show where contestants compete for $50,000 by eating fly-infested fruit and undertaking stunt-style acts of daring. These shows are somewhat reminiscent of the Japanese endurance shows that were broadcast in the UK in youth programming slots late night on Channel 4.

11 The logical extension of reality TV's fascination with people under stress has been brilliantly satirised in Daniel Minahan's feature film *Series 7: The Contenders* (2000) in which six contestants, selected by programme makers without their consent, have to kill all their opponents in order to survive.

12 The material generated by the CPU has appeared in various formats; some of which aim to connect individual experience and national issues such as *Nation Goes to the*

Polls and *One Day in Scotland*, and others which are themed such as *Life, Death, God and Everything*.

13 For a detailed discussion of the possibility of access as exposition see Myra MacDonald (1998).

14 Stated on *Big Brother, Small World* (C4, 2001).

15 'Nasty Nick' Bateman became notorious for 'breaking the rules' by attempting to influence housemates' nominations in *Big Brother 1*. The rest of his housemates confronted him with the accusation 'you're so sick' and he was roundly humiliated and driven from the set. Bateman's defence that he was playing in a 'game show' seems reasonable enough but in the context of British culture, at least, he committed the crime of overtly trying to win. On the other hand, viewers seemed to take the eventual winner Craig Phillips to their hearts. The Liverpudlian builder reciprocated by donating all of his winnings to charity and thus demonstrating that he could really 'play the game'.

16 The fact that Channel 4 was happy to promote programmes using their 'working titles' is designed to appeal to and perhaps flatter a youth audience who appreciate the rough-cut quality of reality programming and the idea of factual television as off-the-cuff work-in-progress.

17 Quoted in 'Tv Insider' column in the *Radio Times,* 19–25 July 2003, 100.

18 Stated in *Big Brother, Small World* (C4 2001).

19 In fact one of the earliest invitations for audiences to survey the subject's personal space was afforded through web-based sites such as 'Jennicam' which surveyed the bedroom activities of Jennifer Ringley via a video camera attached to the computer in her college dormitory. The site was launched in 1996 and became a pay site from June 1997. Here spectators could view not only Ringley's more intimate moments but also the banal everyday activities of her everyday life. As such it would be inaccurate to designate this as pornography since the sexual activity was simply part and parcel of her everyday activities (see Burgin 2002).

20 As Dan Waddell has noted, group-challenge reality programmes are essentially popularity contests and as such, in the British context at least, class continues to be a divisive issue. In *Survivor Panama* teacher Susannah Mofat was continually quizzed about her 'posh' upbringing and it was suggested that she, least of all, needed the money. She never successfully combated their criticisms as her accent and vocabulary established an 'almost insurmountable barrier' (2002: 233). These scenes of conflict based on social difference are roundly de-politicised since they are articulated in a highly individualised context. As Mike Wain notes, 'the trick of popular culture is to draw on and allude to the social dimension of signs and meanings and then, in a sleight of hand, fill up those meanings with notions of individual agency and responsibility' (1994: 55).

21 It is certainly the case that no matter how well film subjects are prepared they may well not fully understand the extent of their responsibilities to the reality project. Dan Waddell notes that in the second series of *Survivor* set in Panama survivors were dismayed to discover they were going to be filmed 24/7, 'something that came as a shock to some members of the group ... [who] were of the bizarre opinion that they would only be filmed for an hour or two a day ... the constant filming was not

welcomed by a number of the survivors – some of whom seemed to think that it would be a free holiday in paradise, a view that did not last long' (2002: 28).

22 The term 'photographic image' here denotes a whole range of images which, 'originating in the camera', also includes 'images which share some of the mechanical, lens-based and analogue features of the chemical photographic process but which are registered by electromagnetic means: broadcast television and video' (Lister 1995: 3–4).

23 Kevin Robins' (1996) discussion of image technologies and visual culture was a valuable source for this opening commentary.

chapter 2

1 A number of critics trace the lineage of reality TV back to these movements. See, for example, Brenton & Cohen 2003: 21–5; Barnfield 2002. See also John Dovey's discussion of the relationship between these movements and factual television in *Freakshow* pp. 29–30 and pp. 51–2.

2 For an extended discussion of the theoretical approaches to film realism see Lapsley & Westlake 1988: 156–80.

3 Jon Dovey (2000: 29) provides an example of the long-term influence of Direct Cinema's belief in the minimum impact of film crew on more recent observational documentaries. Apparently Roger Graef, whose series such as *Police* (1982) employ the Direct Cinema method, instructed his crew to wear black and avoid direct eye contact with film subjects during a shoot.

4 For a discussion of the controversies around the film and their impact on its exhibition see Winston 2000: 85–6.

5 For a full list of the films screened for all six Free Cinema programmes see Dixon & Dupin 2001: 30.

6 For an account of Anderson's contribution to the development of British art cinema see Erik Hedling 1997.

7 There was also a politicised aspect to Jennings' work. For example, in a letter co-authored by Jennings published in the *New Statesman and Society* (1937) promoting the efforts of Mass Observation, the authors contended that the behaviour of ordinary people needed to be charted 'so that their environment may be understood and thus constantly transformed … the knowledge of what has to be transformed is indispensable. The foisting on the mass of ideals or ideas developed by men apart from it, irrespective of its capacities, causes misery…' (in M.-L. Jennings 1982: 17).

8 As Erik Barnouw (1993: 234–5) explains that, up until this point, the use of synchronous sound was in any case extremely difficult to achieve for technical reasons. The cumbersome equipment required meant that documentarists emphasised movement with people actively doing things for the camera rather than speaking to it – the commentary therefore dominated as a way of fixing meaning to filmed action. The Free Cinema group certainly employed sound more innovatively by allowing ordinary people to speak more but their stance in relation to the film subjects was also more ambivalent since they tended not to comment on these voices.

9   For a discussion of the British New Wave influence on *Coronation Street* see Richard Dyer 1981.

10 Tim O'Sullivan's interviews with people who acquired their sets between 1953–58 supports this. One interviewee commented, 'If you had a car and a TV set, you'd really arrived' (1991: 166).

11 The father of this family was quoted as saying, 'The tellie keeps the family together. None of us ever have to go out now' (Young & Willmott 1957: 143). There is still work to be done on the role of early television as a disciplinary technology in working-class life. The usage and financial costs of television, together with the lack of pubs and clubs around the new isolated council estates, helped alter masculine and feminine working-class behaviour. Women were more confined to the immediate area, further from their extended families and men, who had less money and less opportunity to go to the pub after work became more home-oriented. Overall the family became more self-contained (Young & Willmott 1957: 143–6), which fostered the perfect conditions for television viewing.

12 The growing importance of television as a form can be seen in the fact that it was a televised extract of *Look Back in Anger* that helped to make it a resounding popular and critical success (Jacobs 2000: 157–8).

13 Documentary drama is only one variant of a range of documentary forms that employs either dramatised reconstruction or the filmic codes and conventions of drama. In fact documentary appears in so many hybrid formats that a taxonomy undertaken for its own sake would not be especially useful. Readers should note, however, that debates about 'drama documentary' often occur alongside discussion of 'documentary drama' which is distinguishable by its greater emphasis on the documentary style or technique (Kilborn & Izod 1997: 147–8). To add to the confusion writer Jeremy Sandford referred to *Cathy Come Home* as 'dramatised documentary' (in Paget 1998: 160). In this book we choose to use the term 'documentary drama' to refer to any format that marries extensive dramatisation with documentary style or conventions.

14 *Z Cars*, screened from 1962, was set in Liverpool and filmed at the same time and in the same locations as the New Wave film *A Kind of Loving*. One of the originators of the series, John McGrath, has commented, 'the series was going to be a kind of documentary about people's lives in these areas and the cops were incidental – they were the means of finding out about people's lives' (in Lacey 2000: 119; see also Laing 1991).

15 In fact Granada, the production company for *Coronation Street*, has consistently refused to refer to the series as 'soap opera' (Geraghty 1991: 4).

16 The traumatic realism of this scene was effected by filming it with a hidden camera; so that the expressions on the faces of the members of the public passing by, as the children were dragged away by social workers, were authentic (Fuller 1998: 23).

chapter 3

1   The fact that Woolcock becomes deeply involved in the community should not suggest that the film's subjects always approve of the completed film. Woolcock has described,

on a number of occasions, how she had to cope with the consternation and disapproval of local people following the screening of *When the Dog Bites*, for example.

2 This kind of viewing fascination is also invoked by the British comedy *The Royle Family* and the Amercian docusoap featuring the chaotic lives of heavy metal star Ozzy Osbourne and his wife and two children (*The Osbournes*, MTV). The latter family, excessive and carnivalesque, seem very far from the normative ideal and yet at the same time they invite recognition in that despite their celebrity lifestyles they play out scenarios of parenting, neighbour relations and domesticity.

3 *Neighbours from Hell* is an ITV series that uses mainly amateur footage to recount tempestuous and sometimes aggressive neighbourly disputes. The series is very popular and in 1999 was listed by BARB in the top twenty programmes for terrestrial channels in the UK with an audience of 12.8 million.

4 The growing performativity of observational documentary is even more apparent in Watson's later documentary *The Queen's Wedding*. Here the central subject, a gay man who also works as a drag queen, addresses the camera in both personas, each one often contradicting the other and undermining the 'truthfulness' of the documentary project.

chapter 4

1 Michael Renov locates Clarke's work alongside that of ethnographer/filmmaker Jean Rouch whose breakthrough work in the 1960s helped inspire the Direct Cinema movement in the US and the *nouvelle vague* in France. Rouch's African work was characterised by novelties such as 'shared anthropology' and 'ethno-fiction' and is noted for an embrace of daily life and the imagination of a new generation of Africans (http://www.frenchculture.org/cinema/festival/rouch/rouch1.html accessed 13.09.03). Rouch's interactive explorations from the late 1950s revealed a fascination with the encounter between filmmaker and subject and had explored the role of film and confession. In an interview in 1969, Rouch responds to an interviewer querying the camera's influence: 'Yes, the camera deforms, but not from the moment that it becomes an accomplice. At that point it has the possibility of doing something I couldn't do if the camera wasn't there: it becomes a kind of psychoanalytic stimulant which lets people do what they wouldn't otherwise do' (in Renov 1999: 91).

2 For a discussion of this work in context of Warhol's video ventures see Callie Agnell's account (2002: 278–81).

3 See for example Allie Light's discussion of her 3-minute sequence *Dialogues with Madwomen* (in Stubbs 2002: 199–206).

4 See Bill Nichols (1994: 92–106) for a discussion of these performative documentaries.

5 As John Corner has noted, 'The extent to which a concern with formal attractiveness "displaces" the referential to make the subject itself secondary to its formal appropriation has been a frequent topic of dispute' (1996b: 123).

6 Ian Goode has similarly noted the shift in documentary between 'looking through' and 'looking at' as a binary which structures documentary practice and critique. He argues that, 'any pure sense of "looking though" reproduces the fallacy of transparent access

... although a temporary sense of unmediated access continues to be a powerful and necessary feature of many documentary sequences'. On the contrary, he argues that, 'a pure commitment to "looking at" blocks the documentarist's engagement unless it occurs only as one element or movement in a larger referential design' (2003: 98).

7   See preview for 'First Person' series on Magic Lantern's website: http://www.magic lanternpr.com/clients/Errol_files/FirstPerson.html:p1.

8   Cited in Gamson (2000) 'First Person Singular', http://www.prospect.org/print/V11/ 11gamson-j.html, p. 1.

9   Shawn Rosenheim gives a detailed analysis of this and a number of *Interrotron Stories* (1996).

10 Philippa Campey (2002) 'Errol Morris' *Stairway To Heaven*: An exploration of the first person narrative', http://www.sensesofcinema.com/contents/01/13/cteq/stairway.html.

11 As John Ellis notes in *Seeing Things*, 'Witness is a new form of experience; it arrived with the development of mechanical media which accord with how we perceive everyday reality ... Only in the second half of the twentieth century did commentators begin to explore its specific nature allowing us to experience events at a distance, safe but also powerless, able to over-look but under-act' (2000: 15).

12 Here, Bill Nichols' use of the term 'voice' to signal both the physical voice and the authorial imprint of the filmmaker is relevant to Morris' technique. See Nichols in Stella Bruzzi (2000: 164).

chapter 5

1   Kate Boorstein, a lesbian transsexual who has appeared on *Geraldo*, *Donahue* and *Jane Whitney*, has argued that whilst the talk show may be an extension of the nineteenth-century freak-show circus, it now provides the oppor-tunity to represent her specific identity publicly: 'What's different now is that we, as freaks, are doing the speaking. It isn't the barker telling the story for us' (in Shattuc 1997: 93).

2   Here I am indebted to Robins' discussion of the worlds of virtual reality (see 1996: ch. 2).

3   The term 'Trauma TV' has been coined by Jon Dovey, who defines it as: 'Individual tragedies which would once have remained private but which are now restaged for public consumption' (2000: 21–2).

4   The factual information on the Apology Line was taken from Jonathan Freedland's interview with 'Mr. Apology' in the *Guardian*, 30 July 1994, 27.

5   See, for example, Ulrich Beck's *Towards New Modernity* (1992) and Anthony Giddens' *Modernity and Self-Identity* (1991).

chapter 6

1   I have used Susan Moeller's (1999) phrase 'compassion fatigue' which is developed in her account of media constructions of war, famine, pestilence and death.

2   Jane Shattuc (1997: 113–21) outlines the way ego psychology gained precedence in post-war America and illustrates US talk shows use of therapeutic concept of rational self-actualisation.

3   See also Bill Nichols' account of the documentary insistence on the presence of the body to substantiate the magnitude of historical or social events and of historical or narrative agency (1991: 229–66).

4   See also Sonia Livingstone and Peter Lunt's (1994: 64) account of Kilroy's therapeutic performance.

5   Langer's analysis is concerned primarily with news narratives but the description of the victim overcome with unexpected misfortune compares with the accounts of trauma on many talk shows.

6   See http://www.johnwalsh.tv/html/meet.html, 1, accessed 4 August 2003.

7   The story of Walsh's loss of his child has been dramatised in two films – the 1983 NBC television movie *Adam* and the 1986 sequel *Adam: His Song Continues*.

8   See http://www.etonline.com/celebrity/a6852.htm, 1, accessed 4 August 2003.

9   As Cathy Caruth has argued: 'The story of trauma, then, as the narrative of a belated experience, far from telling of an escape from reality – the escape from a death, or from its referential force – rather attests to the endless impact on a life' (1996: 7).

10 In the last week of April 2003, *Get a New Life* (BBC2) scored 2.8 million viewers, *Escape to the Country* (BBC2) 2.3 million and *Home Front* (BBC2) 2.1 million, *Selling Houses* (Channel 4) 3.2 million and *Location, Location, Location* (Channel 4) 4.2 million. Jon Plunkett noted in the *Observer* (4 May 2003) that, at their peak, house re-style programme *Changing Rooms* and garden re-style *Ground Force* were so popular they were moved from BBC2 to BBC1 where they were watched by 12 million viewers. In April 2003 they were rating around 7 million viewers, http://media.guardian.co.uk/Print/0,3858,4661192,00.html, 1, accessed 14 August 2003.

11 In the *Guardian* review, 'C4 drives audiences over the limit' (11 June 2003), Deans notes that both *Reality Check* and *The Dinner Party Inspectors* lost audience shares to more conventional documentaries running on rival stations. http://media.guardian.co.uk/overnights/story/0,7965,975203,00.html, accessed 12 August 2003. See also Mark Lawson's comment on these programmes in the preceding Monday's *Guardian* (9 June 2003), http://www.guardian.co.uk/avantgostory/0,6347,103689-4686799,00.html, accessed 12 August 2003.

12 Under their factual programming category Talkback Productions list a number of extremely successful lifestyle/makeover shows all screened in 2003: *How Clean Is Your House* (Channel 4), *Jamie's Kitchen* (first screened November/December 2002, Channel 4), *Property Ladder* (Channel 4), *Escape to the Country* (BBC2), *Grand Designs* (Channel 4), *Apply Immediately* (under production in summer 2003 for BBC), *Other People's Houses* (Channel 4), *Your Money or Your Life* (BBC2), *Life Doctor* (Channel 5), *Would Like to Meet* (BBC2) and *Dinner Party Inspectors* (Channel 4). See http://www.talkback.co.uk/intro2.html, accessed 22 August 2003.

chapter 7

1   For an insider's view of the filming of emergency services documentaries see Currie 2001 and Docherty 2001.

2   Surveys and classroom discussion with younger male students showed this to be

the case. We are indebted to students on the 'News, truth, power' course at Bucking-hamshire Chilterns University College for sharing with us their perceptions of this programme and its audience appeal. Kathleen Curry has also demonstrated in her sociological audience study of crime television that part of the interest for viewers in these kinds of scenes resides in their sense of the 'other'; that these crimes occur in other social settings than their own (2001: 179). So another line of enquiry might ask whose social space is being filmed here and how does it relate to the space of the viewer?

3   Caplin quoted in the *Radio Times*, 4–10 March 2000: 103.

4   Ariella Azoulay (2001) examines these new alignments of power and space with great clarity in her chapter on the video footage of Yitzhak Rabin's assassination. Here she examines the role of the camera in that event and the ways in which it is not merely a technology of witness but an interventionist protagonist in its own right.

5   The saturation of public space by CCTV is exemplified by the statistic that the average city dweller is likely to be filmed between eight and three hundred times in the course of a day (Carter 2001).

6   Terry Honess and Elizabeth Charman found in their research into public awareness and perceptions of CCTV that the majority of people were only really aware of CCTVs in places such as shops and banks (rather than on housing estates, for example) (1992: 6). A substantial number of respondents ascribed this awareness to television programmes such as *Crimewatch UK*. This, and other crime detection programmes therefore, may have fostered the perception that all cameras are set up to *prevent* and *detect* crime. In fact many camera recordings are not viewed at all but stored on tapes only to be reviewed as evidence well after the crime has taken place.

7   This virtual police presence through scopic technology is doubly underlined in the three part television series *Shooting the Crime* (15 November 2001, ITV). Here 'shooting' refers to the use of police photography and video footage as weapons in the fight against crime. The stories covered in this series are both authorised and effectively authored by the police, as they use police sources to portray a variety of 'crimes' from hostage situations to anti-capitalist demonstrations.

8   The phrase 'carnival of crime' is taken from Presdee (2000), who draws on Mikhail Bakhtin's work in order to think through the operation of law-breaking as the 'second life' of citizens lived out in the interstices of the ordered society.

chapter 8

1   We are drawing on Douglas Kellner's definition of media spectacle: 'phenomena of media culture that embody contemporary society's basic values, serve to initiate individuals into its way of life, and dramatise its controversies and struggles, as well as its modes of conflict resolution' (2003: 2).

2   Factual programming such as documentary has also become increasingly explicit in its representations of suffering, physical trauma and the body. See, for example, the series *Body Shock* and the documentary *The Boy Whose Skin Fell Off* (25 March 2004 – all Channel 4). The latter charted the decline and death of a man suffering from a rare

and dreadful skin condition that finally precipitated the cancer which was to kill him. His decline and death was filmed in explicit detail leading one doctor to observe, 'that there will never be a final frontier for the media when it comes to dealing with human suffering' (McKie 2004: 6). The programme was akin to the Blaine event in that its screen counter noted time passing in a countdown to the film subject's death. See also Blacker 2004.

3   Interviewed in 'Above the Below', directed by Harmony Korine, 2003. On the Channel 4/ Sky 1 broadcast Korine's film was shown intercut with the live broadcast entitled *David Blaine: Above the Below*.

4   Interviewed in 'Above the Below' (Korine 2003).

5   'Hang on in there: Blaine holds a mirror up to Britain', leader in the *Observer*, 21 September 2003.

6   For extended discussions of ordinariness and celebrity in reality TV and popular culture more broadly, see Littler 2003.

7   'Above the Below' (Korine 2003).

8   'The odd couple' at: http://www.guardian.co.uk/arts/fridayreview/story/0,12102, 1049361,00.html, accessed 26 September 2003.

9   Guy Debord (1967) notes in paragraph 18 of *Society of the Spectacle*: 'the spectacle as a tendency to *make one see* the world by means of various specialised mediations … naturally finds vision to be the privileged human sense … [spectacle] is the opposite of dialogue.'

10 Extensive media coverage of the Atkins diet's celebrity advocates, in particular, helped form a strong discursive relationship between star glamour and bodily morbidity. Such was the growing speculation about the diet's 'unhealthiness' and its unpleasant side effects that Hollywood star Catherine Zeta-Jones threatened to sue anyone who associated her with it.

11 Blaine had bulked up his weight before the event, so that even with this weight loss, his body appeared reasonably normal.

12 The only condition more private than illness or suffering is death itself. Foucault notes that as power has adopted the role of administering life (bio-politics) 'death is power's limit, the moment that escapes it; death becomes the most secret aspect of existence, the most "private"' (1976: 138). In the light of this observation it makes more sense that some critics of the event would only be satisfied with Blaine's death; although this, of course, would also have been unrepresentable.

13 Blaine's major set pieces have much in common with what is usually referred to as 'performance art' in that they are usually live theatrical pieces and frequently motivated by a redemptive belief in the transformative capacity of art and/or a radical merging of life and art (Jones 1998: 13).

14 Comment made in the film *Vertigo* (Jacob Septimus and Michael Dimich, 2002).

conclusion

1   We are choosing to use the term 'celebrity' in its broadest sense of people who are objects of pronounced media attention over which they may have only a limited

amount of control. We are also excluding elite persons who, for example, first come to the attention of the media and are newsworthy through their work in the traditional 'masculinised' public sphere of politics, big business or the City.

2   See, for example, Vivian Nicholson's well-known autobiography *Spend, Spend, Spend* (with Stephen Smith, 1978), which chronicles her football pools win and the subsequent notoriety that made her a media celebrity. The National Lottery was established in Britain in 1994. For accounts of lottery winners and their encounters with the media see Hunter Davies 1996.

3   Photospreads of the characters from the series have, appropriately enough, appeared in *Hello!*, 14 January 2003, 14–18.

4   Ex-*Mirror* editor Piers Morgan described Victoria Beckham, for example, as 'the new Diana' (*Tabloid Tales*, BBC1, 2003).

5   Not only achievement but also dramatic failure will bring individuals into the celebrity matrix. Most recently the attempt by Charles and Diana Ingram and their accomplice Tecwen Whittock to defraud the British quiz show *Who Wants to be a Millionaire* transformed them from celebrity winners to celebrity criminals. The documentary *Millionaire: A Major Fraud* (ITV1), which broadcast the show and revealed the frausters' methods, shown on Monday 21 April 2003 attracted nearly 17 million viewers, the biggest audience ever for a factual television programme on ITV.

6   *Pop Idol* won the prestigious Golden Rose of Montreux in 2002. It was cited by the judges as 'perfect television' (http://www.elstree.co.uk). Will Young and runner-up Gareth Gates both were given recording contracts with BMG.

7   The appeal of the competition and its lure as a springboard to celebrity status are illustrated by the number of applications to audition for the 2003 *Pop Idol*. The programme-makers Thames TV/19 TV Production received over 20,000 applications just prior to the 28 February 2003 closing date. See *Pop Idol* official website, http://www.itv.com/popidol/, accessed 18 March 2003.

8   Elstree Studio website, http://www.elstree.co.uk/, accessed 3 October 2002.

9   'A case for expulsion: *Big Brother's* challenge for Channel 4', *Guardian*, 31 July 2002, http://MediaGuardian.co.uk/bigbrother/story/0,7531,766576,00.html, accessed 3 October 2002.

Bibliography

Addley, Esther (2002) 'Sinisa's Story', *Guardian*, 26 July, G2.

Agnell, Callie (2002) 'Andy Warhol – Inner and Outer Space', in Thomas Levin, Ursula Frohne and Peter Weibel (eds) *CNTRL [SPACE]: Rhetorics of Surveillance from Bentham to Big Brother*, Karlsruhe: ZKM/MIT, 278–81.

Aitken, Ian (1997) 'The British documentary film movement', in Robert Murphy (ed.) *The British Cinema Book*. London: BFI, 58–67.

Alberoni, Francesco (1972) 'The powerless elite: theory and sociological research on the phen-onmena of the stars', in Dennis McQuail (ed.) *Sociology of Mass Communications: Selected Readings*. Harmondsworth: Penguin.

Allen, Douglas (2002a) 'Big Brother Turkish Style', *Media Education Journal*, 31, 21–2.

___ (2002b) 'Big Brother 2 Questionnaire', *Media Education Journal*, 31, 23–5.

___ (2002c) 'Big Brother 2', *Media Education Journal*, 31, 26–8.

Anderson, Lindsay (1954) 'Only connect: some aspects of the work of Humphrey Jennings', *Sight and Sound*, April–June, reprinted in M.-L. Jennings (1982) (ed.) *Humphrey Jennings: Film-maker, Painter, Poet*, London: BFI/Riverside Studios.

Anderson, Lindsay (1977) 'National film theatre programme notes – Free Cinema (1 and 2)', at: http://www.bfi.org.uk/features/freecinema/archive/anderson-77prognotes.p.

Andrejevic, Mark (2003) 'Sadistic? Yes, but ambush TV is also fresh', at: http://www.newsday.com/templates/misc/printstory.jsp/slug+ny-vpand293392275jul29&.

___ (2004) *Reality TV: The Work of Being Watched*. Oxford: Rowman and Littlefield.

Ang, Ien (1982) *Watching Dallas: Soap Opera and the Melodramatic Imagination*. London: Routledge.

Asthana, Anoushka (2003) 'I'm starving says Blaine', *Observer*, 21 September.

Austin, Suzy (2003) 'Blaine "a week away from lasting damage"', *Metro*, 29 September, 21.

Azoulay, Ariella (2001) *Death's Showcase: The Power of Image in Contemporary Democracy*, trans. R. Danieli. Cambridge, MA: MIT Press.

Bakhtin, Mikhail (1968) *Rabelais and His World*, trans. Hélène Iswolsky. Bloomington: Indiana University Press.

Baldwin, Elaine, Brian Longhurst, Scott McCracken, Miles Ogborn and Greg Smith (2004) *Introducing Cultural Studies*. London: Pearson Education (2nd edn).

Barker, Paul (1992) 'The Rise of Camcorder Culture', in Kevin Macdonald and Mark Cousins (eds) [1996] *Imagining Reality*. London: Faber and Faber, 352–7.

Barnfield, Graham (2002) 'From Direct Cinema to car wreck video: reality TV and the crisis of content', *Institute of Ideas*, 47–66.

Barnouw, Eric (1974) *Documentary: A History of the Non-Fiction*. New York: Oxford University Press.

____ (1993) *Documentary: A History of the Non-Fiction Film* (2nd edn.). Oxford: Oxford University Press.

Barthes, Roland (1972) 'The Face of Garbo', in *Mythologies*. London: Paladin, 56–7.

Baudrillard, Jean (1968) 'Structures of interior design', in Ben Highmore (ed.) [2002] *The Everyday Life Reader*. London: Routledge, 308–17.

____ (2002) 'Telemorphosis', in Thomas Levin, Ursula Frohne and Peter Weibel (eds) *CNTRL [SPACE]: Rhetorics of Surveillance from Bentham to Big Brother*. Karlsruhe: ZKM/MIT, 480–5.

Bazin, Andre (1967) 'The myth of total cinema', in Leo Baudry and Marshall Cohen (eds) [1974] *Film Theory and Criticism: Introductory Readings*, 199–202.

Beck, Ulrich (1992) *Risk Society: Towards a New Modernity*. London: Sage.

Berger, John (1957) 'Look at Britain', *Sight and Sound*, available at: http://www.bfi.org/features/freecinema/archive/berger-lookatbritain.htm

Berry, David (2000) 'Trust in media practices', in David Berry (ed.) *Ethics and Media Culture*. Oxford: Focal Press, 28–51.

BFI (2001) 'Free cinema interviews', at: http:bfi.org.uk/showing/nft/interviews/freecinema/12-audience.html.

Bignell, Jonathan, Stephen Lacey and Madeleine Macmurraugh-Kavanagh (eds) (2000) *British Television Drama: Past, Present and Future*. Basingstoke: Palgrave.

Bird, S. Elizabeth (2000) 'Audience demands in a murderous market: Tabloidisation in US television news', in Colin Sparks and John Tulloch (eds) *Tabloid Tales: Global Debates Over Media Standards*. Boston: Roman and Littlefield Publishers, 213–28.

Biressi, Anita (2001) *Crime, Fear and the Law in True Crime Stories*. London: Palgrave.

____ (2004a) '"Above the Below": body trauma as spectacle in social/media space', *Journal for Cultural Research*, 8, 3, 335–52.

____ (2004b) 'Inside/out – private trauma and public knowledge in true crime documentary', *Screen*, 45, 4, 401–12.

Biressi, Anita and Heather Nunn (2003a) 'Video justice: crimes of violence in social/media space', *Space and Culture*, 6, 3, 276–91.

____ (2003b) 'The especially remarkable: celebrity and social mobility in reality TV', in

Mediactive 'Celebrity', 2, 44–58.

Blacker, Terence (2004) 'Death has become the latest fashion', *Independent*, 24 March, 31.

Blue, James (1964) 'The Maysles Brothers interviewed', in Kevin Macdonald and Mark Cousins (eds) [1996] *Imagining Reality*. London: Faber and Faber, 258–64.

Brenton, Sam and Reuben Cohen (2003) *Shooting People: Adventures in Reality TV*. London: Verso.

Brockes, Emma (2001) '*The Experiment*', *Guardian*, 16 October, available at: http://www.guardian.co.uk/Archive/0,4273,4277992,00.html.

Brooks, Libby (2003) 'I don't really know why I did it', *Guardian*, 4 December.

Bruzzi, Stella (2000) *New Documentary: A Critical Introduction*. London: Routledge.

Bunbury, Stephanie and Karen Heinrich (2002) 'Retro reality', *The Age*, 18 June, 1–4, http://www.theage.com.au/cgi-bin/common/printArticle.pl?path=/articles/2002/06/18/102.

Burgin, Victor (2002) 'Jenni's room: exhibitionism and solitude', in Thomas Levin, Ursula Frohne and Peter Weibel (eds) *CNTRL [SPACE]: Rhetorics of Surveillance from Bentham to Big Brother*. Karlsruhe: ZKM/MIT, 228–35.

Butler, Judith (1990) *Gender Trouble: Feminism and the Subversion of Identity*. London: Routledge.

Callen, Anthea (2002) 'Ideal masculinities: an anatomy of power', in Nicholas Mirzoeff (ed.) *The Visual Culture Reader* (2nd edn.). London: Routledge, pp. 603–16.

Campbell, Beatrix (1993) *Goliath: Britain's Dangerous Places*. London: Methuen.

Carter, H. (2001) 'Eye Spy', August. *Guardian Unlimited Archive* at: http://www.guardian.co.uk/Archive/Article/0,4273,4231169,00.html.

Carter, Meg (2000) 'From the man who gave you *Big Brother*', *Independent*, 5 September, Features section, 8.

Caruth, Cathy (1996) *Unclaimed Experience*. Baltimore, MA: Johns Hopkins University Press.

Caughie, John (1980) 'Progressive television and documentary drama', *Screen*, 21, 3, 9–35.

___ (2000) *Television Drama: Realism, Modernism and British Culture*. Oxford: Oxford University Press.

Cavender, Gary and Lisa Bond-Maupin (1993) 'Fear and loathing on reality television: an analysis of *America's Most Wanted* and *Unsolved Mysteries*', *Sociological Inquiry*, 63, 3, 305–17.

Clark, Bernard (2002) 'The box of tricks', in *Institute of Ideas*, 1–16.

Collins, Michael (2000) 'The Arts: the camera never lies', *Independent*, 24 March.

Conomos, John (2000) 'Errol Morris and the New Documentary', available at: http://www.senseofcinema.com/contents/00/8/sfferrol.html.

Conrad, Peter (2000) 'The all-seeing eye that understands nothing', *Guardian*, 10 December.

Corner, John (1991a) 'Documentary voices', in John Corner (ed.) *Popular Television in Britain: Studies in Cultural History*. London: BFI, 42–59.

___ (ed.) (1991b) *Popular Television in Britain: Studies in Cultural History*. London: BFI.

___ (1996a) 'Mediating the ordinary: the "access" idea and television form', in John Corner and Sylvia Harvey (eds) *Television Times: A Reader*. London: Arnold, 165–74.

___ (1996b) '*Cathy Come Home*', in *The Art of the Record: A Critical Introduction to Documentary*. Manchester: Manchester University Press, 90–107.

___ (2002) 'Performing the real: documentary diversions', *Television and New Media*, 3, 2,

255–70.

___ (2003) 'Television, documentary and the category of the aesthetic', *Screen*, 44, 1, 93–100.

___ (2004) 'Afterword: framing the new', in Su Holmes and Deborah Jermyn (eds) *Understanding Reality Television*. London: Routledge.

Couldry, Nick (2002) 'Playing for celebrity: *Big Brother* as ritual event', *Television and New Media*, 3, 2, 283–94.

Currie, Mary (2001) 'Crime, causality and consent: making a documentary', *Criminal Justice Matters*, 43, Spring, 46.

Curry, Kathleen (2001) 'Mediating *Cops*: an analysis of viewer reaction to reality TV', *Journal of Criminal Justice and Popular Culture*, 8, 3, 169–85.

Davies, Alistair and Peter Saunders (1983) 'Literature, politics and society', in Alan Sinfield (ed.) *Society and Literature 1945–1970*, 13–50.

Davies, Hunter (1996) *Living on the Lottery*. London: Warner.

Debord, Guy (1967) *Society of the Spectacle*. Detroit: Black and Red.

Dixon, Bryony and Christophe Dupin (2001) 'Soup dreams', *Sight and Sound*, March, 28–30.

Doane, Rex (2000) 'A Conversation with Errol Morris', *Salon*, available at: http://archives. salon.com/people/feature/2000/01/Morris/index1.html.

Docherty, Chris (2001) 'Spread the word: the media and crime reduction', *Criminal Justice Matters*, 43, Spring, 48–50.

Dodd, Kathryn and Philip Dodd (1996) 'Engendering the nation: British documentary film, 1930–39', in Andrew Higson (ed.) *Dissolving Views: Key Writings on British Cinema*, London: Cassell, 38–50.

Dovey, Jon (2000) *Freakshow: First Person Media and Factual Television*. London: Pluto.

Drew, Robert (1983) 'Narration can be a killer', in Kevin Macdonald and Mark Cousins (eds) [1996] *Imagining Reality*. London: Faber and Faber, 271–3.

Dunkley, Christopher (2002) 'It's not new and it's not clever', *Institute of Ideas*, 35–46.

Dyer, Richard (ed.) (1981) *Coronation Street*. London: BFI.

Edgar, David (1988) 'Theatre of fact: a dramatist's point of view', in Alan Rosenthal (ed.) [1999] *Why Docudrama?: Fact-Fiction on Film and TV*, Carbondale and Edwardsville: Southern Illinois University Press, 174–87.

Elliott, Anthony (1996) *Subject to Ourselves: Social Theory, Psychoanalysis and Postmodernity*. Cambridge: Polity Press.

Ellis, John (ed.) (1977) *1951–1976: British Film Institute Productions*. London: BFI.

___ (1992) *Visible Fictions: Cinema, Television, Video*. London: Routledge.

___ (1996) 'The quality film adventure: British critics and the cinema, 1942–1948', in Andrew Higson (ed.) *Dissolving Views: Key Writings on British Cinema*, London: Cassell, 66–93.

___ (2000) *Seeing Things: Television in the Age of Uncertainty*. London: I. B. Tauris.

Elsaesser, Thomas (1996) 'Subject positions, speaking positions: from *Holocaust*, *Our Hitler*, and *Heimat* to *Shoah* and *Schindler's List*', in Vivian Sobchack (ed.) *The Persistence of History: Cinema, Television and the Modern Event*. New York and London: Routledge, 145–83.

___ (2001) 'Postmodernism as mourning work', *Screen*, 42, 2, 193–201.

Farrell, Kirby (1998) *Post-traumatic Culture: Injury and Interpretation in the Nineties*.

Maryland: Johns Hopkins University Press.

Fetveit, Arild (1999) 'Reality TV in the digital era: a paradox in visual culture?', *Media, Culture and Society*, 21, 787–804.

Feuer, Jane (1995) *Seeing through the Eighties: Television and Reaganism*. London: BFI.

Fiske, John (1987) *Television Culture*. London: Methuen.

Flitterman-Lewis, Sandy (1992) 'Psychoanalysis, Film, and Television', in Robert C. Allen (ed.) *Channels of Discourse, Reassembled* (2nd edn.). London: Routledge, 203–46.

Foucault, Michel (1975) *Discipline and Punish: The Birth of the Prison*. Harmondsworth: Penguin.

___ (1976) *The History of Sexuality: Vol. I: An Introduction*. London: Penguin.

___ (1980) 'The eye of power', in Colin Gordon (ed.) *Power/Knowledge: Selected Interviews and Other writings 1972–1977*. New York: Pantheon, 146–65.

___ (1982) 'The subject and power', in Hubert Dreyfus and Paul Rabinow (eds) *Michel Foucault: Beyond Structuralism and Hermeneutics* (2nd edn.). Chicago: Chicago University Press.

___ (1988) 'The dangerous individual', in Laurence Kritzman (ed.) *Politics, Philosophy, Culture: Interviews and Other Writings 1977–1984*. London: Routledge.

Freedland, Jonathan (1994) 'The man who's glad that you're sorry now', *Guardian*, 30 July, 27.

Freud, Sigmund (1912–13) 'Totem and Taboo: some points of agreement between the mental lives of savages and neurotics', in Angela Richards (ed.) [1985] *The Origins of Religion, Pelican Freud Library Vol. 13*. Harmondsworth: Pelican.

___ (1921) 'Group Psychology and the analysis of the ego', in Angela Richards (ed.) [1985] *Civilisation, Society and Religion, Pelican Freud Library Vol. 12*. Harmondsworth: Pelican.

___ (1925) 'Negation', in Angela Richards (ed.) [1984] *On Metapsychology: The Theory of Psychoanalysis, Pelican Library Vol. 11*. Harmondsworth: Pelican.

Frohne, Ursula (2002) '"Screen Tests": Media narcissism, theatricality, and the internalised observer', in Thomas Levin, Ursula Frohne and Peter Weibel (eds) *CNTRL [SPACE]: Rhetorics of Surveillance from Bentham to Big Brother*, Karlsruhe: ZKM/MIT, 252–77.

Frosch, Stephen (1991) *Identity Crisis: Modernity, Psychoanalysis and the Self*. London: Macmillan.

Fuller, Graham (ed.) (1998) *Loach on Loach*. London: Faber and Faber.

Garnett, Tony (2000) 'Contexts', in Jonathan Bignell, Stephen Lacey and Madeleine Macmurraugh-Kavanagh (eds) *British Television Drama*. London: Palgrave, 11–23.

___ (2001) 'Working in the Field', in Sheila Rowbotham and Huw Beynon (eds) *Looking at Class: Film, Television and the Working Class*. London: Rivers Oram Press, 70–82.

Geraghty, Christine (1991) *Women and Soap Opera*. Cambridge: Polity Press.

Giddens, Anthony (1991) *Modernity and Self-Identity*. Cambridge: Polity Press.

Glynn, Kevin (2000) *Tabloid Culture: Trash Taste, Popular Power and the Transformation of American Television*. Durham: Duke University Press.

Goode, Ian (2003) 'Value and television aesthetics', *Screen*, 44, 1, 93.

Goodwin, Andrew (1993) 'Riding with ambulances: television and its uses', *Sight and Sound*, 3, 1, 26–8.

Gorman, Lyn and David McLean (2003) *Media and Society in the Twentieth Century*. Oxford:

Blackwell.

Gray, Chris (2000) 'Most hated man in Britain is found guilty – of breaking the rules of a television game show', *Independent*, 18 August, 7.

Greer, Germaine (2001) 'Watch With Brother', *The Observer: Review*, 24 June.

Grindstaff, Laura (1997) 'Producing trash: class, and the money shot: a behind the scenes account of daytime TV talk shows', in James Lull and Stephen Hinerman (eds) *Media Scandals: Morality and Desire in the Popular Culture Marketplace*. Cambridge: Polity Press, 164–202.

Hajimichael, Mike (2002) 'Unearthing Napa: Exploring the impact of reality TV show techniques on Ayia Napa', conference paper at 'Crossroads in Cultural Studies: Fourth International Conference', 29 June–2 July, Tampere, Finland.

Hall, Stuart (1971) 'Technics of the medium', in John Corner and Sylvia Harvey (eds) [1996] *Television Times: A Reader*. London: Arnold, 3–10.

Hanson, Barry (2000) 'The 1970s: regional variations', in Jonathan Bignell, Stephen Lacey and Madeleine Macmurraugh-Kavanagh (eds) *British Television Drama: Past, Present and Future*. Basingstoke: Palgrave, 58–63.

Hartley, John (1992) *The Politics of Pictures: The Creation of the Public in the Age of Popular Media*. London: Routledge.

Hartmann, Geoffrey (2000) 'Tele-suffering and testimony in the dot com era', in Barbie Zelizer (ed.) *Visual Culture and the Holocaust*. New Brunswick, NJ: Rutgers University Press, 111–51.

Harvey, Sylvia (2000) 'Access, authorship and voice: The emergence of community programming at the BBC', in John Izod and Richard Kilborn (eds) *An Introduction to TV Documentary: Confronting Reality*, Manchester: Manchester University Press, 159–72.

Hattersley, Roy (2003) 'Is this the sickest stunt yet?', *Daily Mail*, 3 October.

Hawkins, Gay (2001) 'The ethics of television', *International Journal of Cultural Studies*, 4, 4, 412–42.

Hedling, Erik (1997) 'Lindsay Anderson and the development of British art cinema', in Robert Murphy (ed.) *The British Cinema Book*. London: BFI, 178–86.

Highmore, Ben (ed.) (2002) *The Everyday Life Reader*. London: Routledge.

Higson, Andrew (1996) 'Space, place, spectacle: landscape and townscape in "kitchen sink" film', in Andrew Higson (ed.) (1996) *Dissolving Views: Key Writings on British Cinema*. London: Cassell, 133–56.

Hill, Annette (2000a) 'Fearful and safe: audience response to British reality programming', in Richard Kilborn and Matthew Hibberd (eds) *from grierson to Docusoap: Breaking the Boundaries*. Luton: University of Luton Press, 212–22.

____ (2000b) 'Crime and crisis: British reality television in action', in Edward Buscombe (ed.) *British Television: A Reader*. Oxford: Oxford University Press, 218–34.

____ (2001) '*Big Brother* 2000: the Real Audience', in Vincent Porter (ed.) *Ethics and Mass Communication in Europe*. London: Centre for Communication and Information Studies, University of Westminster, 36–50.

Hill, John (1986) *Sex, Class and Realism*. London: BFI.

Hoggart, Richard (1957) *The Uses of Literacy*. Harmondsworth: Penguin.

Holland, Patricia (1997) 'Sweet it is to scan…: personal photographs and popular photography', in Liz Wells (ed.) *Photography: A Critical Introduction*, London: Routledge, 103–50.

Holmes, Su and Deborah Jermyn (eds) (2003) *Understanding Reality Television*. London: Routledge.

Honess, Terry and Elizabeth Shandler (1992) *Closed Circuit Television in Public Places: Its Acceptability and Perceived Effectiveness*, Crime Prevention Unit Series: Paper No. 35. London: Home Office Police Department.

Houlihan, Joe (2000) 'Docusoap? Wash your mouth out: once a ratings winner, now it's a dirty word', *Independent*, Features Section, 22 February, 10.

Houston, Penelope (1963) *The Contemporary Cinema*. Harmondsworth: Penguin.

Hughes, Gordon, Eugene McLaughlin and John Muncie (eds) (2000) *Crime Prevention and Community Safety: New Directions*. London: Sage.

Hunt, Leon (1998) *British Low Culture: From Safari Suits to Sexploitation*. London: Routledge.

Institute of Ideas (2002) *Reality TV: How Real is Real?* London: Hodder and Stoughton.

Jacobs, Jason (2000) *The Intimate Screen: Early British Television Drama*. Oxford: Oxford University Press.

___ (2003) *Body Trauma TV: The New Hospital Dramas*. London: BFI.

Jennings, Marie-Louise (1982) (ed.) *Humphrey Jennings: Film-maker, Painter, Poet*. London: BFI/Riverside Studios.

Jones, Amelia (1998) *Body Art: Performing the Subject*. Minneapolis: University of Minnesota Press.

Jones, Janet (2000) 'The postmodern guessing game', *Journal of Media Practice*, 1, 2, 75–84.

___ (2004) 'Emerging platform identities: *Big Brother UK*', in Ernest Mathijs and Janet Jones (eds) *Big Brother International: Formats, Critics and Publics*. London: Wallflower Press, 210–31.

Kavka, Misha and Amy West (2003) 'Conceptualising time in reality TV', in Su Holmes and Deborah Jermyn (eds) *Understanding Reality Television*. London: Routledge.

Keighron, Philip (1993) 'Video diaries: what's up doc?', *Sight and Sound*, 3, 10, 24–5.

Kellner, Douglas (2003) *Media Spectacle*. London: Routledge.

Kember, Sarah (1995) 'Surveillance, technology and crime: the James Bulger case', in Martin Lister (ed.) *The Photographic Image in Digital Culture*. London: Routledge, 115–26.

Kilborn, Richard (1994) 'How real can you get?: recent developments in "reality" television', *European Journal of Communication*, 9, 421–39.

___ (1996) 'New contexts for documentary production in Britain', *Media, Culture and Society*, 18, 141–50.

___ (2003) *Staging the Real: Factual TV Programming in the Age of Big Brother*. Manchester and New York: Manchester University Press.

Kilborn, Richard and John Izod (1997) *An Introduction to TV Documentary: Confronting Reality*. Manchester: Manchester University Press.

Kilborn, Richard with Matthew Hibberd (eds) (2000) *From Grierson to the Docu-soap : Breaking the Boundaries*. Luton: University of Luton Press.

Kilborn, Richard, Matthew Hibberd and Raymond Boyle (2001) 'The rise of the docusoap:

the case of *Vets in Practice*', *Screen*, 42, 4, 382–95.

Lacey, H. (2000) 'Marry on screen, repent at leisure', *Independent on Sunday*, 26 March.

Lacey, Stephen (1995) *British Realist Theatre: The New Wave in its Context 1956–1965*. London: Routledge.

La Fontaine, Jean (1998) *Speak of the Devil: Tales of Satanic Abuse in Contemporary England*. Cambridge: Cambridge University Press.

Laing, Stuart (1991) 'Banging in some reality: The original *Z Cars*', in John Corner (ed.) *Popular Television in Britain: Studies in Cultural History*. London: BFI, 125–44.

Lambert, Gavin (1956) 'Free Cinema', *Sight and Sound*, Spring, 173–7, reprinted in Kevin MacDonald and Mark Cousins (eds) [1996] *Imagining Reality*. London: Faber and Faber, 211–14.

Langer, John (1992) 'Truly awful news on television', in Peter Dahlgren and Colin Sparks (eds) (1992) *Journalism and Popular Culture*. London: Sage Publications,113–29.

____ (1998) *Tabloid Television: Popular Journalism and the 'Other' News*. Routledge: London.

Laplanche, Jean and Jean-Bertrand Pontalis (1988) *The Language of Psychoanalysis*. Trans. Donald Nicholson-Smith. London: Karnac Books/The Institute of Psychoanalysis.

Lapsley, Robert and Michael Westlake (1988) *Film Theory: An Introduction*. Manchester: Manchester University Press.

Lasch, Christopher (1978) *The Culture of Narcissism*. New York: W. W. Norton.

Lesage, Julia (2002) 'Space/Place as represented in travel media: some theoretical reflections', conference paper, 'Media in Transition 2: Globalisation and Convergence', Massachusetts Institute of Technology, Cambridge, MA, 10–12 May.

Levin, Thomas, Ursula Frohne and Peter Weibel (eds) (2002) *CNTRL [SPACE]: Rhetorics of Surveillance from Bentham to Big Brother*, Karlsruhe: ZKM/MIT.

Light, Allie (2002) 'Allie Light: Searching for Metaphor', in Liz Stubbs (ed.) *Documentary Filmmakers Speak*. London: Allworth Press, 195–207.

Littler, Jo (2003) 'Making fame ordinary: intimacy, reflexivity and "keeping it real"', in *Mediactive* 'Celebrity'. London: Barefoot Publications, 2, 8–25.

Lister, David (2000) 'Big Brother offers lessons in life', *Independent*, 19 August.

Lister, Martin (ed.) (1995) *The Photographic Image in Digital Culture*. London: Routledge.

Livingstone, Sonia and Peter Lunt (1994) *Talk on Television: Audience Participation and Public Debate*. London: Routledge.

Loch Hill, Lawrence (n.d.) 'Live from the ministry of truth: reality soaps return to the early promises of live television', *M/C Reviews* online journal, available at: http://reviewes.media-culture.org.au/sections.php?op=viewarticle&artid=115.

Lovell, Terry (1981) *Pictures of Reality: Aesthetics, Politics, Pleasure*. London: BFI.

Lumby, C. (2001) 'Sylvania Waters', available at: http://www.mbcnet.org/ETV/S/htmlS/sylvaniawate/sylvaniawate.htm.

Lyotard, Jean-Francois (1984) *The Postmodern Condition*. Minneapolis: University of Minnesota Press.

Macdonald, Kevin and Mark Cousins (eds) (1996) *Imagining Reality*. London: Faber and Faber.

MacDonald, Myra (1998) 'Politicising the personal: women's voices in British television documentaries', in Cynthia Carter, Gill Branston and Stuart Allan (eds) *News, Gender and*

Power. London: Routledge, 105–20.

MacMurraugh-Kavanagh, Madeleine (1997) '"Drama" into "news": strategies of intervention in "The Wednesday Play"', *Screen*, 38, 3, 247–59.

MacMurraugh-Kavanagh, Madeleine and Stephen Lacey (1999) 'Who framed theatre? The "moment of change" in British TV drama', *New Theatre Quarterly*, 15, 1, 58–74.

Mamber, Stephen (1972) 'Cinéma Vérité in America: Part II – Direct cinema and the crisis structure', *Screen*, 13, 3, 114–36.

Mapplebeck, Victoria (2002) 'The money shot', *Institute of Ideas*, 17–34.

McKie, Robin (2004) 'TV's diary of death is "too graphic"', *Observer*, 21 March, 6.

McLaughlin, Lisa (1998) 'Gender, privacy and publicity in "media event space"', in Cynthia Carter, Gill Branston and Stuart Allan (eds) *News, Gender and Power*. London: Routledge, 71–90.

McLean, Gareth (2001) 'Exposing the Truth', *Guardian*, TV Review, 31 July.

Midgley, Carol (2000) 'A living hell?', *The Times*, 17 July.

Morley, David (1992) 'Where the global meets the local: notes from the sitting room', in *Television, Audiences and Cultural Studies*. London: Routledge, 270–89.

Nicholls, Bill (1991) *Representing Reality: Issues and Concepts in Documentary*. Bloomington and Indianapolis: Indiana University Press.

____ (1994) *Blurred Boundaries: Questions of Meaning in Contemporary Culture*. Bloomington: Indiana University Press.

Norris, Colin and Gary Armstrong (1997a) *Categories of Control: the Social Construction of Suspicion and Intervention in CCTV Systems*. Hull: Centre for Criminology and Criminal Justice.

____ (1997b) *The Unforgiving Eye: CCTV Surveillance in Public Space*. Hull: Centre for Criminology and Criminal Justice.

Nunn, Heather (2004) 'Errol Morris: documentary as psychic drama', *Screen*, 45, 4, 413–22.

O'Dell, Kathy (1998) *Contract with the Skin: Masochism, Performance Art and the 1970s*. Minneapolis: University of Minnesota Press.

Ogle, T. (2002) 'Lord of the fly-on-the-walls', *Observer*, January 27.

O'Hehir, Andrew (2000) 'Mr Death', in *Salon*, available at: http://archive.salon.com/ent/movies/review/2000/01/14/death/.

O'Sullivan, Tim (1991) 'Television memories and cultures of viewing 1950–65', in John Corner (ed.) *Popular Television in Britain: Studies in Cultural History*. London: BFI, 159–81.

Owen, Jenny (1999) 'Documentary and citizenship: The case of Stephen Lawrence', in Jane Stokes and Anna Reading (eds) *The Media in Britain: Current Debates and Developments*. London: Macmillan, 201–7.

Palmer, Gareth (2004) *Discipline and Liberty: Television and Governance*. London: Manchester.

Palmer, Paul (2003) 'Revealed: How Blaine could be out in days', *Evening Standard*, 22 September, 18–19.

Paget, Derek (1990) *True Stories? Documentary Drama on Radio, Screen and Stage*. Manchester: Manchester University Press.

____ (1998) *No Other Way To Tell It: Dramadoc/Docudrama*. Manchester: Manchester University Press.

Paget, Derek (1999a) '"Cathy Come Home" and "accuracy", in British television drama', *New Theatre Quarterly*, 15, 1, 75–90.

___ (1999b) 'Tales of cultural tourism', in Alan Rosenthal (ed.) *Why Docudrama?: Fact-Fiction on Film and TV*. Carbondale and Edwardsville: Southern Illinois University Press.

Parker, Ian (1997) *Psychoanalytic Culture: Psychoanalytic Discourse in the West*. London: Sage.

Peters, John Durham (2001) 'Witnessing', *Media, Culture and Society*, 23, 707–23.

Plunkett, Jon (2003) 'Auntie decides what not to wear', *Observer*, available at: http://media.guardian.co.uk/Print/0,3858,4661192,00.html.

Presdee, Mike (2000) *Cultural Criminology and the Carnival of* Crime. London: Routledge.

Radstone, Susannah (2001) 'Trauma and screen studies: opening the debate', *Screen*, 42, 2, 188–93.

Renov, Michael (1993) *Theorizing Documentary*. London and New York: Routledge.

___ (1999) 'New Subjectivities: Documentary and Self-Representation in the Post-Verité Age', in Diane Waldman and Janet Walker (eds) *Feminism and Documentary*. Minneapolis: University of Minnesota Press, 84–94.

Richards, Barry (1994) *Disciplines of Delight: The Psychoanalysis of Popular Culture*. London: Free Association Books.

Ritchie, Jean (2003) *Big Brother 4: Up Close and Personal*. London: Channel 4 Books.

Robins, Kevin (1996) *Into the Image: Culture and Politics in the Field of Vision*. London: Routledge.

Rogers, Daniel (2001) 'Marketing reality TV', *Guardian*, 29 May, available at: http://www.media.guardian.co.uk/Print/0,3858,4194119,00.html.

Root, Jane (1986) *Open the Box*. London: Comedia.

Rose, Mandy (2000) 'Through the eyes of the *Video Nation*', in John Izod and Richard Kilborn (eds.) *An Introduction to TV Documentary: Confronting Reality*. Manchester: Manchester University Press, 173–84.

Rose, Nikolas (1990) *Governing the Soul: The Shaping of the Private Self*. London: Routledge.

___ (1998) *Inventing Ourselves: Psychology, Power and Personhood*. Cambridge: Cambridge University Press.

Rosenheim, Shawn (1996) 'Interrotroning history: Errol Morris and the documentary of the future', in Vivian Sobchack (ed.) *The Persistence of History*. New York and London: Routledge, 219–34.

Rosenthal, Alan (ed.) (1999) *Why Docudrama?: Fact-Fiction on Film and TV*. Carbondale and Edwardsville: Southern Illinois University Press.

Ross, Nick and Sue Cook (1987) *Crimewatch UK*. London: Hodder and Stoughton.

Rowbotham, Sheila (1997) 'The subversive who surprises: Ken Loach', in Sheila Rowbotham and Huw Beynon (eds) [2001] *Looking at Class: Film, Television and the Working Class*. London: Rivers Oram Press, 83–7.

Rowbotham, Sheila and Huw Beynon (eds) (2001) *Looking At Class: Film, Television and the Working Class*. London: Rivers Oram Press.

Rowe, Kathleen (1995) *The Unruly Woman: Gender and Genres of Laughter*. Austin: University of Texas Press.

Roy-Leven, G. (1969) 'Jean Rouch interviewed', in Kevin Macdonald and Mark Cousins (eds)

[1996] *Imagining Reality*. London: Faber and Faber, 264–8.

Russo, Mary (1994) *The Female Grotesque: Risk, Excess and Modernity*. London: Routledge.

Scannell, Paddy (2002) *'Big Brother* as a television event', *Television and New Media*, 3, 2, 271–82.

Scarry, Elaine (1985) *The Body in Pain*. Oxford: Oxford University Press.

Scott, Ann (1996) *Real Events Revisited: Fantasy, Memory and Psychoanalysis*. London: Virago.

Seltzer, Mark (1998) *Serial Killers: Death and Life in America's Wound Culture*. London: Routledge.

Schlesinger, Philip and Howard Tumber (1996) 'Television, police and audience', in John Corner and Sylvia Harvey (eds) *Television Times*. London: Arnold, 66–74.

Scraton, Phil (1999) *Hillsborough: The Truth*. Edinburgh: Mainstream Publishing Projects.

Shandler, Jay (2000) 'The man in the glass box: Watching the Eichmann trial on American television', in Barbie Zelizer (ed.) *Visual Culture and the Holocaust*. New Brunswick, NJ: Rutgers University Press, 91–110.

Shattuc, Jane (1997) *The Talking Cure: TV Talk Shows and Women*. London: Routledge.

Shubik, Irene (2000) *Play for Today: The Revolution of Television Drama* (2nd edn.). Manchester: Manchester University Press.

Sigesmund, B. (2003) 'Just Blaine crazy?', *Newsweek*, 28 August.

Silverstone, Roger (1994) *Television and Everyday Life*. London: Routledge.

Smith, Rupert (2002) 'The price of fame', *Guardian*, 18 November,15–17.

Sparks, Richard (1992) *Television and the Drama of Crime*. Buckingham: Open University Press.

Spigel, Lynn (2001) *Welcome to the Dreamhouse: Popular Media and Postwar Suburbs*. Durham: Duke University Press.

Stallybrass, Peter and Allon White (1986) *The Politics and Poetics of Transgression*. London: Methuen.

Steedman, Carolyn (1989) *Landscape for a Good Woman*. London: Virago.

Stratton, Jon and Ien Ang (1994) *'Sylvania Waters* and the spectacular exploding family', *Screen*, 35, 1, 1–21.

Street, Sarah (1997) *British National Cinema*. London: Routledge.

Stuart, Julia (2000) 'The year of living dangerously: A group of strangers volunteered to spend 12 months together on a storm-lashed island', *Independent*, 17 January.

Tagg, John (1988) *The Burden of Representation: Essays on Photographies and Histories*. London: Macmillan.

Undercurrents (1997) 'Caught on camera', available at: http://tv.cbc.ca/undercurrents/1997_1998/week01/.

Van Loon, Joost (2000) 'Enframing/revealing: on the question of ethics and difference in technologies of mediation', in David Berry (ed.) *Ethics and Media Culture*. Oxford: Focal Press, 54–70.

Waddell, Dan (2002) *Survivor Panama*. London: Carlton Books.

Wayne, Mike (1994) 'Television, audiences, politics', in Stuart Hood (ed.) *Behind the Screens: The Structure of British Television in Nineties*. London: Lawrence and Wishart, 43–64.

Wexler, Haskell (1971) 'Filming Torture Victims', in Kevin Macdonald and Mark Cousins (eds)

[1996] *Imagining Reality*. London: Faber and Faber, 298.

Wheatley, Helen (2001) 'Real crime television in the 8–9 slot – consuming fear', in Charlotte Brundson, Catherine Johnson, Rachel Moseley and Helen Wheatley, 'Factual Real crime entertainment on British television', *European Journal of Cultural Studies*, 4, 1, February, 29–62.

Williams, Linda (1998) 'Mirrors without Memories', in *Documenting the Documentary*. Detroit: Wayne State University Press, 379–96.

Williams, Raymond (1977) 'A lecture on realism', *Screen*, 18, 1, 61–74.

Winston, Brian (1995) *Claiming the Real: the Documentary Film Revisited*. London: BFI Publishing.

___ (1996) *Technologies of Seeing: Photgraphy, Cinematography and Television*. London: BFI Publishing.

___ (1998) 'The tradition of the victim in Griersonian documentary', in Alan Rosenthal (ed.) *New Challenges for Documentary*. Berkeley: University of California Press, 269–87.

___ (2000) *Lies, Damn Lies and Documentaries*. Berkeley: University of California Press.

Woodhead, Leslie (1981) 'The Guardian lecture: dramatized documentary', in Alan Rosenthal (ed.) [1999] *New Challenges for Documentary*. Berkeley: University of California Press.

Yesil, Bilge (undated) 'Reel pleasures: exploring the historical roots of media voyeurism and exhibitionism in the USA', in *M/C Reviews* online journal, available at: http://reviewes.media-culture.org.au/sections.php?op=viewarticle@artid+116.

Young, Alison (1996) *Imagining Crime*. London: Sage.

Young, Michael and Peter Willmott (1957) *Family and Kinship in East London*. Harmondsworth: Pelican.

Žižek, Slavoj (2002) 'Big Brother, or, triumph of the gaze over the eye', in Thomas Levin, Ursula Frohne and Peter Weibel (eds) *CNTRL [SPACE]: Rhetorics of Surveillance from Bentham to Big Brother*, Karlsruhe: ZKM/MIT, 224–7.

Index